WINNING OUR ENERGY INDEPENDENCE

WINNING OUR ENERGY INDEPENDENCE

{AN ENERGY INSIDER ✳✳✳ SHOWS HOW}

S. DAVID FREEMAN

Gibbs Smith, Publisher

TO ENRICH AND INSPIRE HUMANKIND

Salt Lake City | Charleston | Santa Fe | Santa Barbara

First Edition
11 10 09 08 07   5 4 3 2 1
Text © 2007 S. David Freeman

Published by
Gibbs Smith, Publisher
P.O. Box 667
Layton, Utah 84041

Orders: 1.800.835.4993
www.gibbs-smith.com

Designed by Blackeye Design
Printed and bound in China

Library of Congress Cataloging-in-Publication Data
Freeman, S. David.
  Winning our energy independence : an energy insider shows how / S. David Freeman. — 1st ed.
     p. cm.
  Includes index.
  ISBN-13: 978-1-4236-0156-2
  ISBN-10: 1-4236-0156-4
  1. Renewable energy sources. 2. Energy conservation. I. Title.

TJ808.F74 2007
333.79'4—dc22
                        2007011579

To my grandchildren—

Lisa and Karen Hopkins, and Nate, Alex, Tess, Kelsey, Ben, Tim, and Carolyn Freeman

CONTENTS

✳✳✳

ACKNOWLEDGMENTS

✳ ✳ ✳

THIS BOOK WOULD NOT HAVE BEEN POSSIBLE WITHOUT the inspiration of Gibbs Smith and his wife, Catherine, who were persistent over many months in persuading me to write it.

Even so, I would not, and did not, write it alone. Rachel McMahon was my constant partner in endless conversation that critically examined the book's contents. She did all the research, some of the writing, and the preliminary editing. Perhaps of greatest value, she encouraged me to express my opinions with my life-long style of "straight talk" and humor. For all this, Ms. McMahon has my gratitude and heartfelt appreciation.

I wish to also acknowledge the major contribution by two of my friends. Laurie Kaufman, in a very short period of time, edited the rough draft of the book so well that my editor-in-chief, Leslie Stitt, was impressed. And best of all, our friendship survived the editing process.

Arjun Makhijani reviewed the manuscript and made invaluable contributions, especially on the various clean-energy technologies and the nuclear section. The opinions are mine, but Arjun helped me explain the technologies more precisely and more accurately.

No book is a success without a world-class editor. Leslie Cutler Stitt is in that class and her suggestions went far beyond the usual. The consumer action elements of the book and personal anecdotes are Leslie's inspiration, for which I am most appreciative.

INTRODUCTION

✳✳✳

THIS BOOK FOCUSES ON the United States, but it really is about the 6 billion people on earth. The essential truth documented herein is that the United States can move swiftly to a predominantly renewable energy future. The exciting fact is that if it can happen in this country, it can happen in China, India, Indonesia, and almost anywhere on earth. And by starting an energy revolution, the United States will set an example that regains the respect and admiration of the rest of the world.

As I complete this book, I find my ideas reinforced almost on a daily basis by reports of the growing dangers of global warming, oil dependency, and nuclear proliferation. But the hopeful signs are a flood of support for renewable energy and recognition by the auto industry that the use of renewable electricity to power motor vehicles is the wave of the future. I hope this book will help the American people understand why sustaining this momentum can lead to success in what is a life-or-death struggle by this high-energy civilization.

The hopeful prospect of a pollution-free and sustainable energy future can provide an outlet for the emerging grassroots desire of most Americans. The American people, through their purchasing power and the power of their votes, can make it happen.

The United States can, I hope, launch and sustain a moon-shot effort that will bring excitement, joy, and purpose to this nation and, in turn, to the 6 billion people on earth. And as we take action, the American dream of being a world leader will again become a reality.

This book expresses opinions formed by 50 years of practical experience in the field of energy as an active participant. I'm not a scientist, an economist, or a political analyst offering learned opinions, nor do I represent any one interest group. I've been on the firing line on both sides of many of these issues and formed my opinions from deep involvement and a demanding teacher called experience.

I'm now eighty-one years old and believe the opinions I have formed can help the American people see through the self-serving propaganda of the energy industry and the timidity of today's political and business leaders.

I was the first person in the U.S. government with responsibility for energy policy under President Johnson way back in 1967. I drafted the very first energy message that a president sent to Congress, delivered by President Nixon in 1971. To my embarrassment, it featured the nuclear breeder reactor. But, at my initiative, it contained the first energy efficiency measure—a directive to the Federal Housing Administration (FHA) to require proper insulation in FHA-financed homes.

In addition to my early energy responsibility, I also had the privilege of working on the foundation of our nation's environmental policy. Along with Doug Costle, a fellow staff member, we "sold" the idea of an independent Environmental Protection Agency (EPA) to the Nixon administration and worked on the initial clean air and clean water laws.

I believe I can fairly say that from 1970 to 1971, I was a participant in creating the nation's first energy and environmental policies. It was an exciting time to be involved in government.

I left the Nixon administration in 1971 and led the Ford Foundation's first comprehensive study of energy policy that featured conservation and renewables.

I then worked for the U.S. Senate Commerce Committee and was the staff person who led the successful effort to enact better mileage standards for motor vehicles in 1975.

In 1977, President Carter named me to lead the Tennessee Valley Authority (TVA), which had the nation's largest nuclear power program. My vote was responsible for stopping eight large reactors already under construction in the homeland of the atomic bomb. It was not a popular move—especially because I was born and raised in Tennessee—but the nuclear plants cost way too much money and resources, and had the potential to do greater harm than good. We implemented a conservation program that was much cheaper on all fronts.

After TVA, I was the CEO of a "little TVA" in Austin, Texas, called the Lower Colorado River Authority (LCRA) from 1986 to 1990. I got that job because Bob King, a friend from my TVA days, called my name to LCRA's attention. I first had to clean up a scandal called "Trailergate," then I stopped a lignite mine before it destroyed Fayette County, even though the mining equipment had already been purchased. The lignite was not only very dirty, it was also very expensive to produce. LCRA nowadays is doing fine.

I next moved to California in 1990 to manage the electric system in Sacramento, the state's capital. The utility was in real trouble with a recent history of rate increases, fired managers, and a nuclear plant that worked on average every other day. They hired me and we "fired" the nuclear plant and stopped raising rates. Conservation and smaller plants did the trick. And we initiated one of the state's first solar energy programs. We also defeated an attempt by Pacific Gas and Electric to take us over.

We were successful enough that I was urged to run for the California state legislature. But Peter Bradford, a former nuclear regulatory commissioner and good friend, brought my name to Governor Cuomo's attention. He offered me the job of leading the New York Power Authority, and I accepted. Then just to confound my critics, I "nursed" a nuclear power plant back to "health" and initiated major conservation efforts, including solar power and electric cars, which Governor Pataki continued and indeed strengthened after I left New York in 1996.

I returned to California at the invitation of Governor Wilson's staff, and Dan Fessler, then president of the California Public Utilities Commission, and Chuck Imbrecht, then president of the California Energy Commission. They all asked me to be the trustee of the funds available to assure that the infrastructure for the new electric deregulation initiative in the state was completed in a timely fashion. It was. However, the policy itself was fatally flawed, but we didn't realize that at the time.

My job in setting up the infrastructure for deregulation in California was completed in 1997. Another dear friend, Ralph Cavanagh, a leader in the Natural Resources Defense Council, helped me get my next job. He introduced me to Ruth Galanter, then chair of the city council committee that oversaw the Los Angeles Department of Water and Power. As a result, I was hired by the City of Los Angeles in 1997 to be the general manager of its city-owned electric system, the largest public power distributor in the nation.

Here again, the utility was in serious trouble, fearing bankruptcy if it couldn't meet the oncoming competition from the Enrons in the new world of electric deregulation.

I took advantage of the fear. I reduced the oversized workforce at L.A.'s utility by over 1,000 people as part of a cost-cutting effort that made

L.A. very competitive and ensured its success. We beefed up our power supply through conservation and adding small plants and thus survived the California energy crisis of 2001 with no blackouts, no rate increases, and reduced debt.

We also initiated programs for solar and other green power and began reducing our use of coal—a dirty, nonrenewable energy source.

The worst years of my long career as a public servant were from 2001 to 2003. I was "drafted" by Governor Gray Davis to assist the state in dealing with the electric power shortages that were manipulated by the deregulated generating companies. We stopped the rip-off with a strong conservation effort and long-term contracts that financed new power plants. But the damage was already done and no one involved escaped intact.

I returned to L.A. in 2003 and am now the president of the commission overseeing the Port of Los Angeles. We recently announced the most aggressive clean air action plan in the nation.

I served in World War II in the Merchant Marine and graduated from Georgia Tech with a degree in civil engineering in 1948. I graduated first in my class from the University of Tennessee law school in 1956. In addition to the Ford Foundation report previously mentioned, I authored *Energy: The New Era*, published in 1974.

1 THE HEART OF THE STORY

{AMERICA CAN BECOME
ENERGY INDEPENDENT} ✳✳✳

I AM ENCOURAGED TO WRITE THIS BOOK because my own experience has taught me that one person can make a difference. In 1974, a team I led released a report funded by the Ford Foundation titled "A Time to Choose." It documented why conservation of energy and renewables should be our nation's future policy. We sent a copy to the governor of each state. Jimmy Carter was one of those governors.

I later learned from Omi Walden, who was then Jimmy Carter's energy aide, what happened when the then-governor of Georgia received my Ford Foundation report on energy policy. "The governor brought the report to me and asked me to read and summarize it," Walden said. "I saw that some pages had been torn out in the front." It was the executive summary that preceded the study. "I wondered what was going on," she continued. "I completed the summary and after the governor read it, he pulled the torn-out pages from inside his desk and said, 'Omi, your summary agrees with theirs, so the report must back up the executive summary. I agree with just about everything they say in here. This will be our energy policy from now on.'"

I hope that this book will have the same effect on people in all walks of life. I hope the result will be to change our way of life and our government policies.

THE BIG PICTURE

In 2006, as the price of gasoline shot up above three dollars a gallon, a giant iceberg reared its ugly head above the ocean and came into clear view. And, believe me, the totality of the energy problems that haven't yet hit us are as huge as an iceberg. Fortunately, we have the renewable resources and technology to steer around the iceberg—and I mean all of it, not just the part we can see. But it won't happen if we stay on automatic pilot. The price of oil grabbed the attention of the American people because it inflicted pain, a pain that affects people's day-to-day lives and standard of living. It is something tangible.

The lesson to be learned is that it's too late to avoid pain if we wait until we're already feeling it. It is no comfort to hear government officials concede that the pain of higher gasoline prices is not going away. But it is comforting to believe this is a wake-up call. Three dollars a gallon for gasoline was a warning of deeper trouble that includes worldwide shortages of oil, and power and growing influence to oil producers such as Iran, Saudi Arabia, Russia, and Venezuela. And we are facing threats even more dangerous than terrorists—threats that concern life on this planet as we now know it.

It's time to be bold, and look deeper. We must not react to the high price of oil in an unthinking manner by embracing solutions that have their own devastating side effects and will create more problems than they can allegedly solve. We do not need to resort to inadequate and dangerous solutions when we have cleaner, safer, and cheaper alternatives that will be well documented in this book.

President George W. Bush stated in a speech in 2006 that the American people are addicted to oil. The truth is that we are addicted to our cars and their mobility that has become our way of life. The American people would be more than happy to kick the oil habit if they were offered a homegrown clean fuel for driving their cars.

As we focus our attention and common sense on the energy issue, we will find that all our energy can come from the sun, the wind, plants we can grow here in the U.S., and the trash we throw away, combined with huge increases in efficiency. And these homegrown sources of energy can be far cheaper than petroleum.

In 1973, my Ford Foundation report "A Time to Choose" documented the case for greater efficiency and renewables. At that time the U.S. embraced greater efficiency, but it is fair to say that, for renewables, the last thirty years have been "a time to snooze." Our snoozing time must and can end. The global environmental and security impacts of burning fossil fuels and the failure of nuclear power have put us in a position of domestic and international crisis. There is still a last clear chance to make a spirited and determined transition to a renewable world. But we have no time to lose. A continued massive use of fossil fuels and nuclear power is an almost certain path to havoc and destruction of the high-energy civilization we enjoy.

I do not make these statements lightly. I have spent my adult life as the CEO of major publicly owned electric utilities that have burned large quantities of coal and utilized nuclear power. I know from personal experience that many professionals in those industries resist change as much as a little boy resists a bath, but I also know that this resistance can be overcome with common sense and strength of purpose. Change we must and change we can.

THE PROBLEM

This country is in a heap of trouble because we are overly dependent on oil from a group of folks who are terrorizing the world. Oil money is at the heart of what is financing terrorism as well as Iran's nuclear program. Remember that Osama bin Laden originated from Saudi Arabia, and it is Saudi Arabian oil money that has financed his terrorism. We help fund the terrorists every time we buy a gallon of gasoline. The United States' ability to make peace in the world is badly constrained by our fear of the "oil weapon" being used by nations such as Saudi Arabia and Iran. It is commonly understood that we are at war in Iraq, and fought in Kuwait, in large part to preserve our oil lifeline.

David L. Bosco, senior editor of *Foreign Policy Magazine*, and Joseph Cirincione, senior vice president for national security at the Center for American Progress, reported the results of a survey of the nation's top security experts on June 28, 2006. The respondents to this survey voted overwhelmingly that to reduce terror threats, reducing reliance on foreign oil is the number one issue to which the U.S. government ought to give top priority.[1]

The price of oil is forty dollars a barrel more than its cost to most producing nations. Oil producers overseas and in the U.S. are benefiting from the largest transfer of wealth in history. Russia, Venezuela, Iran, and Saudi Arabia have become financial giants. It is disturbing to me, having lived through the Cold War, that Russia is becoming more confrontational than friendly.

Our other large and life-threatening fossil fuel is coal. We now realize that the burning of oil, coal, and other fossil fuels creates a greenhouse effect that has caused the earth to warm at a very rapid rate, a worldwide average increase of 1 degree Fahrenheit in the past 100 years. Unless we change our ways, this trend will get worse and worse.[2]

We stand in imminent peril within the next decade or two of seeing more severe hurricanes, floods, and glacial ice melt, causing the seas to rise and our coastal areas to become inundated with water. If our high-energy civilization continues the large-scale burning of fossil fuels, it will constitute the most severe security problem that this nation and the world face. Terrorists can kill thousands of people at a time, but the consequences of Mother Nature can—and will—ruin the lives of hundreds of millions.

THE SOLUTION

Let us take a moment and lift our faces up and see this planet as it is. The most prominent force on Earth is the power of the sun. The overwhelming supply of energy on Earth comes free of charge from Mother Nature in the form of the sun's rays and the power of the winds and the natural growing system that we call biomass. Renewable energy that is possible from a combination of the sun, wind, waterpower, and biomass is immense in comparison to the fossil fuels and nuclear power from our light-water reactors fueled with uranium.

There are breakthroughs in new technology that promise to make the cost of solar power as low as that of coal, nuclear, and oil. Almost simultaneously in South Africa and the Silicon Valley in the United States, companies are building huge new solar factories to manufacture a paper-thin solar coating that can generate electricity that could actually *lower* our electric bills. These breakthroughs reflect decades of research. Investors are betting over $100 million that they will pay off. These breakthroughs promise solar power at 75 percent less than today's price. They are the best news ever in the field of energy because we now can use the sun to fuel our lifestyles—the cleanest and largest source of energy in the world.

This book will demonstrate that it is entirely practical and feasible to get all our energy from renewable resources and to do so with today's technology. We don't need to wait for decades in order to get started. The day that the United States commits itself to a sustainable march to an all-renewable energy economy is the day the world changes. It will change in these dramatic ways:

* We will become freer to assert a sane foreign policy without fear of blackmail by oil-producing nations.
* Suddenly the whole outlook toward the environment will change. The oceans will get cleaner, the air in our cities will become breathable and, most importantly, we will begin to reduce our carbon emissions rather than watching them increase. The damage from global warming, which may already be irreversible, will at least be contained and the worst may not happen.
* Our balance of trade numbers will get better and more of our money that formerly went overseas will be spent at home to create new green jobs and more economic growth in America.
* We will no longer debate over whether to drill in the areas we wish to preserve because we won't need the oil. We will use less and less oil each year.

The fact that it may take twenty or thirty years for a complete transition from fossil fuels and nuclear to renewables is not a reason to throw up our hands or delay. Quite the contrary, it means that it is important to lay out a thirty-year program with action starting now. We suffer today from the failure of our political and business leaders to plan and act prudently over the past thirty years.

Our impatient modern culture demands and expects results that are immediately tangible to the individual. Yet, two or three decades are a blink of an eye in the span of time for our children and grandchildren's generations and all those beyond. And it will go by in a flash if we don't begin today with a strong, steady effort to make progress toward our goal every year.

The problem that we face in the energy field is not the lack of renewable resources or the lack of the technology to utilize them. It is not well known to consumers that all our energy could come from renewables utilizing known technology, and at a lower cost to the public. Most people do not know where and how they could get renewable energy to drive their cars and light and heat their homes and offices, and they are unsure of how to proceed once they become aware of these facts. Educating the general public becomes the key component.

> I am reminded of Bill Clinton's favorite story. He went into a bar and saw a sign that said "Free Beer Tomorrow." He came back the next day and the sign still said "Free Beer Tomorrow." There is no waiting until tomorrow because it will never come unless we act today.

And there is a related problem. The scientific world shows little interest in applying what we already know and putting it into operation. It took 2,000 years to connect the wheel with luggage. Scientists love to invent new things and to tackle the toughest possible problem because that is what is most challenging. But the less interesting task of making use of what we know is often neglected. Let me illustrate.

Solar power is delivered to the earth's surface free of charge and can be converted to electricity with technology developed in the space program called photovoltaic cells. These cells have no moving parts and last a long time. And they work. The initial cost for photovoltaic cells is relatively high compared to other technologies, but the fuel cost (the sun) is zero. So, with the price of petroleum going up like a rocket, you would think that scientists would focus on promoting solar power and improving the known technology. Instead, the scientific research community is much more interested in fusion power. Fusion requires, believe it or not, that we duplicate the heat of the sun here on Earth, contain it, and learn how to make electricity from it. This research has been going on for more than fifty years and has not achieved scientific feasibility, not 1 kilowatt hour (kWh) net out of a fusion project. More than $10 billion has been spent on developing fusion technology since 1950.

THE SOLAR POWER ON THIS LAND COULD GENERATE ELECTRICITY THAT, IF CONVERTED TO HYDROGEN, COULD COMPLETELY REPLACE GASOLINE AND DIESEL

Research to utilize solar power here on Earth has, relatively speaking, had much less attention. But because of the space program, the technology does exist and there has been some technological and commercial development of photovoltaic cells. And at long last, private capital appears to be funding a solar revolution.

Although small-scale rooftop installations of photovoltaic cells can be a growing source of electricity, hot water, and hydrogen to fuel our cars, we have yet to focus on what I call "Big Solar." All of the U.S. petroleum needs could be met if we dedicated about 1 percent of the land area in the United States—which equals 4.5 percent of our deserts, or about 39,000 square miles—and erected solar collectors on the land, which would not be harmed one bit. The solar power on this land could generate electricity that, if converted to hydrogen, could completely replace gasoline and diesel. In short, our vast solar and wind potential for electricity, converted to hydrogen, could meet all of our energy needs, from driving our motor vehicles to heating our homes and other uses now being supplied by coal, nuclear, oil, and natural gas.[3] We would have our renewable energy when, where, and however we liked it.

This is how it could be done. With today's technology, we could convert that solar energy into electricity. The electricity would be transmitted by additions to the existing electrical transmission system that runs throughout the nation (also known as the energy grid, or "the grid"). The electricity can replace oil in the plug-in hybrid and all-electric cars that can be built with today's technology. In a few years some of the solar electricity could be converted into hydrogen with a machine that separates water into its two components, hydrogen and oxygen, using a process called electrolysis. With a pipeline system, we could transport the hydrogen across the nation over time. Or, we could use renewable power from the grid to make hydrogen at fueling stations.

People will say, "Well, what about the costs?" The oil people have given us an answer with their greed. We now need to focus on the price that consumers pay, which has little relation to cost. It's the price to the consumer at the pump, and not the actual cost of petroleum, that wins huge excess profits for oil companies, oil company executives, oil company major shareholders, and oil-producing nations. As I shall demonstrate, electricity to run a plug-in hybrid or an all-electric car is far cheaper for the consumer than gasoline pumped from the ground.

What about national security? What is it worth not to send young American men and women to the Middle East to defend our oil interests with their lives? The value of the lives lost is incalculable. However, one measurable cost is what we spend each day defending our oil lifeline to the Middle East—a cost that could be avoided if we had our own domestic energy supply. If you make even a rough estimate of the health and defense costs, you will find an amazing fact. Solar and wind electricity is the cheapest fuel for America today. The problem is that our accounting system for pricing fuels doesn't count the things that are valued the most in this world—health and security. And, therefore, we make the wrong decisions for the public and the right decisions for the profits of the coal, nuclear, and oil companies and the people who run them.

The fundamental route to change is to educate the people of the United States to the true facts about energy and to help them recognize there is not just a false hope that we may be able to move to a clean energy future.

The reality is that a renewable future is available if we can only muster the willpower to do what is in the interests of the people, rather than the interests of the oil lobby and their allies.

The solar power alone dwarfs our needs, but we need not put all of our eggs in a solar basket. Technology is much more advanced today in utilizing our wind resource, and the United States is home to one of the best wind resource areas in the world, the Midwest states of North and South Dakota, Nebraska, Kansas, Montana, Iowa, and Oklahoma.[4]

It's time for America to wake up. We can generate more than our annual electricity needs from the huge wind source in the United States.[5] To be specific, the wind potential in the United States has been very conservatively estimated at 500 million kW[6] onshore and 900 million kW offshore.[7] I am not suggesting that large parts of the United States be razed and covered with wind farms. These farms could be distributed throughout the vast wind resource areas in the nation, as well as off the coasts, and they would not even be noticed by 99 percent of the American people.[8] Grazing and farming could take place right up to the wind towers. We could easily replace a substantial portion of our coal- and nuclear-fueled plants in a couple of decades.

Geothermal energy is another reliable and renewable source of electricity. Geothermal plants can operate around the clock, providing us with a cleaner, reliable source of power.[9] Geothermal resource areas are mostly concentrated in the western states, and could provide more than 20 million kW of additional electric generating capacity. This is only a small percentage of national needs, but it is significant in the West, where geothermal resources are concentrated. This is just what is *presently* economic. If we dig deeper, the earth becomes hotter and hotter, and the energy potential becomes even greater. Scientists predict that there could be up to five times the current amount—100 million kW—as additional resources are discovered.[10]

There is also a huge source of renewable energy in the wastes that are leftover in the forests, in agriculture, and from municipal waste. Right now, about 90 percent of the ethanol produced in the United States comes from corn crops. In 2004, ethanol production claimed about 11 percent of the corn harvest in the United States, and experts say that this can be increased to a maximum of 20 percent before corn-based food supplies are disrupted, which would equal about 6 percent of our gasoline consumption.[11] This is not the big ticket we need. There is much talk of ethanol from sugar. That's great if you live in Brazil. But sugar-based ethanol in the United States means we're back in the import business, since America is too far north to grow large quantities of sugar. However, other products in the United States are currently being studied for their ability to make ethanol.

Forest residues and agricultural wastes can also help supply ethanol. But compared to the market for gasoline, they can add only another 5 or 10 percent to the solution. They alone cannot supply the solution, but it all adds up.

There is more good news in the huge potential to create ethanol and other biofuels from our nation's trash, about 280 million tons of which is usble for this purpose.[12] New technologies can be used to create biofuels and convert municipal waste in an environmentally satisfactory manner. Here again is another 5 to 10 percent substitute for gasoline.

Our path to 100 percent renewable energy will span several decades and incorporate a mixture of these resources. No one today can predict which member of the renewable family will dominate. It is enough to know that usable renewable resources are over twice as large as what we may need and, if used efficiently, can eliminate all the threats we face from existing sources.

But the unifying force needed to tap the potential of these resources and options has yet to coalesce. Consumers, angry over gasoline prices, are largely unaware of the plug-in hybrid. The "carbon only" environmentalists concerned about global warming don't give equal weight to the dangers of imported oil. Many concerned about oil dependency ignore the dangers of nuclear power. Others who focus only on nuclear proliferation and contamination don't talk much about the renewable alternatives.

These factions need to join together in the common solution to these problems. A unifying solution exists to control consumer costs, protect the security of this nation, combat the awesome threat of global warming, reduce the existing health menace of local air pollution, and decrease the radioactive dangers of nuclear power. Such a solution, advanced by a unifying coalition, could move us away from the energy sources that poison the environment and tie the hands of government to a dangerous foreign policy.

> **IT IS ENOUGH TO KNOW THAT USABLE RENEWABLE RESOURCES ARE OVER TWICE AS LARGE AS WHAT WE MAY NEED AND, IF USED EFFICIENTLY, CAN ELIMINATE ALL THE THREATS WE FACE FROM EXISTING SOURCES**

> You can take action yourself by buying the most fuel efficient car, air conditioner, or refrigerator, and by asking your utility to sell you green power. You can install solar panels on your roof and tell your elected representative to vote for the policies set forth in detail in this book.

BACK IN THE NIXON ADMINISTRATION, WE USED TO JOKE ABOUT GIVING THE ENVIRONMENTAL- ISTS "THE MUSIC" AND THE INDUSTRY "THE ACTION." THE TIME HAS COME TO GIVE THE PUBLIC INTEREST SOME ACTION

Back in the Nixon Administration, we used to joke about giving the environmentalists "the music" and the industry "the action." The time has come to give the public interest some action.

Never in the history of our energy policy have the combined problems become as critical and as potentially lethal as they have today. And it's not just because of the price of oil. This is the great American wake-up call. The environmental and foreign policy threats are no longer theoretical, and neither is the solution. The American people need their leaders to tell them that we are taking our future, and our children's future, into our own hands.

The giant glaciers in the Arctic and Antarctic are melting. Air pollution is causing epidemics of cancers and childhood breathing disorders throughout the high-energy world.

Our government has got its hands tied and is unable to carry out its foreign policy for fear of retaliation by governments of oil-producing nations.

Polar bears struggle to survive in a shrinking ice environment. Worldwide polar bear population is expected to plummet over the next fifty years. Source: World Prout Assembly

The world oil market is so fragile that any terrorist action, inflammatory speech, large hurricane in the Gulf of Mexico, or breakdown in the supply chain causes the price of oil to jump. Think what would happen if there were an industrial accident. Don't believe for a minute that terrorists don't consider oil as a weapon to our domestic security.

The threat, the danger, the reality of it all is very clear. What is not clear is the exciting fact that we have the resources from Mother Nature and the technology developed by humanity to relieve us of these poisons and this dependency. We can create a high-energy global civilization where each nation has its own homegrown, carbon-free renewable source of energy. This is not just a hope or a dream. It is a reality waiting to be implemented by the combined action and voice of ordinary people.

It is time for the common sense, can-do approach of the American people to move front and center and take over this issue. It's time to brush aside the false propaganda of the peddlers selling us air poisoned by oil and coal and radioactive trash, accompanied by the possibility of deadly releases of radioactivity from nuclear power.

This book documents that the solar world we live in is available to heat and cool our homes, run our cars, power our factories, and do all the things that our civilization requires. I am not talking about solutions that include brownouts or shortages. Indeed, these shortages will continue to get worse if we rely on the relatively scarce amount of petroleum and fossil fuels. We need to hitch our future to the only source of energy that makes life possible on this planet—the sun and its ancillary forces in the wind and the cycle of growing plants from Earth.

This book hopefully provides the foundation for a renewal of the American spirit that can solve our energy problems starting today, not tomorrow.

***

1   Center for American Progress, "The Terrorism Index: A Survey of the U.S. National Security Establishment on the War on Terror," panel presented by the Center for American Progress and *Foreign Policy Magazine* (June 28, 2006).
2   Intergovernmental Panel on Climate Change, "Climate Change 2001: Synthesis Report: Summary for Policymakers."
3   See calculations in chapter 4, "We Live in a Solar World."

4 Christina Archer and Mark Z. Jacobson, "Evaluation of Global Wind Power" (Stanford, CA: Department of Civil and Environmental Engineering, Stanford University, 2004).

5 U.S. Department of Energy (DOE), Energy Efficiency and Renewable Energy, Wind, and Hydropower Technologies Program (Sept. 8, 2006). http://eereweb.ee.doe.gov/windandhydro/wind_potential.html.

6 D. L. Elliot and M. N. Schwartz, "Wind Energy Potential in the United States" (Richland, WA: Pacific Northwest Laboratory, September 1993). http://www.nrel.gov/wind/wind_potential.html.

7 U.S. Department of the Interior, "Technology White Paper on Wind Energy Potential on the U.S. Outer Continental Shelf" (May 2006). http://ocsenergy.anl.gov/documents/docs/OCS_EIS_WhitePaper_Wind.pdf.

8 There are wind farms operating in twenty-six states from coast to coast in the United States.

9 Charles F. Kutscher, United States National Renewable Energy Laboratory, "The Status and Future of Geothermal Power" (August 2000). http://www.nrel.gov/geothermal/pdfs/28204.pdf. Geothermal plants operate 90 percent of the time, compared with an average of 60 to 70 percent for coal and nuclear plants.

10 Ibid.

11 Eric Heitz and Patrick Mazza, "The New Harvest: Biofuels and Windpower for Rural Revitalization and National Energy Security" (San Francisco CA: The Energy Foundation, November 2005).

12 Environmental and Energy Study Institute, "Ethanol, Climate Protection, Oil Reduction," 9 (May 25, 2000).

2 RAISING THE BAR

{A Stronger Effort Is Needed} ✳✳✳

IN A RECENT PRIVATE CONVERSATION WITH SI RAMO—the R in TRW, a huge industrial company—ninety-two-year-old Mr. Ramo said that he was optimistic about America's future. I asked why. He said things were now so bad that America would do something about them. He pointed out that Americans were not good at preventing trouble but when the danger to our country became unmistakable, we had a pretty good track record of turning things around.

I share that optimism. But we Americans need to be sure that the actions we take are designed to deal decisively with our energy problems. We will cure our energy troubles once we set in motion programs that will start a decline in the use of fossil fuels and nuclear power. We need to get on a path to obtain most of our energy from renewables by thirty years from now, one year at a time.

The current debate reveals a growing awareness of runaway prices at the gasoline pump and higher and higher utility bills. Americans are also aware of local air pollution, global warming, and oil dependency. The American people are frustrated and would support serious action, which their common sense tells them is necessary and possible. But many have the feeling that our leaders are being misled by the big industries. In my view, the common-sense gut feeling of ordinary people is more correct than the experts who say we must expand the use of "clean" fossil fuels and "safe" nuclear power. We, the people, know better.

Frankly, the reform proposals of even the advocates of change fall far short of the path to victory over the growingly expensive life-threatening poisons we now use. For example, neither the consumer advocates nor the regulators are "raising the bar" high enough for efficiency or renewables in the current energy debate. We are bogged down in a seemingly endless struggle over bits and pieces of what is needed to really fix the problems. Even the good guys are not seeking the whole strong package of what is needed to secure our energy future.

There seems to be a serious lack of urgency by President Bush and Congress. Everyone knows America can build cars that use less energy. But the big campaign contributions of the auto industry and the political

power of their allied unions have stopped the legislation to require it done. Once the cars are built, most folks are stuck with what they have purchased for years. Investments in efficiency would actually increase economic growth because they are lower in cost than the fuel they displace. This is particularly true in the case of inefficient automobiles, as half of the money for purchasing oil goes overseas to the producing nations and we have little or no control over the price.

Smog is a familiar sight in American cities. The American Lung Association of California reports that nearly 100 million Americans live in areas that do not meet federal ozone standards. Source: DOE/NREL

STEP ONE: FEDERAL EFFICIENCY PROGRAMS

The first step in "raising the bar" is to have federal government-mandated efficiency programs for utilities, auto companies, manufacturers of energy-using equipment, and home builders that will achieve additional energy savings each year.

We can easily provide enough saved energy to fuel the growth in the American economy required to meet increased demand. American consumers would continue to have the same choices in cars, homes, appliances, and so on; they just wouldn't need as much gasoline or electricity to fuel their lifestyle choices.

The energy debate is not being presented to the American people in a straightforward, common-sense manner. Instead, we are left with the impression that renewables can supply at best 20 percent of our electricity years from now, and that ethanol and other biofuels are what environmentalists are really proposing. Biofuels can help, but in the small numbers that exist today and even tomorrow, they don't come near to solving our problems.

Typical of what Americans hear and see on television was a segment on MSNBC's *Meet the Press* on Sunday, June 18, 2006, devoted to "Pain at the Pump" and alternatives. Who were the guests? The CEOs of three major oil companies! And what was their answer? We need to drill offshore of California and Florida, we need to drill in the Arctic, and then we need to dig up the tar sands in Canada and the shale oil in the West. No mention of global warming, local air pollution, or destroying what's left of America the beautiful. And what did the host throw out as an alternative? Not plug-in hybrids or all-electric cars or hydrogen, but our old enemy nuclear power, as though it were a new idea.

A great number of books discuss the world's running out of oil. In my view the greatest danger to humanity and the planet is our finding and using more and more oil. That would certainly assure further devastation from global warming, more health concerns from local air pollution, and continued dependence on the governments that support terror on this earth. Remember, the last thirty years of oil extraction have shown that we have "drained America first."

THE FIRST STEP IN "RAISING THE BAR" IS TO HAVE FEDERAL GOVERNMENT-MANDATED EFFICIENCY PROGRAMS FOR UTILITIES, AUTO COMPANIES, MANUFACTURERS OF ENERGY-USING EQUIPMENT, AND HOME BUILDERS THAT WILL ACHIEVE ADDITIONAL ENERGY SAVINGS EACH YEAR

A favorite trick of the energy establishment is to say our problems are so big that we have to try everything—extract oil wherever the oil people want to drill, build nuclear reactors, and strip mine coal. Of course, they mention solar and conservation to appear to be open minded. But by doing so they ignore the fact that coal, oil, and nuclear cause the problems while renewables are the solution and are fully capable of meeting all our energy needs. The energy industry is, in effect, cleverly saying we must continue using oil, coal, and nuclear solutions because there isn't enough renewable energy to do the job. They are wrong, but they are getting away with it. With such one-sided, misleading presentations to the American people it is no wonder we are confused as to what to do.

It is true that renewables are now a fashionable theory to favor "for the future." Even the oil companies and President Bush are giving renewables some music. But the serious question is, "Where is the beef" in today's federal

The Trans-Alaskan Pipeline System transmits oil 800 miles overland to then be shipped to the lower forty-eight states. Source: Arctic Power

programs? Where is the path that will steadily reduce oil consumption? It's not there, but it can be.

Just as the warming of the earth and the melting ice in the Arctic and Antarctic is proof that global warming is real, it is the price of gasoline—the "pain at the pump"—that has brought home to the American people that we need something else. We now have environmental and foreign policy concerns joined by a concern that's very real and current— prices are beyond America's control.

Windfall profits are going to oil companies and oil-producing nations. This is a tax that we can't even vote on. It is proof that this problem can be cured only by a homegrown alternative. And fortunately, that's just what we have.

STEP TWO: PHASING OUT COAL AND NUCLEAR POWER PLANTS

As I stated in chapter one, we obtain 75 percent of our energy today from what I call the three poisons—coal, oil, and nuclear power. So the second step in raising the bar is to have federally mandated laws that force the retirement of fossil fuel and nuclear power plants, which will be replaced by renewable resources. Currently there is no program being advocated in any serious way to assure the three poisons will ever be replaced by renewables. But they can be replaced. Here's how.

The electric power industry could make the transition to renewables if we simply outlaw new coal or nuclear plants, place a reasonable retirement age on the existing plants, and replace them with renewable alternatives—sun, wind, geothermal, biomass, and municipal waste.

Most of our coal and nuclear plants are old. The law should require that a gradual retirement of coal and nuclear be completed in thirty years. We would, of course, do it on a timetable providing a five-year period to build efficiency improvements and renewable resources as a replacement. As a former utilities executive, I know the power system must be reliable. The cleanest of the fossil fuels—natural gas plants—should be allowed to continue to generate power, together with storage options, to assure reliability during hours when the renewables are not available.

The Sacramento Municipal Utility District's first solar array, PV-1, the first utility-scale solar array in the nation, sits in the foreground of the cooling towers at the decommissioned Rancho Seco Nuclear Station. Since PV-1 was constructed in 1984, five more arrays have been built at the site, producing 3.2 megawatts, enough electricity to power about 2,200 single-family homes. Source: www.smud.org

That approach can work for the current uses of electricity. But as we shall later discuss, electricity from the grid can be a growing source for running our cars. The hybrid car has an electric motor and, when it has a plug-in feature, its batteries can be charged by electricity from the grid when it is parked at homes (overnight) and businesses (during the day). This electric current can power cars most of the time and can be a major replacement for gasoline. It will require renewable electricity in excess of today's electric loads.

This basic understanding makes clear that what I suggest is practical, doable, and economical as the cost of fossil fuels skyrockets and the dangers of nuclear power escalate. A requirement of steadily increasing portfolio standards for utilities may be the best way to implement this solution.

The major point here is that phasing out coal and nuclear is doable and practical. These fuels are used almost exclusively to make electricity, and the utilities are largely regulated. This basic approach would outlaw any new coal and nuclear production plants and set forth a timetable to go steadily from the 9 percent renewables[1] used today to 60 percent by 2037, with the rest of the portfolio supplied by natural gas.

STEP THREE: REDUCE AMERICA'S DEPENDENCY ON OIL

The third step for raising the bar is to reduce America's dependency on oil.

There is not yet even a foundation or platform for "winning" the battle to replace oil, where the danger is most acute. Oil is polluting the air, warming the earth, and has the U.S. in a straitjacket because of our dependency on imports from nations and regions that draw us into war and fund terror organizations with oil money. To add insult to injury, the price of oil has now itself become a serious threat to our ability to pay our bills.

The argument that renewables are too expensive is now answered at the gas pump and in utility bills. Oil prices are set by a world market that America has no way of controlling. As millions of people in China and India begin to have the resources to buy cars, the price of oil is apt to continue on an upward spiral.

In contrast, renewables, once the initial investment is made, are virtually fixed in price. Electricity from the sun and wind has no fuel costs and requires very little labor after renewable stations are built. Their costs remain stable.

THE THIRD STEP FOR RAISING THE BAR IS TO REDUCE AMERICA'S DEPENDENCY ON OIL

It should be clear that switching to renewables will stabilize the future cost of energy. It will keep the money in America, create more jobs, and alleviate environmental and foreign policy concerns.

The stakes are high. The enormous amount of oil that the U.S. consumes must be reduced. The alternative fuels programs to replace oil must be aggressive and steady.

Today's consumers know that cars with better mileage are available. They have seen advertisements and read about them in scientific magazines. But there are no programs, incentives, or requirements in place that would make more than a dent in reducing our oil consumption. Most people don't even have an overall understanding of how we can "put sunshine in the gas tank." In fact, some Americans have never even heard that gasoline could, in fact, be replaced—they have only the fear of a gas shortage and the reality that prices are out of control.

In total, America's petroleum consumption is more than 7 billion barrels of oil per year, 20 million barrels per day; 67 percent of which is used for ground transportation. Aircraft usage is 9 percent, home heating 5 percent, and the rest goes to industry.[2]

All this oil can be replaced by homegrown energy in four forms:

* Cars with better mileage
* Electricity made from renewables for plug-in hybrid cars
* Biofuels
* Hydrogen made from renewable electricity and water

The auto industry has steadily made its engines more fuel efficient. But for the last fifteen years, instead of improving mileage for consumers, they have used extra energy to make their cars bigger (SUVs) with more add-ons and luxuries.

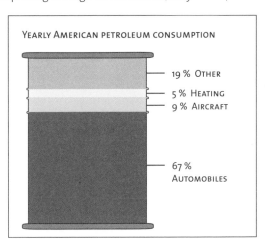

YEARLY AMERICAN PETROLEUM CONSUMPTION

19 % OTHER

5 % HEATING

9 % AIRCRAFT

67 %
AUTOMOBILES

We now face a crisis. Even the American auto companies are feeling the pain, in large part because they have promoted cars that many Americans can no longer afford to run and are not interested in buying. It is in the national interest—and it is an act of patriotism—for the current legal requirement of 27.5 mpg (miles per gallon) for cars and 20.7 mpg for trucks and SUVs to be raised one mpg each year indefinitely. That means that in twenty-four years, gasoline consumption in cars would be cut in half for the same number of cars. There will, of course, be more people and more cars, but higher gasoline prices, better mass transit, and motor vehicles that use very little or no oil can achieve a massive reduction in oil consumption.

The achievement of a 50 percent reduction in gasoline consumption through steady reduction over the next twenty-four years becomes believable as we recognize the role that plug-in hybrid and flex-fuel cars can play. The hybrid car is already being manufactured, and the plug-in feature will be added in this decade. It provides an early and easily achievable way to substitute renewable electricity for gasoline.

It is entirely feasible for most American cars to be plug-in hybrids within the next ten to fifteen years. But it will take the combination of stronger overall efficiency standards and tax incentives for this to happen. Replacing passenger cars with plug-in hybrids for all car models will enable America to cut gasoline consumption in half within the next twenty years. Buses

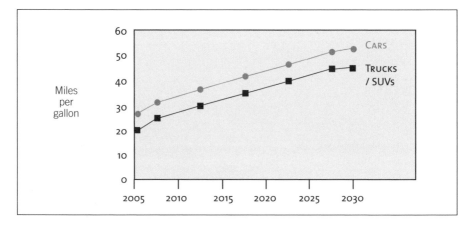

Projected fuel efficiency of vehicles

and trucks will also benefit from hybrid technology and natural gas, and could cut in half their consumption of petroleum over the same twenty-year period.

As renewable hydrogen becomes available, hybrid vehicles can become zero-oil vehicles. It is possible to completely replace petroleum in cars within thirty years if we decide to do it. Within a thirty-year timeframe, airplanes can fly, and fly farther safely, on renewable hydrogen. As oil furnaces are replaced in future years, home heating can be converted to natural gas and biogas from municipal waste. Biofuels can play a significant role, reducing petroleum a further 50 percent, or down to 20 percent of today's usage.

All of these efforts need to be launched at once, and if they are, we can start reducing our use of petroleum this year and every year thereafter. We're in a battle and the frontlines are here, at home, and every man, woman, and child can help America win.

The battle is already taking shape. When gas prices rose in 2006, the consumption of gasoline actually leveled off. And it's no wonder. Americans had very little choice but to cut back on their mobility in order to balance their household budgets. But most people are stuck with the cars and trucks they own, so the major reaction to higher prices is shock and awe at the pump. But the long-term reaction is that the next motor vehicle most people will buy will be more fuel efficient. That's already happening, and that's significant.

The high price of petroleum has now emerged as perhaps the strongest force for renewables. Consumers can't make their own cars. But they can tell the car companies that "I want my next car to be a plug-in hybrid." Hopefully the federal and state governments will enact tax credits to off-set the higher first cost of the plug-in hybrid (about $5,000–$10,000) so that plug-ins soon become the standard car.

The alternatives to gasoline are here. What is needed is the will of the people to be channeled into a series of governmental actions and individual choices that enable us to march steadily ahead in reducing our oil dependence and emissions of carbon at the same time.

* * *

1 Hydro 6.8 percent, other renewables 2.3 percent. U.S. Department of Energy, Energy Information Administration (U.S. DOE EIA), "Summary Statistics for the United States" (November 9, 2006), http://www.eia. doe.gov/cneaf/electricity/epa/epates.html.
2 U.S. DOE EIA, "Petroleum Navigator: Product Supplied" (October 2, 2006), http://tonto.eia.doe.gov/dnav/pet/pet_cons_psup_dc_nus_mbbl_a.htm.

3 THE THREE POISONS

{THE DANGERS OF OIL, COAL, AND NUCLEAR} ✳✳✳

LET'S EXAMINE THE MAJOR ENERGY SOURCES we use today, one at a time, and why we must stop using them as quickly as possible and transition to renewable sources.

NUCLEAR

In his State of the Union address on January 31, 2006, President George W. Bush stated emphatically that America needs to "kick the oil habit."

That thought has not been lost on the atomic power industry, which has now emerged from its market-driven grave to announce its availability to save the day.

The concern now in an age of terror is that an atomic power plant complex has the destructive power of a bomb if terrorists hit it with a missile or a large airplane. The nuclear industry must concede that the risk to society is greater than zero.

This time around, the atomic power proponents are also a bit more modest than their "too cheap to meter" opening line almost fifty

> The nuclear crowd has always been good at propaganda. When I first became director of the Tennessee Valley Authority in 1977, the staff gave me a T-shirt that said, "Nuclear power is safer than sex." This was supposedly based on a study at Oak Ridge National Lab that showed more radiation was emitted when two human bodies rubbed together than the routine emissions of a nuclear power plant. The decades since then have shown that both nuclear power and sex can be dangerous—quite dangerous, in fact, with the known perils of massive releases of nuclear radiation and the AIDS epidemic. I'll leave it to the reader to decide which, nuclear power or sex, he or she wishes to do without.

years ago. They really don't speak much about cost. They advance nuclear as a clean alternative to imported oil but fail to even mention that we use almost no oil in making electricity.

Back in the 1960s, atomic power was considered the wave of the future. In 1965 I was retained briefly by the Peabody Coal Company to make plans for creating more public power agencies in the West. The idea was to lower the cost of coal-fired plants. This stemmed from the fear that nuclear power was going to take all of Peabody's business. And, for a while, business did shift toward nuclear energy. But nuclear power failed to deliver on its promises. In 1978 the power industry stopped building and buying nuclear energy. Today's nuclear power lobbyists act as though everyone has forgotten their failures. Well, I haven't.

NO ONE, NOT THE PRESIDENT OR ANY SCIENTIST, CAN ACCURATELY CALL A FORM OF ENERGY "SAFE" THAT IS INHERENTLY CAPABLE OF RELEASING MASS DOSES OF CANCER-CAUSING RADIATION AND CREATING RADIOACTIVE WASTES THAT WE DON'T KNOW WHAT TO DO WITH

Back in the 1970s, I often said that the commonsense concern that the average American had about nuclear safety would turn out to be more accurate than the opinions of the so-called scientific experts who pronounced it safe. Those concerns were brought to the living rooms of all Americans by television during the Three Mile Island meltdown. This catastrophe, coupled with huge cost overruns, stopped the nuclear stampede thirty years ago.

President George W. Bush said on May 24, 2006, "Nuclear power is safe." No one, not the president or any scientist, can accurately call a form of energy "safe" that is inherently capable of releasing mass doses of cancer-causing radiation and creating radioactive wastes that we don't know what to do with. And when the wastes are reprocessed, as the president proposes, the plutonium will separate into a usable form that can fuel a bomb.

The president and the nuclear lobby can certainly express their opinion that the risks are low and the U.S. should take that risk rather than harness the sun and the wind. They are entitled to their opinion. But they are wrong. President George W. Bush and the nuclear lobby would do well to listen to Mikhail Gorbachev, who was president of the Soviet Union at the time of the Chernobyl accident. He, like myself, has had hands-on experience with nuclear power. In 2006, Mr. Gorbachev said, "Nuclear power is neither the answer to modern energy problems nor a panacea for climate change challenges. You don't actually solve problems by finding solutions that create more problems down the track. It doesn't add up economically, environmentally, or socially."[1]

I have been an active participant in the electric power industry over the last forty years. I've been a regulator, a policymaker, and the CEO of a number of large public power systems. I know of no failure as clear and dramatic as the failure of nuclear power on both public safety and economics.

Historically, nuclear power has built up high expectations from the American public but has followed up with only a series of failures. Fifty years after the first commercial nuclear reactor began service in Shippingport, Pennsylvania, in 1957, the nuclear industry has failed on all counts:

* Failed to find a safe place to store its wastes
* Achieved the largest cost overruns in utility history
* Failed to perfect any of the fundamentally safer reactor concepts
* Failed to develop the breeder reactor that would make nuclear a large source of usable energy
* Failed so miserably in the marketplace that no nuclear plants have come online in ten years, and no new ones have been ordered in thirty years
* Failed to be safe or economically viable enough to even afford its own insurance after more than five decades and billions of dollars in research

My insight into nuclear safety was formed during the 1973 oil embargo when a group of reporters from around the U.S. came to Washington, D.C., to be briefed by "us experts." Before I started speaking, a reporter from Iowa raised his hand and said, "Mr. Freeman, I have an observation that I'd like you to comment on. We were just briefed by Mr. Milton Shaw of the Atomic Energy Commission and he explained in great detail how a nuclear power plant worked. He is obviously a very skilled person. My observation is that Mr. Shaw might be able to operate a nuclear plant quite well, but I wonder if he isn't about the only one who can. It seemed awfully complicated."

I replied, "Sir, that's the problem. Nuclear power demands perfection in its manufacture, its operations, and its maintenance. It also demands instantaneous reaction to trouble. Given those challenges, if we build enough of them, America is going to have a lot of trouble."

Yet the advocates of nuclear power have launched a new initiative that fails even to address the failures of the past. Instead, they stress that nuclear energy is carbon free and is the sure cure for global warming.

Spare me the cure. All radiation—including the routine emissions referred to by the pseudo-magical term "low-level" radiation—can cause cancer. There is no threshold below which radiation emitted routinely by

nuclear power plants is absolutely safe.[2] In addition, radioactive tritium has leaked into the groundwater at twelve operating nuclear reactors.[3] And radioactive wastes are dumped into waste dumps not licensed for that purpose.

It is important that the large number of younger Americans who have not heard about nuclear dangers and failures are told the truth. The truth will not come from the federal government of 2006, which is more pronuclear than at any other time since 1975. But the information is out there.

In a hospital in Kiev, April 6, 2006, a Ukrainian woman who was exposed to radiation from the Chernobyl nuclear power plant explosion rests after her cancerous thyroid was removed.
Source: Corbis

The Dangers

Let's examine some of the very real and specific dangers of nuclear energy.

The nuclear reactor's potential for massive destruction is an immediate danger. Nuclear plants are vulnerable to accidents. The younger generations don't remember Chernobyl and Three Mile Island, but those older than forty-five should. Those were terrifying days for the entire world, and the lessons learned should never be forgotten.

Nuclear power plants have now become a prime target for terrorists. Terrorists have the opportunity to hit the U.S. with the radioactive force of a massive atomic bomb without even having to smuggle weapons across our borders. Make no mistake, these nuclear plants, especially the pools full of radioactive fuel, while well fortified and policed, can be penetrated by an airplane or missile attack. It would take only one.

The atomic power cycle provides the means and excuse for politically unstable and unfriendly nations—as well as terrorists—to build an atomic bomb.

Nuclear power generation creates "spent fuel" that remains highly radioactive for hundreds, even thousands of years. It won't go away; there is no safe grave or burial site. This is the "forever" problem. Not only have individual states passed laws about not having radioactive waste deposited within their boundaries, but several have passed laws that assure that the radioactive waste will not even be transported across their state lines! There must be something wrong with these waste products if no one wants them in their backyards. This shortsightedness is an immoral radioactive legacy we leave our descendants. Alone, this is enough reason to stop making more nuclear waste. (See Nuclear-Waste Storage Sites Map in map insert section.)

The mining of uranium exposes miners to lung disease and leaves behind radioactive wastes in the form of mill tailings that remain dangerous for hundreds of thousands of years.

It is not necessary to agree on the size of the nuclear risk. Even the nuclear industry must agree that it is much greater than zero! Why take such a risk when there are benign alternatives? No sane nation in a war with terrorists would consider building more and more nuclear plants. The George W. Bush administration, Congress, and, oddly, some in the environmental movement are trying to do just that. It is bad enough that we are stuck with old, decaying nuclear power plants. New nuclear facilities will just increase the risks of accidents and provide more targets for deliberate meltdown by terrorists.

The Costs

Now for the costs. As mentioned earlier, despite all these safety risks, nuclear power also has failed economics. No U.S. utility has ordered a new nuclear plant since 1973, and this market failure is not a mystery. Nuclear was hyped in the 1960s as being "too cheap to meter" and ended up in the 1980s as "too expensive to build."

Nuclear power is a poor economic risk because no private insurance is available for an accident that causes billions of dollars of damage. No utility is willing to take the risk without such insurance. The cost is too high. Without the subsidy of federal insurance, the nuclear option is dead. The federal government—meaning the American taxpayer—takes the

NUCLEAR POWER IS A POOR ECONOMIC RISK BECAUSE NO PRIVATE INSURANCE IS AVAILABLE FOR AN ACCIDENT THAT CAUSES BILLIONS OF DOLLARS OF DAMAGE

TENNESSEE VALLEY AUTHORITY

President Carter appointed me director and chairman of the TVA in 1977. I was responsible for a utility that had three large atomic power units operating and fourteen under construction at the time. My vote was decisive in stopping construction of eight of these units. It was not the safety concerns that stopped the building of those units, as serious as they were, but rather the skyrocketing costs that triggered rate increases for customers. TVA would almost certainly have been bankrupted long ago had I not shut the nuclear power plants down. I shut them down because they cost too much.

I found that even the cost just to complete the partially built plants would result in higher electricity costs than that of the available alternatives. We stopped construction on eight large one-million-kW units and we had to lay off thousands of construction workers. This was not an easy decision to make. Tennessee is my home state and everyone there loved nuclear power. The Oakridge, Tennessee, high school football team was called "The Bombers." But to continue pouring good money into bad ideas would have been ruinous for the TVA ratepayers and for TVA itself.

Author listening to concerns of residents who lived near the Sequoia nuclear plant during his time as general manager of TVA.

risk. It is ironic that the federal government, and particularly the Bush administration, which preaches the virtues of the free-market economy when it comes to regulating pollution and deregulating the price of electricity, is able to overcome its economic principles when it comes to nuclear power.

Subsidizing the risk inherent in nuclear power is only the first basic assist that the federal government gives the nuclear industry. Between 1948 and 1998, Congress approved $66 billion on nuclear power research and development. The Energy Policy Act of 2005 approved over $4 billion in tax breaks.[4] These amounts dwarf the puny incentives for solar energy. In addition, and of growing proportions, are the costs of protecting atomic power plants with aerial surveillance and added homeland security. The nuclear waste problem is largely viewed as a safety concern. However, if there is radioactive trash that will be lethal for many thousands of years, there is a cost to keeping it reasonably safe. These costs will go on and on and on. They are large and pretty much incalculable. We can be sure of only one thing—our kids and grandkids will pay the bill.

In the recent attempt to resurrect the nuclear option, no one seems to be mentioning the total cost of running and maintaining the existing nuclear plants.

My experience at TVA was that nuclear energy costs over ten cents/kWh. This was based on costs of construction twenty years ago. Cost information for new plants is conspicuous by its absence. None have been built for decades. The estimates for new nuclear facilities, with all their risks, are more expensive than the development of wind, solar, geothermal, or biomass facilities, which don't carry the life-and-death risks.

Author meeting with President Jimmy Carter in the Oval Office in 1977.

Atoms for Peace, Atoms for War

It is useful to recall that the entire "peaceful atom" program began out of an American guilt trip over dropping the bomb on Japan. We felt duty bound, as President Truman said, to "make a blessing out of it." President Eisenhower felt the same way and gave a famous "Atoms for Peace" speech at the United Nations in which he said, "If the fearful trend of atomic military build up can be reversed, this greatest of destructive forces can be developed into a great boon, for the benefit of all mankind."[5]

The current light-water reactors were never supposed to be the end result—they were supposed

Right after I left TVA in 1984, I was honored as Conservationist of the Year by the National Wildlife Federation. It was the result of TVA's new programs in soil and energy conservation. It's a very prestigious award. I think it was highly unusual for a utility executive to get it.

At about that time I also received an honorary degree from Williams College, an Ivy League school in New England, for our work in energy efficiency and shutting down nuclear power plants. I remember receiving the award in a ceremony that also recognized U.S. representative Morris Udall (D-Ariz.) and Amory Lovins, a noted energy conservationist. I felt honored to be in their company.

to be just the first step toward the breeder reactors, which were promised to the public as a truly huge source of power. The idea was to take the spent fuel from the light-water reactors and reprocess it to extract the plutonium to fuel the breeders and then bury the wastes in the ground somewhere.

The problem is that the breeder reactors failed both economically and operationally here in the United States., in France, and elsewhere. The Bush administration wants to resume the reprocessing of spent fuel, as is currently done in France. Reprocessing creates plutonium, the material atomic bombs are made of, and has no place to be stored safely. Over $100 billion, in 1996 dollars, has been spent by nations trying to commercialize breeder reactors that use reprocessed plutonium. All they've created are nuclear proliferation concerns, with no commercial success.

Loose plutonium becomes a principal concern for the proliferation of atomic bombs that can be made by terrorists or rogue nations. Don't forget that enriching uranium is another path to the bomb and is part of the same technology used to make fuel for a reactor.

America has sold other nations on an "Atoms for Peace" program. This program is based on the agreement that "If you promise not to make a bomb, America will help you make electricity out of the atom." Now we

THE FRENCH EXPERIENCE

The French nuclear program is often held out by American nuclear advocates as an example of success. The first point to recognize is that the French program is cited because the U.S. experience has been a failure. France has a government-controlled nuclear monopoly—one manufacturer and one utility. Their regulatory process has only recently been open to serious public participation. Yet it is true that at present they do generate most of their electricity with nuclear reactors.

We do know that there is strong opposition to new nuclear plants in France, and we know that the French breeder program failed. We also know they reprocess their spent fuel and that of Japan. They have about 80 metric tons of surplus plutonium in storage in La Havre, France.[6]

The French plutonium stockpile is a tempting source for terrorists to gain the material to make a bomb or export to other nations that may someday wish to add to nuclear proliferation. In addition, France stores liquid high-level wastes in tanks that require constant cooling. They too are vulnerable to accidents and terror attacks. The whole French economy is vulnerable because they are just one accident away from nuclear disaster.

French electric rates are at the same level as the U.S. so nuclear power doesn't seem to result in lower rates. Perhaps the most telling point is that for the past two years the French have been going gangbusters for wind power. They will have 2 million kW from wind power by the start of 2007 and their target is 13.5 million kW by 2010.[7]

find that we must break that agreement because we know that atomic electric energy is the path for making a bomb and that some countries, such as Iran and North Korea, have notoriously proven themselves not to be trusted with atomic energy. Other countries' stability and trustworthiness is only as good as their current governments.

In truth, there is no such thing as the peaceful atom. We cannot with a straight face pursue atomic programs at home, with all our bombs and nuclear power plants, and then persuade other nations not to make a bomb. Nuclear power plants themselves are inherently dangerous and are huge threats to domestic security. It is time to recognize that atomic energy is a deadly hazard to humanity. "Atoms for peace" is just another name for "atoms for war."

The Alternative

The American people, when asked to compare nuclear with solar, know better than the so-called experts. No one in his or her right mind could prefer a radioactive factory to one that harnesses the sun! As a substitute for oil, coal, and nuclear energy, the sun can replace the three poisons with inexhaustible fuel. By contrast, it must be noted that the uranium supply in the U.S. is a relatively small source of energy. Renewables pose none of the hazards of atomic energy, are far more plentiful, and are much lower in cost to the consumers who ultimately pay all the bills. Rather than granting massive subsidies to resurrect a technology that is inherently dangerous and a failure, let's put American money and ingenuity into advancing a safe and superabundant alternative with costs that are inflation proof (the sun goes up but not its price).

The American people haven't been given the straight talk that they have a choice between renewables and nuclear energy. Nuclear power plants don't replace oil, they are just a man-made attempt to eclipse the sun.

PETROLEUM

Thirty years ago the oil industry had a slogan, "A nation that runs on oil can't afford to run short." They were right. We have found out the hard way. We're overly dependent on oil, and we have been lazy about developing the alternatives. Oil, like nuclear power, is a cause and instrument of war. It also has proven to be destructive of the environment.

The Dangers

Oil does not just beckon big trouble—it is already big trouble today.

The harsh fact is that nearly all of the nation's cars, trucks, railroads, airplanes, and buses run on oil, about two-thirds of which is imported. The United States consumes about 20 million barrels of oil per day, 25 percent of the world's oil consumption.[8] The worldwide demand for oil keeps growing as millions of people in developing countries begin to drive cars. China is even expected to surpass the U.S. as the world's greatest guzzler of oil by 2025. Rather than racing to become the greatest guzzler, I'd like to propose that, as America cuts back on petroleum usage, the race should be to see which country can get off oil the soonest. (See Known Oil Fields in the United States Map in the map insert section.)

The petroleum supply is barely meeting demand today. The market is currently so tight that any oil-producing nation or group of nations can use oil as an economic and political weapon by taking their oil off the market, causing shortages that will drive the price up. This action can literally bring this country and others around the world to a screeching halt. This is not an idle threat. The Arab oil-producing nations in OPEC actually shut off their oil exports to the U.S. in 1973, and cars and trucks had to wait in long lines to get gas. And there was a similar event in 1979.

America is especially vulnerable to attack by the oil weapon not only because we are so grossly dependent on imported oil, but also because

IN MANY WAYS OUR OIL DEPENDENCE HAS ACTUALLY *BECOME* OUR FOREIGN POLICY

many of the oil-producing nations disagree with U.S. foreign policy, such as the war on terrorism, our sending troops to Iraq, and our support of Israel. And, indeed, the extreme fundamentalists disagree with our way of life.

The danger of our oil lifeline being severed is manifold. We could witness a deliberate act to withhold supply by a nation such as Iran, whose government is in serious conflict with us and has openly threatened such action. Or we could suffer from political upheaval. There could be a coup in Saudi Arabia and a government sympathetic to terrorists could take control. They could quickly cut back on their sizable production and jack the price of oil up to double today's price. A more terrifying and perhaps more likely threat is that terrorists could blow up the oil infrastructure in Saudi Arabia, Russia, or America. Of course, terrorists have done just that in Iraq, where oil production is below the levels that it was under Saddam Hussein.

The impact of our dependence on imported oil is a huge anchor on the U.S. ship of state that influences our foreign policy and our domestic economy. In many ways our oil dependence has actually *become* our foreign policy. Let me illustrate.

America's oil dependency puts a limit on our support of Israel, the only real democracy in the Middle East. Our ability to support Israel is restrained because of our fear of offending Saudi Arabia and other Arab oil-producing nations. Politicians fear what may happen if America ever had to choose between supporting Israel or fueling our cars. Remember, it was our support of Israel that caused the 1973 oil embargo.

America does not have a free hand as long as the Arab nations have the power to stop our ability to drive to work. Would America have sold advanced fighter planes to Saudi Arabia if we didn't need its oil? Would we have gone to war in Kuwait if we weren't worried about the Saudi oil fields falling into unfriendly hands? Would we be tolerating the Saudi money going to the terrorists? Oil has tied our hands in the Middle East and demanded our presence to protect our oil lifeline there at huge cost to the U.S. in money and lives lost.

Our dependence on imported oil also inhibits the U.S. in negotiating with Iran. We don't import oil directly from Iran. But they are a large enough producer that if they cut back their oil, it would cause sharp increases in the world price of oil. The tightness of the world's oil market enables Iran to grant favors to other nations who, in turn, refuse to support initiatives by the U.S. to restrain Iran. It is difficult for America to get any nation to partner with us in applying sanctions against Iran to stop their support of terrorists, their threats and funding of Hezbollah to destroy Israel, or their program to build atomic bombs.

Don't be deceived by pro-democracy rhetoric that Americans and Iraqis are being killed in Iraq just to

In 1970, I sat on a task force headed by George Schultz, who later became the secretary of state. This task force published a report concluding that if oil imports outside of the Western Hemisphere exceeded 10 percent, the U.S. had a serious national security problem. It is now thirty-five years later, our imports are about 60 percent of our total oil supply, hugely greater than 10 percent from outside the Western Hemisphere, and our national security is seriously imperiled by our dependence on imported oil. In fact, it is one of the few conclusions that every president since Richard Nixon has agreed on.

ensure a better way of life. There are dictatorial thugs on the African continent presiding over genocide, but we are not invading their countries. We
even support some of them, like the dictatorship in Equatorial Guinea, for
the sake of oil.

The common threat in our policy is oil—our current dependence on it. Oil
production in Iraq is important to world supply—some 2 million barrels a
day—and Iraq is also home to sizeable oil reserves for the future.

Journalist Fareed Zakaria said it best in the *Washington Post*: "Reducing
our dependence on oil would be the single greatest multiplier of American
power in the world."[9]

The Cost

It's not just our foreign policy that is being constrained by oil. People don't
realize the enormous flow of wealth taking place from the U.S. to the oil-
producing nations. In 2005, it was more than $200 billion![10] In 2006, it was
about $300 billion![11] Just think how many jobs that money could create if it
were spent at home on energy efficiency: solar, wind, biomass, and conversion to hydrogen. To be sure, some of the money is returned in exchange
for U.S. military equipment. Wouldn't the world be better off if this money
were invested in solar collectors and wind turbines instead?

The Russians have over $200 billion in gold and hard currency in the
bank and are enjoying the power of petrol-dollars. They see no need to be
our ally to advance democracy or even help us prevent Iran from making
a nuclear bomb.

That "great sucking sound"—as Ross Perot used to say—is the billions of dollars flowing from the United States, Europe, Japan, and many
poor nations in Africa and Asia to the rich and increasingly powerful
oil-producing nations and oil companies.

The harsh truth is that all of the current oil-related problems will get
worse unless we take strong measures immediately to use less oil each
year. The world does not have enough oil in places where it is environmentally acceptable to produce it to sustain our growing addiction much
longer. Tapping sources such as our shale oil is an environmental disaster, and it perpetuates the idea that the answer to the oil crisis is to find
more oil reserves, not to cut back. Some say oil production will peak in
three decades, some say one decade. Some say oil production has already
peaked. The bottom line is that, unless we kick the habit, oil is not going to
get cheaper or more available; it is going to continue to get more expensive as the resources get scarcer. Unless the U.S. leads the world in cutting

back rather than guzzling more, there won't be enough to satisfy global needs at or even near today's prices.

Business as usual could easily result in oil wars among nations competing for supply and currying favor from oil-producing nations. We must face these facts, not in panic, but as an impetus for immediate action.

Reducing our consumption of oil offers the greatest double bargain on earth. It will reduce a major cause of global warming, air pollution, and contamination of our oceans in addition to alleviating the foreign policy and economic troubles just discussed.

The Dangers to the Environment

It is an unhappy fact that the places where additional oil in the U.S. might be found are places of extreme beauty that most Americans believe ought to be left alone. I refer to the Arctic National Wildlife Refuge and the offshore areas of California and Florida. America is an old oil patch and most of the oil in the lower forty-eight states has been discovered long ago and is mostly consumed.

The price for expanding oil production is destroying much of what's left of America the beauti-ful. Oil rigs are now in pristine forests, landscapes, and off our coasts.

In March 1989, the Exxon Valdez oil tanker spilled millions of gallons of oil into Prince William Sound, killing hundreds of thousands of animals and nearly all the plankton supply. Source: Exxon Valdez Oil Spill Trustee Council

All of that oil will not feed our oil habit for long, but the beauty and safety of these places is being destroyed forever. That's just too high a price.

As ocean explorer and educator Jacques Cousteau vividly showed us, oil is contaminating the oceans, spill by little-noticed spill. The younger generations may not even have heard of the giant Santa Barbara oil spill and the disaster of the Exxon *Valdez*; those were major ecologic disasters. Not noticed at all are the small day-in and day-out spills from large tanker traffic as it moves oil from the Middle East and other faraway places to feed the American love of mobility.

Oil spills are a growing menace to the fish that live in the ocean. This is yet another of the unnoticed dangers of our oil-based economy that can only grow worse and worse as ocean traffic increases to serve the 6.5 billion people on earth. We can reverse the trend by developing an alternative that need not traverse and contaminate the oceans.

Serious air quality problems result from refining crude oil into gasoline and heating oil. No community is going to sit still and permit a new refinery to be built. As a result, no new refineries have been built in America for thirty years, and none is likely to be built in the future. So shortages are inevitable if we continue on the present destructive oil-growth pattern.

The really serious environmental problems with oil take place when we burn it in planes, cars, trucks, buses, and railroad locomotives, and use it for heating homes. First, there is the local air pollution from motor vehicles that occurs largely on the streets and freeways of American cities where we travel and breathe.

The brew of toxins emitted when petroleum is burned in a motor vehicle is partially regulated. Although the regulated pollution per vehicle has gone down, the number of vehicles keeps going up. After thirty years of regulation, the air in Los Angeles, Houston, Atlanta, and other major cities is still unhealthy. This situation is causing health hazards that shorten lives and tally untold billions of dollars in medical bills. Until we run our country on zero-polluting energy, thirty years of history suggest the air will continue to be dirty and unhealthy and our families, especially our children and elderly, will continue to suffer.

Air pollution control agencies have only recently begun to identify, much less deal with, what may be the most persistent killer in the air. I refer to tiny particles from the combustion of coal and petroleum that are too small to see—the ultrafine particles that currently go unregulated. These particles lodge in the deep recesses of our lungs and enter the heart and the bloodstream.

I was a staff member in the White House with Doug Costle, who later headed the EPA under President Carter. We helped sell the idea of a standalone environmental agency. I recall some of the early discussions about the serious hazard of those tiny microscopic particles. I warned about them in the Ford Foundation report that I led. To this date, there are no regulations that control them. And we are now learning that the technology to control the larger-sized small particles releases vapors that, in cold weather, become ultrafine particles. We don't have any technology that will contain them.

What we know is that today's epidemics of asthma and cancer are caused in significant part by the burning of over 7 billion barrels of oil a year in close proximity to most Americans. Think for just a moment how different our cities would be if all those vehicles ran on renewable electricity that emitted zero pollution, or hydrogen with by-products of water and a tiny bit of oxides of nitrogen (NOx) that could be controlled. Imagine air with no particulates or pollution. It would be the difference between light and grey. The cities would glisten in the light. The air would be fit to breathe. The streets would be free of the oil spills from cars and trucks that pollute nearby waterways.

Global Warming
Within the past thirty years or so, as humanity has gained knowledge of the impact of burning fossil fuels, we have discovered a more fundamental problem. We now realize that the carbon in fuels, never considered a pollutant in the past, is triggering global warming that seems likely to change the face of the earth. Global warming can make all the natural events—hot summers, cold winters, floods, hurricanes—more severe. It can also cause the oceans to rise and inundate areas where hundreds of millions of people now live.

The debate over whether global warming exists is now over. If you are still in doubt, watch Al Gore's movie, *An Inconvenient Truth*, or read his book by the same name. The only issue left is how fast it will get warmer and what damage it will do. Today we know the following facts:

* The earth's surface temperature has, in fact, been getting warmer in recent years.
* Polar ice is melting at an alarming rate in both the Arctic and Antarctic. There is a real danger that the oceans may rise as much as twenty feet as early as a decade from now. The ice in Greenland is one mile thick. In Antarctica, it is two miles thick. They both contain such huge quantities of water that it is easy to understand how their melting could raise ocean levels by twenty feet.
* The island lifestyles of many people (the Arctic Inuits, for example, and the residents of the tiny island nation of Tuvalu) are being dramatically changed by warming and rising oceans.
* Climate change has caused birds, insects, and animals to adapt their behaviors, which has changed their interactions within food chains and habitats. A prime example is that of the mountain pine beetle, which has been devouring huge forests

in British Columbia faster than logging companies and forest fires. This has been attributed to climate change because the insect is rapidly adapting and spreading northward into regions that it would have found uninhabitable before.

* The destructive hurricanes from the Gulf of Mexico over the past few years are a result of the warming of gulf water; hurricanes gain strength over warm water.

* All of these factors add up to great risk to our American society from global warming. One can argue about likelihood and severity, but no one can rationally claim that the risk is zero. In a typical risk assessment, a prudent person, business, or nation takes out an insurance policy. But our best insurance policy is to stop the progress of global warming by finding an alternative to carbon-based energy.

In summary, oil poses five major threats to America:

1. It is the main obstacle to cracking down on nations that promote terrorism.
2. It is picking the pockets of American consumers by billions of dollars per year.
3. It pollutes our oceans.

4. It poisons the air in our cities and causes major health ailments.
5. It is a major cause of global warming, which, in turn, is the cause of other environmental catastrophes.

Coal reserves in the United States contain one-quarter of the world supply. The burning of coal is a huge source of toxic air pollution and greenhouse gas emissions. Source: DOE/NREL

COAL

The phrase "clean coal" is an insult to human intelligence. There is no such thing. Coal is inherently dirty and is an unhealthy source of energy throughout every stage of its mining and use. I say this based

My first professional experience with coal was as a young lawyer working for TVA in the late 1950s. Someone had sued TVA claiming the effluent from the coal-fired Kingston Steam Plant in eastern Tennessee was killing the nearby white pine trees. This was before we started calling it "acid rain." The TVA power people planted a test stand of white pine trees up in the Smoky Mountains, and these trees also died even though they weren't near the steam plant. This was offered as proof that TVA's steam plant did not cause the damage. In the course of preparing for the trial for the defense, I discovered that the white pine trees near a coal power plant in Pennsylvania were also dying. The theory of the TVA staff was thus debunked, and I learned an important environmental lesson. I never again believed at face value the claims of those responsible for using fossil fuels or nuclear power. They will clutch at any superficial evidence to try to convince people that coal is clean or nuclear is safe. But believe me, they aren't. Anyone visiting the Smokies these days can see the haze and blight from acid rain.

on my experience as the former head of the TVA, which bought and burned more than 30 million tons of coal a year. I was deeply involved in the strip mining, underground mining, trucking, and most importantly, the burning of huge quantities of coal. No one who has been deeply involved with coal can rightfully say it is clean.

Let's look at each stage of coal's development. Coal mining is a dirty and dangerous job. The death of underground coal miners gets attention only when the deaths occur in sizable numbers. What goes unnoticed are the deaths and injuries that occur one or two at a time and the infection of the miners' lungs from breathing coal dust underground, resulting in massive incidents of black lung disease.

What also goes unnoticed in much of the country is subsidence of the earth over deep mines and the devastation to the surface of the earth from strip mining, which has turned countless mountain areas into wastelands that resemble the face of the moon. Chopping off the tops of mountains is sanctioned by

Trees in Mount Mitchell, North Carolina, are stripped of their foliage by acid rain. Source: Corbis

loopholes in the surface-mining laws. In 2004, more than 1 billion short tons of coal were extracted from 1,379 mines in the United States.[12] About 60 percent of the coal mined in the U.S. is collected through strip mining, which requires huge amounts of land and has devastating impacts on the environment and surrounding communities. In the last thirty years, at least 400,000 acres—about 625 square miles—of forest in Kentucky, Virginia, and West Virginia have been dedicated to, and destroyed by, strip mining.[13] According to the EPA, roughly 700 miles of natural streams have been completely buried, wiped out by strip mining.[14] Further, 12,000 miles of streams have been contaminated with heavy metals and toxic drainage from coal

Our thirst for allegedly "cheap" coal is also a huge, though largely unseen, environmental justice issue due to its devastating impact on Native American reservations with coal mines or plants nearby. The Mohave Generating Station, for example, fed energy-hungry Southern California.[16] Coal slurry (a toxic cocktail of 50 percent water and 50 percent coal) was transported to a plant in Nevada by a 273-mile pipeline from the coal mine on the Hopi and Navajo Black Mesa reservation in Arizona. The water used for this operation was taken from an aquifer created in the last ice age and is the only potable source of water in that remote, arid desert region. It has been depleted to dangerously low levels. An alternate water source for coal production has been discussed for years, but none has been secured.

The Mojave Generating Station in Laughlin, Nevada, ceased operations on December 31, 2005. Attempts to restart the plant have failed.

In addition, the Mohave Generating Station and the Navajo Generating Station in Arizona were both targeted with lawsuits by environmental groups as major contributors to the haze in the Grand Canyon. The Mohave Plant has now been shut down. The scrubbers that were put on the Navajo Generating Station in Arizona did a lot to reduce haze-forming pollutants (SO_2), but they ironically also had the effect of increasing the amount of the toxic pollutant NOx on the Hopi and Navajo lands. It seems there is no winning with coal.

mining.[15] That is about the same length as the nation's longest rivers—the Missouri, Mississippi, Yukon, Rio Grande, St. Lawrence, and Colorado—combined. (See Coal Fields Map in map insert section.)

The mining of coal is just the beginning of coal's damage to the earth and to the physical, economic, and mental health of the communities nearby. The real trouble begins as we burn the coal. For thirty years, we have been tightening air quality standards for the burning of coal, but advances in scientific knowledge of the dangers far outstrip our ability to control pollution from coal.

Laws have been passed over the years to require cleanup of lands contaminated by coal mining. The federal Clean Air Act and Clean Water Act forced companies to reduce their release of pollutants into the air and water. Nevertheless, no matter how well sulfur and oxides of nitrogen or mercury are controlled, coal is still dirty because of the ultrafine particles that are too small even to measure, as previously discussed with petroleum. Coal has perhaps an even greater proportion of these uncontrolled, cancer-causing by-products because the particles arise in proportion to carbon content. Coal is carbon rich, the worst of the fossil fuels for global warming. Some suggest that carbon can be sequestered from the discharge of burning coal and stored in the earth. But that is simply talk. No one is sequestering coal today or even advocating that laws be enacted to order it done. There are no demonstration projects. Anyone with a broad knowledge of geology knows the extent to which the earth shifts below the surface. No geologist can assure us

> When I was a kid growing up in Chattanooga, Tennessee, we had a coal furnace in our home and we also lived near the railroad tracks. The white shirts my father, an umbrella repairman, wore on Sunday would be grey by noon from all the soot in the air. As time passed, hydropower from the TVA hydroelectric dams powered our homes. This renewable energy helped clean the air.

that carbon injected into the ground will stay there over any long stretch of time, and, to truly be a solution, it would have to stay there forever.

While the need to reduce carbon emissions becomes more urgent by the day, the electric utility is speeding along with plans to build 150 new coal plants. These plants would increase the total U.S. carbon emissions by 10 percent. None of those plants even propose carbon sequestration.[17] There is a clear and present danger of major expansion of a power source that will bring the havoc of global warming sooner and with greater severity.

A change of policy to ban new coal and nuclear plants is needed now. Our nation has substituted natural gas for coal for home heating for one main reason: it is cleaner. The American people know from experience that coal is dirty and no amount of sexy, witty, or pseudo-green advertising about clean coal can change this truth. Even so, we still burn lots of coal, but mostly where people can't see it. There are remote electric power plants where some of the pollutants are controlled and others are not.

It is irrefutable that the carbon in coal, when burned, goes into the atmosphere and contributes to the greenhouse effect that could destroy much of life as we know it on this planet. It is time to "say no" to nuclear power, petroleum, and coal and apply our common sense to use the truly clean energy Mother Nature delivers free of charge, forever.

***

1   Warren McLaren, "Gorbachev Sounds Off on Nuclear vs. Renewables," (April 27, 2006) http://www.treehugger.com/files/th_exclusives/celebrities/index.php?

2   "Health Risks from Exposure to Low Levels of Ionizing Radiation," (National Academy Press, 2005).

3   *Los Angeles Times* (August 18, 2006), B-1.

4   The 2005 Energy Policy Act includes the following provisions: 1) production tax credit of 1.8 cents/kWh up to $125 million per year for 8 years, 2) $1.25 billion to fund a prototype advanced nuclear plant, and 3) cost overrun support of $2 billion for 6 new nuclear plants. Nuclear Energy Institute, http://www.nei.org/documents/Energy_Bill_2005.pdf.

5   Dwight D. Eisenhower, "Atoms for Peace," General Assembly of the United Nations on Peaceful Uses of Atomic Energy (New York City, December 8, 1953).

6   David Albright and Kimberly Kramer, "Plutonium Watch: Tracking Plutonium Inventories," (Institute for Science and International Security, June 2004).

7   "Arrêté du 7 juillet 2006 relatif à la programmation pluriannuelle des investissements de production d'électricité," Décrets, arrêtés, circulaires, Textes généraux, Ministère de l'économie, des finances, et de l'industrie—industrie, *Journal officiel de la République française*, Texte 17 sur 65, 9 juillet 2006.

8   U. S. Central Intelligence Agency (2003). CIA World Fact Book. http://
www.cia.gov/cia/publications/factbook/.

9   Fareed Zakaria, "Mile by Mile, Into the Oil Trap," *Washington Post* (August
23, 2005).

10 According to the U.S. EIA, the average imported oil price was $47.70 per
barrel in 2005. About 4.9 billion barrels were imported in 2005, for a
total of about $233 billion spent on imported oil in 2005.

11 At the time of this writing, the U.S. had imported about 2 billion barrels
of oil in the first five months of 2006 at an average price of about $57
per barrel, for a total of about $114 billion. Assuming that the price of oil
remains at about $62 per barrel, at a total of 5 billion barrels for 2006,
the U.S. will spend about $300 billion on imported oil.

12 U. S. DOE EIA, "Coal Production and Number of Mines by State and Type"
(2003). http://www.eia.doe.gov/cneaf/coal/page/acr/table1.html.

13 Jack Spadaro, "Mountaintop Removal: Mining Practices must change or
the ecosystem will be destroyed," *Charleston Gazette* (February 21, 2005).

14 Eric Reece, "Moving Mountains: The Battle for Justice Comes to the Coal
Fields of Appalachia," *Orion* (January 9, 2006).

15 U.S. Bureau of Mines (1995).

16 The Mohave Generating Station was shut down on December 31, 2005,
because of failure to comply with the retrofits required by the settle-
ment of a lawsuit filed by environmental groups in 1999. The plant con-
tributed to about 40 percent of the air pollution in the Grand Canyon.

17 U.S. Public Interest Research Groups (PIRG), "Making Sense of the Coal
Rush: The Consequences of Expanding America's Dependence on Coal"
(July 2006).

WE LIVE IN A SOLAR WORLD

{RENEWABLES ARE THE LARGEST SOURCES OF ENERGY}   ✳✳✳

MOST PEOPLE BELIEVE that we fuel our civilization with poisonous power sources because they are cheaper than renewables. Another myth is that renewable sources are so diffuse and remote that they are not a significant enough alternative source of power generation. The essential truth is just the opposite. Renewables are a cheaper, feasible, practical alternative and a huge one at that. They include:

* ✳ The sun that makes all life possible on Earth
* ✳ The winds, which are perpetual in nature
* ✳ All sorts of plant life, from sugar and corn to rotting trees to agriculture waste
* ✳ Garbage that would otherwise be burned or tossed into our bulging landfills

These abundant fuels can all be harnessed and put to use with existing technology and at a lower cost to the health of the earth and the pocketbook of consumers.

One might ask, "If all that is true, why are we still relying on the poisons?" The answer is that the folks who sell oil, coal, and nuclear reactors spend tremendous amounts of money convincing the American people that what they sell is economical, safe, and clean. They contribute huge sums of money to the politicians who repeat their propaganda. How often have you heard phrases such as "clean coal," "safe nuclear power," "clean diesel," or "low-level radioactive waste"?

These phrases are images invented by highly paid, highly skilled advertising firms. But these claims are lies. There are even ads on TV and in the

WHEN DAVID YARNOLD, ENVIRONMENTAL DEFENSE'S EXECUTIVE VICE PRESIDENT, WAS ASKED IN MAY 2006 WHY HIS GROUP WASN'T OFFERING SOLUTIONS MORE DRAMATIC THAN WHAT CONGRESS WAS CONSIDERING, HE REPLIED, "WHY WOULD YOU WANT TO LOBBY FOR SOMETHING THAT CAN'T GET DONE?"

newspapers featuring pristine landscapes and young, freshly scrubbed spokespeople advertising coal as a clean energy resource. This is ridiculous. Coal is inherently filthier than dirt itself. The current energy industry has quite masterfully succeeded in lulling many Americans to sleep on the dangers of the poisons they sell while portraying renewables as a distant dream.

Well, folks, it is time to speak the truth to the powers that be. The high price of gasoline at the pump is telling the American people the truth about the price of oil. That's only a preview of what's coming.

Quite frankly, our environmental leaders have inadvertently helped mislead Americans by conceding that renewables are more expensive and lobbying for goals that make renewables only a small part of our supply. For example, those of us who advocated to raise our renewable electricity mix to 20 percent of our electricity in the case of California, have set the bar too low. I do not mean to criticize those who have helped move the renewable energy bar from zero to 20 percent. These have been important strides that laid the foundation for raising the bar much higher. But the effect of our struggle to gain a foothold for both efficiency and renewables has also helped the energy industry spread the lies that renewable energy can only be a minor source of power.

The problem is that some environmental leaders have become part of the status quo. They seem afraid to advocate bold programs that are needed. They are afraid of failing. Their attitude and activism reflects their fears. When David Yarnold, Environmental Defense's executive vice president, was asked in May 2006 why his group wasn't offering solutions more dramatic than what Congress was considering, he replied, "Why would you want to lobby for something that can't get done?"[1] If a Congress that consistently supports the coal, oil, and nuclear industries sets the bar for what environmentalists propose, we are indeed in a heap of trouble. Environmentalists need to stand up and propose solutions to our problems and help the true interests of the American people get heard. Now is the time to take a stand and put into action the programs that will get the job done—the job of making renewables the primary source for all America's energy.

The driving force will be actions taken by readers of this book and concerned citizens generally, who will demand plug-in hybrid cars, purchase only Energy Star appliances, demand green power from their utility companies, install solar panels on their roof, and lobby senators and representatives to enact the policies set forth in chapter 12.

SOLAR: THE REVOLUTION IS UNDER WAY

We live in a solar world. Mother Nature delivers a superabundance of energy to the earth, free of charge. Every day, the sun delivers five thousand times more energy to the planet's surface than the whole world consumes. Each continent on the planet receives enough energy directly from the sun that—if sufficient collectors were deployed—would negate the need to import fossil fuels, mine coal, or construct dangerous nuclear power plants ever again.

Even today's solar technology could meet all of our energy needs. Even more exciting are the breakthroughs in technology to convert sunlight to electricity that are in the manufacturing stage even as you read this book. Yet today, solar power is not even one-tenth of one percent of our current energy supply.

A true solar revolution more promising than the development of nuclear power is under way that is likely to drop the cost of solar power below the cost of electricity from coal, natural gas, oil, and nuclear power. The breakthrough is the commercialization of an ultra-thin solar-coating material that can, over time, cover anything under the sun and generate electricity with no pollution and no fuel cost. Along with Jim Harding and Roger Duncan, I reported on this breakthrough in the *Seattle Post-Intelligencer* on August 10, 2006:

> While on the White House staff during Lyndon Johnson's administration, I saw to it that the National Science Council, another federal agency, put money into the first grants for solar power research in the country. These modest efforts studied the application of solar power. I remember the first study that came back in 1968 showed that you could economically heat water with solar power.

"MUCH LIKE CELLULAR PHONES HAVE CHANGED THE WAY PEOPLE COMMUNICATE, CHEAP SOLAR CELLS CHANGE THE WAY WE PRODUCE AND DISTRIBUTE ELECTRIC ENERGY."

In separate announcements over the past few months, researchers at the University of Johannesburg and at Nanosolar, a private company in Palo Alto, have announced major breakthroughs in reducing the cost of solar electric cells.

South Africa and California technologies rely on the same alloy—called CIGS (for copper-indium-gallium-selenide)—deposited in an extremely thin layer on a flexible surface. Both companies claim that the technology reduces solar cell production costs by a factor of 4-5. That would bring the cost to or below that of delivered electricity in a large fraction of the world.

A powerful team of private investors, including Google's two founders and the insurance giant, Swiss Re, among others, backs the California team. It has announced plans to build a $100 million production facility in the San Francisco Bay area that is slated to be operational at 215 megawatts in 2007, and soon thereafter capable of producing 430 megawatts of cells annually.

What makes this particular news stand out? Cost, scale, and financial strength. The cost of the facility is about one-tenth that of recently completed silicon cell facilities, the current solar technology.

Second, Nanosolar is scaling up rapidly from pilot production to 430 megawatts, using a technology it equates to printing newspapers. That implies both technical success and development of a highly automated production process that captures important economies of scale. No one builds that sort of industrial production facility in the Bay Area—with expensive labor, real estate, and electricity costs—without confidence.

Similar facilities can be built elsewhere. Half a dozen competitors also are working along the same lines, led by private firms Miasole and Daystar, in Sunnyvale, California, and New York.

But this is really not about who wins in the end. We all do. Thin solar films can be used in building materials, including roofing materials and glass, and built into mortgages, reducing their cost even further. Inexpensive solar electric cells are, fundamentally, a "disruptive technology".... Much like cellular phones have changed the way people communicate, cheap solar cells change the way we produce and distribute electric energy.

The announcements are good news for consumers worried about high energy prices and dependence on the Middle East, utility executives worried about the long-term viability of their next investment in central station power plants, transmission, or distribution, and for all of us who worry about climate change. It is also good news for the developing world, where electricity generally is more expensive, mostly because electrification requires long-distance transmission and serves small or irregular loads. Inexpensive solar cells are an ideal solution.

Meanwhile, the prospect of this technology creates a conundrum for the electric utility industry and Wall Street. Can—or should—any utility, or investor, count on the long-term viability of a coal, nuclear or gas investment? The answer is no. In about a year, we'll see how well those technologies work. The question is whether federal energy policy can change fast enough to join what appears to be a revolution.[2]

Rooftop Solar

The roofs of our buildings provide a large platform for solar panels, even if confined to the parts of America where the sun shines the brightest. According to the National Center for Photovoltaics at the National Renewable Energy Laboratory, we have about 140 million acres of potential off-ground solar resources—residential and commercial roofs and sides, parking lots, and other structures—available to us in the United States. If we installed photovoltaics (PV) on only 7 percent of this area, we could meet all our nation's electricity needs.[3]

Thin solar film. Source: DOE/NREL

Roofs are not the only place solar power can be harnessed. There are many examples of sides of buildings (the sunny side) made of solar collectors, and clever designers and architects are continually finding obvious and subtle ways to incorporate solar power into buildings. Passive solar home designs are as old as civilization. In residential areas, there often is room in neighborhoods for an individual or community solar plant. As we move into using hydrogen to run our cars, a solar panel and small electrolysis system could

Solar rooftop systems generate clean power, lessen dependence on fossil fuels, and give energy back to the power grid during peak demand. Source: DOE/NREL

provide homeowners with their own personal "filling station" that could refill their car while parked at home.

If you are building a new home, ask your architect about a passive solar design and insist on some rooftop solar. Solar panels can also be retrofitted on your existing home. Your phone book should have these products and services listed under such topics as solar products and services, energy management, or alternative fuels. The Internet is also a huge wealth of information about solar products.

Solar power harnessed on rooftops avoids the costs and uncertainties of transmitting and distributing electricity to your home from distant coal, nuclear, and natural gas plants. They must be valued by your utility at the retail price of electricity instead of the cost at a nuclear or coal plant. If solar doesn't have that value where you live, call your state public utility commission and complain. You should ask your electrical company to make net metering mandatory. This means that you would be able to sell the solar power that you don't need back to the utility for full retail price.

The Costs of Solar Power

The cost of an installed solar collector will not go up each year, even if electric rates continue to soar. Consumers, when they learn the truth, will find that solar power is actually a bargain with the subsidies that are now available. The installed cost of solar has gone down 95 percent since 1970,[4] and is expected to go down even more with massive deployment and thin-film technology in the near future. And who can put a cost on the health benefits of cleaner air and the environmental benefits of stopping or at least slowing down global warming?

It is useful to note that in the Sunbelt region of the U.S., and in many other states, solar hot water is now cheaper than heating water with electricity or even natural gas. While the cost of electricity and natural gas will keep increasing in price, the solar heater's cost, once installed, remains fixed. Heating water is the simplest application of solar power and is widely used in Greece, Israel, and other nations.

Solar-heated water could replace a sizeable volume of natural gas used for heating water. Why the need to replace natural gas? The natural gas saved by solar hot water heaters could then be used as a substitute for petroleum in transportation in the coming decade, especially in trucks, to reduce pollution as well as our dependence on imported oil. Shifting natural gas from making hot water and being used as boiler fuel in power plants could be a large step on our path toward the full transition to 100 percent renewable transportation fuels.

Solar Satellites
The famous bank robber Willie Sutton, when asked why he robbed only banks, said, "That's where the money is." The real treasure trove of solar power is in the sky above the clouds and in the Sunbelt, especially in the deserts, where the sun shines the brightest. Up above the clouds the sun is more intense than on earth[5] and shines twenty-four hours a day, 365 days a year.

A NASA rendering of the solar satellite. Source: NASA

The concept of a solar satellite in the sky in geosynchronous orbit around the earth's equator was proposed in the late 1960s and even pursued by the Soviet Union. It was proposed that the sun's rays be converted to electricity by photovoltaic cells on the solar satellite, producing about six to seven times more solar electricity than on earth.[6] The proposed solar collector would have had a surface area of 40 square miles and would have produced about 10 million kW of energy per day, which would have been beamed by microwave 22,000 miles to a receiving station on Earth.[7]

Such a system could easily supply all of the earth's energy with just a few large stations, and it requires no new inventions. As a practical matter, it would be a giant undertaking with serious engineering and environmental problems to be solved. Here are questions that might come to mind: What about airplanes running into the microwave beam? What about the impact on radio signals? What about national security issues? We were assured back then that these concerns could be overcome, but we did not go forward with the project. Remember, thirty years ago nuclear power seemed the wave of the future and oil was three dollars a barrel (that's right, a barrel).

President Nixon's science advisor, Lee DuBridge, said to me when we briefly entertained the idea back in the 1960s, "Dave, I think that's a little far out."

I mention this example of solar power in space only to illustrate the enormity of the solar resource. But we don't need to put all our energy eggs in one big solar basket or to reach for the sky to harness the sun. We can take advantage of the natural delivery system here on land. All it takes is for us to be smart enough to focus our efforts where the solar energy is stacked up like the gold in Fort Knox—the hot spots here on earth.

Big Solar—There is Land Aplenty

The deserts are the hot spots. That's where solar energy is available twelve hours per day (six to seven hours of direct sunlight), 365 days per year. And there are vast expanses of land in the deserts that would not be harmed by locating solar equipment on them. It is in these solar "goldmines" that we can harness the huge quantities of energy the nation needs to meet all its energy requirements in combination with wind power and biomass. (See Solar Resource Map in the map insert section.)

Furthermore, if we put ourselves to the challenge we could obtain all our energy for electricity, transportation (including airplanes), and home heating from renewable hydrogen using our vast solar and wind resources.

More than enough, and that's not even counting our geothermal, biomass, and hydro resources. In the Southwest alone, we have about 53,900 square miles of the world's best solar resources available to us.[8]

Here are a few illustrations:

* An area in the Southwest about 13,000 square miles in size (114 square miles if all in one place), or 25 percent of the best solar potential in the Southwest, could produce enough renewable electricity to supply electric power for the entire country, based on current (2006) U.S. electricity consumption.[9]

* An area of about 23,500 square miles in size, or 43 percent of the best solar land, could supply enough electricity that, if converted to hydrogen, could supply enough hydrogen to replace the current demand for gasoline in our cars and trucks.[10]

* To meet all U.S. transportation-related fuel demand with hydrogen, including airplanes, we would need a land mass of about 39,000 square miles, which amounts to 73 percent of our best solar land resources.[11]

And these are conservative estimates based on currently available technology. Of course, you would not use just one resource, or put it all in one place. What is clear is that renewable resources can do it all.

Fossil fuel and oil advocates try to portray solar power as so diffuse that land requirements alone make it impractical. They are wrong. If you compare solar with coal, we would use less land in the long run because of one simple fact. To feed a coal-fired power plant with strip-mined coal, you have to strip more and more land every year, which wrenches trees from the ground, devours topsoil, and buries fresh water springs and streams under tons of rubble. With solar, you need only the land at the power plant, land that is baking under the hot desert sun. The same land uses the same sun day after day, year after year.

I designed the basement floor for a coal-fired electric power plant at Kingston, Tennessee, built in 1950. That plant has been devouring coal for over fifty years and I'd hate to think how much land has been stripped to feed it with coal over the past five decades. If we took all the land stripped for mining coal and devoted the same acreage to concentrated solar, we would have pollution-free electricity in sufficient quantity to meet 100 percent of America's electricity needs.

Land use is not a good reason to favor nuclear power. Every nuclear power plant contaminates the site it occupies and generates wastes that will contaminate the surrounding land forever. Uranium mining doesn't occur in space. The crucial point is that the land used for nuclear is toxic forever, while solar plants do no harm. Perhaps most telling is the risk of what almost happened at Three Mile Island, which could have left an area larger than all of New England permanently contaminated with radioactivity just as the 1986 Chernobyl accident did in the Ukraine.

Reliable Solar Power Supply

A reasonable person can ask, "What do we do when the sun is down? We need electricity all the time, so how can all of our electricity come from solar power?"

I know firsthand the importance of reliable service. I know from years of personal experience that the electric system can be both largely renewable and reliable.

The answer is manifold:

* Demand for electricity at night is low, and there is surplus natural gas capacity in most systems. For the indefinite future, natural gas turbines used more and more in a combined heat-and-power mode for maximum efficiency will be available to meet peak loads and firm up the solar and wind resources.
* Off-peak rates for the plug-in hybrids will discourage people from recharging them during peak hours when people are doing most of their driving.
* Load management that reduces the demand for electricity during peak hours will also be a participant in reliable electrical service.

I was the senior energy advisor to Governor Gray Davis during the dark days of the California energy crisis in 2001. Brownouts could have been averted if we would have been able to use all the backup generators located in office buildings, hospitals, etc. But we could not use these generators because they ran on diesel fuel and the air quality regulators rightfully would not permit their operation on the hot days when electric demand is highest and the air is the smoggiest. Yet if those generators ran on hydrogen, they could have been used in this time of great need.

A more fundamental solution to the concern that solar and wind are not available around the clock (but solar by day, wind by night, makes a good combination) is that we can store their energy and use it when we need it. Storage devices include batteries, compressed air, and flywheels. Storage for use when needed is the real value of converting solar power and wind power to hydrogen. That is how we will put the sun and wind in the gas tank, so to speak, and use hydrogen instead of fossil fuels to run backup turbines during peak hours when air quality concerns don't permit the use of diesel fuels.

Rather than creating a problem of reliability, a switch to hydrogen could enhance reliability. Let's make solar and wind power available when we really need them, in the form of hydrogen that can be burned without polluting the air.

Solar Conclusions

In summary, the solar resource could replace all need for oil, coal, and nuclear resources in the United States, but it doesn't have to work alone. As you will see, wind, geothermal, and biomass can also play their part in the replacement energy scenario. In addition, solar offers a nondestructive solution to the land that it uses, whereas coal and nuclear taint and contaminate the land they use forever.

> SOLAR RESOURCE COULD REPLACE ALL NEED FOR OIL, COAL, AND NUCLEAR RESOURCES IN THE UNITED STATES, BUT IT DOESN'T HAVE TO WORK ALONE

We have the ability with today's technology to literally "put the sun in the gas tank."

The first step is to manufacture hybrid cars that can plug into renewable electricity (see chapter 8). This is a known feature that can and should be added to the hybrid. The extra benefit of the plug-in model is that you can charge it with electricity plugged into an ordinary socket at home or at work, and reduce your gasoline consumption by between 55 and 100 percent.[12] The cost savings of using electricity to replace gasoline is like buying gasoline at less than one dollar a gallon.

Solar-powered electricity converted into hydrogen by electrolysis of water is another promising option for our cars, trucks, or buses.

The Tehachapi region of Southern California is one of the largest wind resources in the world.

Unfortunately, the "green, clean energy crowd" has not emphasized the opportunities for using renewables for transportation. It needs to be shouted from rooftops and taught in the classrooms that renewable electricity can power a plug-in hybrid or be used in the form of hydro-gen. The public needs to be told solar, wind, hydro, and biomass can all be converted to electricity and hydrogen. This is the way to replace oil as the fuel on which this nation runs.

WIND

While the sun itself can meet all our energy needs, the renewable family has many members. We have a diversity of renewable resources. Just like the sun, wind power alone, over time, could meet all of our electricity needs. The central region of the United States is home to some of the best wind resource sites in the world. To be specific, the wind potential in the United States has been estimated at 500 million kW[13] onshore and 900 million kW offshore.[14] (See United States Annual Average Wind Power Map in map insert section.)

The potential exists to generate more than our annual electricity needs from the huge wind source in the United States[15]—on about 6 percent of our total land area, (about 341,000 total square miles), off our shores and elsewhere in our country[16]—at costs that are quite competitive with today's prices for natural gas. While this is a lot of land, wind has a particular advantage in land use over other methods of generation, renewable and nonrenewable. The height and distance required between turbines means that land used for wind turbines can also be used for agriculture and grazing. In fact, only about 5 percent of the land in a wind farm is actually occupied by the turbines themselves.

Yet it must be recognized that wind projects face opposition. The concern from animal activists is that occasionally birds get caught in the turbines. This does not endanger any particular species that we know of. There is also opposition from people who don't like their looks. The "not in my line of sight" or "not in my backyard" (commonly known as NIMBY) point of view has succeeded in killing many projects, both renewable and nonrenewable.

I understand the NIMBY point of view although I don't agree with it. I think the greater good outweighs the "looks" issue by far. I'd much rather see a wind turbine in my line of sight than have a nuclear power plant contaminating the ground near my home any day. However, the opposition to wind power is not going away. For that reason, I don't count on harnessing all or even most of the wind potential. The wind resource in locations where the wind power can be peacefully transmitted by wire or can be converted to hydrogen at the site is still a tremendous resource. And the electric power industry is already demonstrating that, despite the opposition, wind projects can be developed and their power transmitted into the grid. In fact, installed wind power capacity in the U.S. is now up to more than nine million kW,[17] which generated 23.2 billion kWh in 2005 and will continue growing.[18] For reference, the entire annual consumption of electricity in the U.S. is about 3.6 trillion kWh per year. In 2005, wind power produced a little over one-half percent of the electricity in the country, when it is capable of producing 100 percent.

We can realistically view wind power as a serious partner to the sun, based on its growing use in the United States and in Europe. Even though it is not a 24/7 resource, here in America it can produce a kWh of electricity at about the same cost as natural gas. It is competitive without even counting the added health benefits from reduced air pollution and zero-carbon emissions.

AS WE EMBARK ON THE ROAD OF REDUCING CARBON EMISSIONS AND OIL IMPORTS, WIND POWER CAN PLAY A USEFUL ROLE RIGHT AWAY

Thirty years ago, you could generate a kWh of electricity with natural gas for one-half cent, while wind power cost about one dollar per kWh. Today, natural-gas-fired electricity is over five cents per kWh in the most efficient generators and three times as high in older plants. Wind power is down to the level of the cheapest gas plants, as low as five cents per kWh.[19]

The current competitive price of wind power provides the opportunity to steadily substitute wind power for much of the natural gas used for boiler fuel. In the late 1970s, under President Carter, the nation outlawed the use of natural gas as a boiler fuel. That law was repealed in the 1980s. But the force of environmental necessity and actual cost economics are now combining to achieve the same result—allocate more of our domestic natural gas resource to a higher and better use.

As we embark on the road to reducing carbon emissions and oil imports, wind power can play a useful role right away. Utilities can economically replace natural gas with a cleaner and cheaper source of energy, thus releasing natural gas to run trucks, buses, and even cars to reduce our dependence on imported oil. Existing gas-fired power plants need not run during hours that wind is available.

It is therefore very practical to count on the development of wind power to satisfy a large slice of our electric energy future, especially when people wake up to the truth and insist that the electric industry move aggressively toward more and more renewables.

BIOMASS

A third member of the renewable family is biomass. It is already a significant source of energy in the form of wood for home heating and electric power production.

What is newer and growing at a rapid rate is what I call "food for energy." I call it "food for energy" because as promising and exciting as it is to drive your car on homegrown corn or soybeans, we must remember that we are diverting foodstuffs to fuel the gas tank. This does not necessarily mean we are taking food off the table. Unlike many countries, the United States has the ability and the land to increase its production of foodstuffs needed to create energy, but only by a limited amount. However, there are other sources of biofuels that do not require the use of foodstuffs, but instead use recyclable by-products or other organic material.

Biofuels are organic products that can be mixed with gasoline to fuel our transportation needs. The two most common are ethanol and biodiesel, both of which are gaining in popularity. A less common biofuel is biobutanol, which is a direct substitute for gasoline that doesn't require any separate infrastructure.

Ethanol

Ethanol has commonly been made from corn and, more recently, sugars. To obtain ethanol, we can use about 20 percent of our corn crops for fuel production without disrupting our food supply. This would yield about 8 billion gallons of ethanol per year.

Some have opposed subsidies for ethanol production by claiming that ethanol from any source takes more energy to produce than it actually yields. This is simply not so. Considering the cradle-to-grave energy needs, called "well-to-wheels" in transportation fuel terms, production of ethanol yields a net-energy benefit. An important part of the energy benefit equation comes from the fact that the lignin by-product from ethanol production can be used to generate energy to run the ethanol plant operations.

According to Argonne National Laboratory, as well as a number of other scientific experts who have studied this issue, ethanol production from corn yields 25 percent more energy than the fossil energy used to produce it.[20] Ethanol from corn, therefore, has a net energy benefit of only 25 percent and thus, on a net basis, could supply only 2 percent of our gasoline supply.

But there is another possibility. There is a huge potential to generate ethanol from the cellulose in organic wastes of agriculture and forestry.[21]

BIOFUELS ARE ORGANIC PRODUCTS THAT CAN BE MIXED WITH GASOLINE TO FUEL OUR TRANSPORTATION NEEDS

All together, ethanol from cellulose offers a far greater potential than ethanol from corn. Ethanol potential from forest wastes is estimated at 368 million dry tons a year[22] using existing conversion technologies, yielding about 18.4 billion gallons of ethanol a year. This is the equivalent of about 14 billion gallons gasoline, or about 10 percent of current gasoline consumption.[23] With technological improvements, the potential exists to nearly double these projections.

The energy yields with cellulosic ethanol are much better than with corn. Cellulosic ethanol only uses about one-seventh the energy used to gather and process corn ethanol. So, one unit of cellulosic ethanol only needs one-tenth of one unit of fossil fuels to produce it.

Domestic sugar could also be a biomass resource, though the United States does not produce a lot of it, and certainly not enough to make a huge impact. The U.S. only produces about 6 percent of the world's sugar, 7.7 million tons per year, and we consume about that much.[24] Hawaii is going forward with plans to build a plant to convert sugarcane to ethanol. Florida, our greatest sugar producer, and Louisiana are also looking into sugar fuel conversion.

Biodiesel

Biodiesel is produced using any fat or oil, the most common being soybean oil. Biodiesel can be used in a 100 percent biomass form, or blended with petroleum, such as an 80 percent vegetable oil/20 percent petroleum diesel fuel combination. Biofuel (also known as veggie fuel, veggie oil, or fryer oil) can also be made from recycled cooking oil from restaurants, which requires no combination of petroleum.[25] Biodiesel can meet about 10 percent of current on-road diesel demand with current technology, according to the National Renewable Energy Laboratory.[26] (See Biomass Resources Map in map insert section.)

Plan for Biofuels

The potential for biofuels, both ethanol and biodiesel, from agricultural sources is about 900 million dry tons per year potential, while still meeting food (human and other animal) and export needs.[27] This could produce 40 billion gallons ethanol per year, the equivalent of about 30 billion gallons gasoline, about 21 percent of current gasoline consumption. Again, this is a low-end estimate. With technological improvements, the possibility exists to double this yield.

People are hard at work on this issue.[28] The Oak Ridge National Laboratory's (ORNL) biomass advisory committee has assessed that in order to replace 30 percent of petroleum use with biofuels, we would need 1 billion dry tons of biomass annually. This would take up 450 million acres of U.S. farmland. This acreage is at the upper limits of farmland and counts on such improvements over today as higher crop yields, better residue collection, and switching to switchgrass, a perennial plant, for cellulosic ethanol.[29]

MUNICIPAL WASTE

A huge supply of biomass energy that is just piling up is the nation's garbage. And as long as Americans continue their current lifestyles, it is a never-ending supply. The energy potential in our garbage is huge. Americans dispose of 280 million tons of reusable garbage a year,[30] which could produce about 14 billion gallons of ethanol, the equivalent of 10 billion gallons[31] of gasoline per year, or about 7 percent of our current consumption.

Why then are we in America letting our garbage pile up and make such a stinking mess? Here the story is a bit more understandable. We made a false start twenty-five years ago or so when we tried diverting society's waste into energy. The waste-recycling plants of long ago polluted the air not only with chemicals but also with odor. They were often located near low-income housing, as most residential areas were up in arms about these plants being located in their neighborhoods. The good news is that, just as with solar and wind, the technology for making useful energy from municipal wastes has advanced considerably as has our recognition of environmental justice.

The art and practice of recycling has advanced tremendously. We learned that garbage can and should be separated at the source. Much can be recycled or composted and the rest literally devoured by conversion processes at very high temperatures. One such technology is called the plasma torch, which limits pollution to levels well below existing health standards.

Animal Waste
The use of animal waste is also called manure-to-energy or biodigestion. The potential here is about 106 million gallons per year, but this number should be taken with a big caveat. One of the major issues of biodigestion is the scalability. Let's take the example of a co-digester plant that uses leftovers from an ice cream factory and a salad oil plant to combine with dairy manure. The goal would be to improve the nutrient balance and generate more gas. The dairy, salad oil plant, and factory would need to be in close proximity to each other and be able to produce enough of their waste products to keep a plant of sufficient scale running.[32] This is true for three reasons: transportation feasibility, costs, and minimization of air pollution caused by carrying huge amounts of waste in diesel long-haul trucks. It is not impossible, certainly, but it does narrow the potential.

Biofuels and Municipal Waste Summary

The prospects for biomass becoming a sizeable part the solution are good, but the hype, parochial political support, and exaggerated claims are diverting attention from the larger percent needed to replace our dependence on oil. Ethanol and biofuels on their own can't do it, but they can certainly be a part of the solution and should not be overlooked.

We can cut current petroleum demand about in half, from 20 million barrels a day to less than 10 million barrels a day with efficiency and smart growth measures, according to an analysis by the Natural Resources Defense Council and the Union of Concerned Scientists.[33] It is estimated that we would need at least 1 billion tons of biomass fuel to make enough ethanol to replace 30 percent of U.S. gasoline consumption. According to the Department of Energy, the Department of Agriculture, and other experts, meeting this objective is very much a possibility. Not immediately possible, of course, but over time, certainly so.

In combination, the remains of the forests, ethanol from corn and sugars, the waste oils from our food chain, our garbage, and a variety of plants can all make fuels to run our cars and power our electric generating stations. After the sun and the wind, they rank third in the renewable energy family.

GEOTHERMAL

At the center of the earth is a huge fiery ball. If we drill into the ground, the deeper we drill, the hotter it gets. Geothermal energy—the heat in the earth—is an enormous potential source, but unlike the sun, only a small fraction of the heat reaches the surface of the earth. When it does, it puts on quite a show in the form of geysers, hot springs, and other geothermic activity.

Geothermal steam is today a small but very reliable source of energy to make electricity. There are extensive steam fields where the heat is at or near the surface, making them an economical source of electricity. Although geothermal fields have long lives, any given field is really not renewable. It is considered part of the renewable family because it is an alternative solution to the oil-coal-nuclear dilemma. However, the heat in the earth is so vast that this resource can rightfully be called inexhaustible.

The limiting issue on geothermal is simply economics. Steam fields that have come to the surface and been identified in the U.S. could supply 157.6 billion kWh or about 4 percent of our electricity.[34] This is a useful source but small compared to solar, wind, or even biomass. But remember the existing geothermal resources represent a tiny portion of heat within the earth. As a practical matter, geothermal cannot be counted on for more than what's currently available and economical. But we should remember that if we ever needed more relatively clean homegrown energy, we need only drill down into the earth, and not nearly as deep as we drill for oil and natural gas. Scientists estimate that geothermal potential could be as large as 100 million kW.[35] This would raise the generation potential to about 20 percent of our nation's electricity. (See Geothermal Resource Map in the map insert section.)

A geyser erupting shows geothermal energy in its most basic form. Source: DOE/NREL.

HYDROELECTRIC

The U.S. has undoubtedly built all of the dams that our environment can tolerate. In theory, we could add to our hydropower, but as a practical matter it is the existing hydro that can play a significant role in making our electric power supply renewable and reliable.

The beauty of hydropower is that much of it is stored in reservoirs behind dams and could thus be used when needed to meet peak loads. Some hydro is generated by the run of the river and you use it or lose it. But hydropower stored in reservoirs can be turned on or off at the press of a button and is an ideal partner in an electric system with the wind and sun to firm up the supply at times when the load is greatest. Hydropower today represents 7 percent of our electric supply and is a valuable renewable source.

FUTURE SOURCES

Tidal

Tidal power is a vast resource that has been the subject of much discussion but little action. It is true that if you build a system that allows the tides to come in, and then traps the water and generates power as it flows out, our seacoasts, in theory, could generate huge quantities of power. The amount that can be generated without disturbing the environment and habitat is limited, however.

For example, the tides under San Francisco's Golden Gate Bridge hold the potential to supply about 237,000 kW of power, only 35,000 kW of which could be tapped in an environmentally responsible manner.[36] Projects such as this should not be discouraged, but if we are looking for solutions to our vast electric system, then we shouldn't get too excited about projects as small as 35,000 kW. Such efforts help, but are not the road to salvation.

Fusion

Another fifty-year-old dream is to develop a form of nuclear energy called fusion power that would be so large as to be superabundant. Without going into the intricacies of nuclear fusion—a process in the sun—it seeks to duplicate the heat of the sun here on earth, contain it, and extract net energy from the system.

The research continues and no one can say it will never be a success—it just hasn't succeeded after fifty-five years of effort. Safety problems and the cost of building a fusion power plant have yet to be addressed. I mention fusion power primarily to make it clear that I don't count on fusion power or any form of nuclear energy when I say that all our energy can be renewable.

Magnetic

Magnetic power exists on this earth in huge magnitudes. Many scientists are aware of its existence, and someday it is possible that humans will learn how to harness magnetic power into a nonpolluting significant source of energy. Again, it is nothing that we can count on now.

FUTURE TECHNOLOGY

I mention these enormous sources—the intense sun above the clouds, wind, biomass, the heat in the earth, the tides, fusion, and magnetic power—merely to show how vast and diverse is the energy potential on this earth yet to be seriously explored. The focus of this book is on energy from sun, wind, and biomass, the largest renewable sources whose commercial use is far enough advanced that we know we can make do just fine.

In the last fifty years, mankind has already developed and, in some cases, made commercial the technologies that enable us to transition to an all-renewable energy supply in the next thirty years. Yet it is worth noting that it is possible to add to the renewable family in the twenty-first century.

The march of progress will continue even faster if we make the fundamental decision that all our energy must be renewable for the survival of humanity.

***

1   Katherine Ellison, "Turned Off by Global Warming," *New York Times* (May 20, 2006).

2   S. David Freeman, Jim Harding, and Roger Duncan, "Solar Cells Change Electricity Distribution," *Seattle Post-Intelligencer* (August 10, 2006).

3   U.S. National Renewable Energy Laboratory (NREL), "How Much Land Will PV Need to Supply Our Electricity?" http://www.nrel.gov/ncpv/pvmenu.cgi?site+ncpv&idx=3&body=faq.html (January 2004).

4   Paul Hawken, Amory Lovins, and Hunter L. Lovins, *Natural Capitalism: Creating the Next Industrial Revolution* (Boston: Little, Brown and Company, 1999), 248.

5   For reference, the intensity of solar radiation outside of the atmosphere is about 1.3 kilowatts per square mile, and 1.1 kilowatts per square mile in the southwestern U.S., home to some of the best solar sites in the world.

6   The solar satellite would collect solar energy 24 hours/day, four times more than solar collectors on Earth (6–7 hours/day). Solar insolation on the earth's surface is about 200 watts per square mile, when averaged over 24 hours. Solar radiation outside the atmosphere is 1.3 kilowatts per square mile.

7   S. David Freeman, "Energy: A New Era," (New York: Vintage Books, 1974), 274.

8   Mark Mehos and Richard Perez, "Mining for Solar Resources: U.S. Southwest Provides Vast Potential," National Renewable Energy Laboratory (Summer 2005).

9   To reach this calculation, the following assumptions were used: 1,000 kW/5 acres of CSP capacity = 128,000 kW per square mile. At a 25 percent capacity factor, each $mile^2$ of CSP generates approximately 280,320,000 kWh/year. To meet U.S. electric demand in 2003, 3.6 trillion kWh, we would need an area of about 13,000 square miles, about 114 miles on a side.

10 To reach this calculation, the following assumptions were used: 2003 gasoline consumption is 142 billion gallons gasoline X 115,000 BTU/gallon gasoline = 16 quadrillion BTU = 142 million tons hydrogen (115,000 BTU/kg H_2). 16 quadrillion BTU = 4.8 trillion kWh. Electrolysis of water has electricity to hydrogen conversion of about 75 percent. 4.8 trillion kWh/.75 = 6.4 trillion kWh. Using solar electricity potential (endnote 7), H_2 production needs 1.8 times more land area, which equals about 23,500 square miles.

11 This includes fuel demand from all transportation sources—cars, trucks, buses, airplanes, and so on. The total BTU for all transportation consumption is 28 quadrillion BTU.

12 Electric Power Research Institute, "Comparing the Benefits and Impacts of Hybrid Electric Vehicle Options for Compact Sedan and Sport Utility Vehicles" (July 2002).

13 Elliot and Schwartz, 1993.

14 U. S. Department of the Interior, "Technology White Paper on Wind Energy Potential" (May 2006).

15 U. S. DOE, Energy Efficiency and Renewable Energy, Wind, and Hydropower Technologies Program. http://eereweb.ee.doe.gov/windandhydro/wind_potential.html (September 8, 2006). It should be noted that, due to the intermittency of wind, the maximum percentage of total power mix for wind is generally calculated at about 20 percent. However, deployment of advanced storage could enable wind to be a larger percentage of our electricity supply than the current maximum of 20 percent.

16 Ibid.

17 U. S. DOE, Energy Efficiency and Renewable Energy, "United States—2005 Year End Wind Power Capacity (MW)," *Windpowering America*

(January 25, 2006). http://www.eere.energy.gov/windandhydro/wind-poweringamerica/wind_installed_capacity.asp.

18 U. S. DOE, Energy Information Administration, "Annual Energy Outlook 2006" (December 2005).

19 American Wind Energy Association, "Comparative Cost of Wind and Other Energy Sources," 2001.

20 U.S. DOE (Sept. 26, 2006).

21 Ethanol is derived from the glucose, or natural digestible sugars, found in corn, sugar beets, sugarcane, and other crops. Cellulosic ethanol, on the other hand, is derived from the cellulose in organic matter wastes, including plastics, which is not easily digestible and thus not used for foodstuffs. I, and other experts in the field, believe cellulosic ethanol to be a major energy source in the future.

22 This includes 52 million tons of fuelwood from forests, 145 million tons from wood and paper processing mills, 47 million tons urban wood residues such as construction and demolition wastes, 64 million tons from logging and clearing, 60 million tons from fire treatment operations to reduce fire hazards.

23 Using the conversion technologies with an efficiency of about 43 percent, you can get about 50 gallons ethanol/dry ton cellulosic biomass.

24 U.S. Department of Agriculture, Economic Research Service, http://www.ers.usda.gov/data/. (November 1, 2006).

25 Other feedstocks for biodiesel include rapeseed, sunflowers, animal tallow, and thermal gasification of biomass. To produce biodiesel, the fuel oil reacts with an alcohol to remove the glycerin in a process called transesterification.

26 According to the National Biodiesel Board, 75 million gallons of biodiesel were sold in the U.S. in 2005, up threefold from 2004, in which 25 million gallons were sold. While that sounds like a lot, and it is, bear in mind that diesel accounts for 20 percent of all U.S. transportation fuels consumed. The U.S. consumes about 56 billion gallons of diesel per year, in a number of applications—on-road cars and trucks, farm equipment, backup generators, etc.

27 U.S. Departments of Energy and Agriculture, "Biomass as Feedstock for a Bioenergy and Bioproducts Industry: The Technical Feasibility of a Billion-Ton Annual Supply" (April 2005). This includes 428 million tons crop residue and 377 million tons perennial crops.

28 For example, Nathaniel Greene of the Natural Resources Defense Council (NRDC) estimates that an ethanol industry using environmen-

tally preferable production methods could fully replace the gasoline used in America by mid-century and slash U.S. greenhouse-gas emissions by 1.7 million tons per year, equivalent to 80 percent of current greenhouse-gas emissions from transportation.

29 U. S. Departments of Energy and Agriculture, "Biomass as Feedstock" (April 2005).

30 "Ethanol, Climate Protection, Oil Reduction," 2000.

31 Ethanol has a lower energy content than gasoline—1.3:1.

32 Adapted from a personal conversation with John Shears of the Center for Energy Efficiency and Renewable Technologies.

33 Nathaniel Greene, "Growing Energy: How Biofuels Can Help End America's Oil Dependence," Natural Resources Defense Council, (December 2004).

34 U.S. total electricity consumption in 2003 was 3.6 trillion kWh. This estimate is based on a 90 percent capacity factor and the 20 million kW of known resources in the U.S.

35 Kutscher, "The Status and Future of Geothermal Power," 2000.

36 "System Level Design, Performance, Cost and Economic Assessment— San Francisco Tidal In-Stream Power Plant," Energy Policy Research Institute (EPRI) (June 10, 2006).

THE MAJOR USES OF ENERGY

{How Efficient Use of
Renewables and Natural Gas
Can Supply Them All} ✱✱✱

IT IS A BOLD STAND TO TAKE, claiming that the efficient use of renewables, supplemented by natural gas, can supply all our energy demands and show that the resources and technology are available to do so. A skeptical or even excited person has a right to ask for more detail. Here is how we can do it.

The major sources of total energy in the U.S. are as follows:[1]

* Petroleum—40 percent
* Natural Gas—23 percent
* Coal—23 percent
* Nuclear—8 percent
* Renewables, including hydroelectric—6 percent

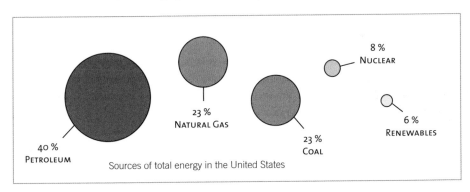

Sources of total energy in the United States

With renewables at less than 10 percent, we do have a challenge. If we continue to use natural gas, the cleanest of the fossil fuels, we still need to replace 71 percent of our energy supply. It's a big challenge but one that can be met over a thirty-year period, if we start now and steadily make the transition one year at a time.

There are three major markets for energy:

* Electricity
* Transportation
* A combination of heating buildings and industrial processes

In terms of units of energy, each of these markets consumes about one-third of the total. Let's examine them one at a time, and how their dependence on the previous sources can be replaced with renewables.

ELECTRICITY

Today our electric systems are run primarily on coal (50 percent), nuclear (20 percent) and natural gas (20 percent), with a small contribution by renewables, including existing hydro (10 percent).[2] As previously noted, the electric power industry uses virtually no petroleum. Therefore, the surest way to slash our oil imports is to build more electric mass transit, electrify the railroads, and develop all-electric cars and plug-in hybrids. If we are to make the transition to renewables we need to use renewables to generate electricity, and we also need to use more of that electricity for transportation.

Today the transition to renewable electricity is moving slowly in a few states and not at all in others. The key to success is a national policy to meet our emerging needs with energy efficiency, decentralized power, and renewables.

Today, about one-third of the electric grid consists of power plants over thirty years old. These old fossil plants are the worst polluters; in fact they are ten times dirtier than new power plants.[3] Coal plants of all ages account for 86 percent of carbon dioxide (CO_2), 95 percent of sulfur dioxide (SO_2), and 90 percent of oxides of nitrogen (NOx) emissions from the power sector.[4] Operating nuclear power plants are all approaching old age. Although their performance has, in fact, improved over the years, they are still first-generation plants, with no previous track record. We are essentially conducting an experiment in the durability of key components that is dangerous and unnecessary. Many of these plants, such as Indian Point, about fifty miles north of New York City, are at sites that would never be approved today because they are too close to large population centers.

The natural gas plants are the "least dirty" of the fossil fuels. Even though some of them are old, we need to keep them as backups for the renewables. These existing central station plants need to be used fewer and fewer hours to make room in the power supply for solar and wind power. Even so, we need them and new decentralized cogeneration plants, which generate both electric and heat energy, to firm up the renewables during those hours when the wind is not blowing or the sun is not shining.

I realize we can't quickly replace the coal and nuclear plants that constitute the bulk of our nation's electricity supply. I also know that over twenty to thirty years, it can be done. But unless there is a fixed timetable to replace them over a thirty-year period, they will still be poisoning the air and threatening our safety thirty years from now. I can say this because as a civil engineer I helped design a coal-fired plant in Tennessee built in 1950 that's still operating and polluting fifty-six years later.

The Joy of Unplugging

I know that electric utilities are companies the customers "love to hate." Customers rightfully expect lights to come on when they flip the switch and rates to stay level. Outages do occur, and rates do go

---

"THE BIG BLACKOUT"

It was 5:11 p.m. Eastern Standard Time on Nov. 9, 1965. I was alone in the chairman's office at the Federal Power Commission. The phone rang. It was a reporter from the Wall Street Journal saying, "Dave, what's going on about the blackout? The lights are out all over New England."

I thought it was a joke. It wasn't. Just about then, every light on the telephone switchboard lit up. The White House called. It seemed that every newspaper in the world called. Our agency had not had an inch of ink in the *Washington Post* in the four years I was there. We bored the hell out of everybody at cocktail parties. Yet all of a sudden the lights were out over much of the northeastern United States and no one knew why. And people wanted answers.

The president directed the Federal Power Commission to take over the investigation. I could barely even get a phone call through to Consolidated Edison, the power company in the area of the blackout, but I was told, "Dave, you have the full force of the federal government behind you. Now find out what's going on and get the lights back on."

It was an exciting time. Within about twenty-four hours, we found out the problem was with the power lines going north from Niagara Falls into Canada. The relays had not been adjusted for years and years. So when the power loads reached a certain limit, they short-circuited the transmission lines. All the power that was designed to head north into Canada from Niagara Falls turned around and went charging down the lines into New York State and knocked out whatever was in its path. It was like a huge wall of water rolling down a river, destroying everything in its way.

In those days, there were no protections built into the system. Afterward, we initiated a huge effort, building in safeguards so such an incident would not knock out power plants again. And we haven't had anything like that happen since then.

The power commission prepared a report that demonstrated how everyone responded to the emergency so peacefully. The moon was out so people could see at night. No airplanes crashed. There was no looting. People got to know each other. The most interesting statistic was that the birth rate shot up nine months later.

up, and if you don't pay your bill, they cut the lights off. There is no love of the utility.

For that reason, it would seem logical that most customers would jump at a chance to "unplug"— to generate some or all of their electricity at a reasonable cost with equipment they own at or near their location. The utilities are very much aware of that threat to their business, an alternative commonly referred to as distributed generation—rooftop solar and smaller generators powered by natural gas or hydrogen fuel cells.

The utilities, without much attention by the public, have designed their rates and service conditions to frustrate and stop any big-scale, distributed-power developments. Since it is really not economical to disconnect completely from the grid, the utilities routinely charge a high backup rate even if no backup power is used, undervalue the price they might pay for surplus power from the consumer, and take forever to agree to reasonable terms.

There is an elegant device called a heat pump that takes the solar heat in the air or the ground and brings it into the home. It can be encouraged or discouraged based on the rate structure of the utility affected.

Even in states where a fair deal for solar is in effect, the amount of solar is limited to a very small percent of the business.

Decentralized power is, of course, more reliable than central stations because it avoids the risks of transmission and distribution lines failing in wind and heat storms.

Also, a decentralized power plant can be located near an industry that needs heat. Thus what is "waste" heat to a large central station plant becomes a valuable replacement for natural gas or oil in a decentralized cogeneration plant. Decentralized power sources coupled with efficiency can provide sizeable replacements for coal and nuclear power.

In order for this option to be viable there must be a national policy of encouraging decentralized power. The kinds of policies I envision are:

* Utilities must be able to charge customers with decentralized power systems for only the actual amount of any backup power that they take from the utility system.
* Extra power from decentralized systems must be purchased by the utility for the price it charges for retail power.
* The utility must make standard connection agreements available and approved within ninety days.

Such a mandate, to be enforced by a state utility commission, must be part of a comprehensive national energy policy.

The path toward an all-renewable electric system is thus pretty straightforward:

* Existing coal and nuclear plants should be retired in harmony with renewable replacement, with the older plants shutting down first.
* No new fossil fuel or nuclear plants should be built.
* The nation should adopt a portfolio standard that requires every publicly and privately owned utility to meet the following standards:
  a. 20 percent renewable by 2017
  b. 40 percent renewable by 2027
  c. 60 percent renewable by 2037
* Utilities should be required to present for approval to their state Public Utilities Commission (PUC) a thirty-year plan to retire their coal and nuclear plants and replace them with conservation, decentralized power, and their choice of the vast array of renewable sources available to them.
* Natural gas plants can continue to supply all the capacity we need while economically cutting back on their output as wind and solar power is developed.
* Plug-in hybrid cars and possibly all-electric cars should be promoted with low off-peak rates and tax credits. These cars should become more numerous in the years ahead, and the beauty is that the extra electricity can come from renewables and natural gas.

The renewable resources are plentiful and the technology is commercial and can only get more and more cost effective with large-scale use. One thing for sure is it will never happen unless we start making these renewable technologies the "main event," and not just a sideshow, as they are today. And with an informed, knowledgeable citizenry, we can and we will.

TRANSPORTATION

Today this country runs on oil. That must and can change and the vehicles we love to drive can be just as sexy, roomy, safe, and comfortable. There are five sizeable sources of fuel combined with efficiency that can reverse the current dependency on imported oil. Used in combination, these methods will steadily reduce oil use down to next to nothing within thirty years.

The five ways are:

1. Efficient motor vehicles
2. Hybrid cars that plug into the electric grid

After our Ford Foundation study was published in the 1970s, I tried to help implement it by going to work for Senator Warren Magnuson (D–Wash.), chairman of both the Senate Commerce and Appropriations Committees. For many years he was known as Mr. Consumer on Capitol Hill. Senator Magnuson allowed me to work with any senator who was interested in energy. I helped out and became friends with people like Senators Walter Mondale (D–Minn.) and Edward Kennedy (D–Mass.) I also got to know consumer advocate Ralph Nader when we were both fighting for price controls on natural gas, economy standards for automobiles, and all the consumer laws that went through the Senate Commerce Committee.

Senator Magnuson asked what was the most important recommendation in my report. I said it was increasing the miles per gallon Americans get from their cars up from 10 to about 20 or 25 mpg. Then Senator Magnuson agreed to focus on that issue.

We persuaded Senator Fritz Hollings (D–S.C.), then a junior member of the Senate Commerce Committee, to hold hearings. We obtained valuable data from the Ford administration, "leaked" by my good friend Bob Hemphill, and put together a bill that became law requiring that American cars increase their miles per gallon. It was the first time Congress told the big automakers to shape up on mileage.

3. Biofuels, including ethanol
4. All-electric vehicles—cars, trains, and mass transit
5. Renewable hydrogen

Efficient Motor Vehicles

It is a technical fact that every existing model of car can be made more fuel efficient. And it is equally obvious that revising the fuel efficiency law to require better mileage is necessary to make it happen. To avoid any question about the auto industry's ability to comply, I propose raising the current average fuel efficiency of 24 mpg by only one mpg per year for the next twenty-four years. That would assure that America would offset the growth from additional vehicles. This option has been delayed because of opposition by the automakers. American voters haven't yet elected a president and Congress committed to better mileage.

Hybrids

An option for more dramatic reductions in oil consumption is hybrid cars that can plug into the electric grid. They will have sufficient batteries to basically run on an electric motor most of the time, backed up by a small internal combustion engine for longer trips. That car can be made today.

Existing hybrids run mostly on gasoline but still get about 40 mpg on average. The big breakthrough will take place if manufacturers incorporate the plug-in feature so that the car batteries can be charged when the car is not running.

It is urgent that we persuade auto companies to mass-produce

> We don't need a multiyear research project to build a plug-in feature into a car or to include a few more batteries than are already in the existing hybrids. In fact, just to prove the point that the auto companies are doing their usual delaying tactics, companies such as EDrive Systems and Hymotion, run by common-sense engineers, are manufacturing a plug-in kit that, without the economies of scale, costs $12,000. It would cost less than $5,000 if it were mass produced and if breakthroughs in lithium ion battery technology came to fruition.[5]

The plug-in feature fits neatly into the trunk of a car.
Source: www.calcars.org

plug-in hybrids in all of their models. We need to apply the purchasing power, political will, and common sense of the American people to make it happen promptly. That's what is required if we are to take our energy woes seriously enough to overcome them before they overcome us.

There was a Congressional hearing on this subject on May 17, 2006, and the resulting headline in the L.A. Times read, "Scientists Urge Congress to Fund Research on Plug-in Hybrids." The auto industry says it's too early to know whether plug-in hybrids could become cost effective. They have said much the same thing about seat belts, air bags, and pollution controls.

A plug-in hybrid can achieve 80 to 100 miles per gallon.
Source: www.calcars.org

The auto industry sells millions of cars each year on the merits of everything but price. But when it comes to fuel economy—the one thing that would save consumers money—the industry claims it costs too much.

We are at war and the oil weapon is our enemies' strongest weapon. No one in charge is telling the American people the facts or reflecting the urgency. A nation that put a man on the moon can add a plug-in feature and a few more batteries to a hybrid car. We need the voice of the American people to convince the scientists and the automakers that plug-in hybrids are what they want to drive, and they want to drive them NOW!

The plug-in hybrid would achieve the gasoline equivalent of 80 to 100 mpg. And there is no reason why, in a few short years, all the makes and models of hybrids today could not be plug-in hybrids. This option alone could easily cut gasoline consumption in half or more within a fifteen-year period.[6] The technology exists. The cars would have an additional cost of perhaps $5,000 more for the plug-in feature and the batteries, a cost that would be recovered in fuel savings, health, and defense costs, costs already being paid for by consumers. Tax credits to make this happen will be discussed in chapter 12.

The plug-in hybrid could become a zero-oil car by using ethanol, other biofuels, or hydrogen to power the internal combustion engine needed to supplement the electric motor to give the car the necessary range.

Biofuels

Biofuels today only really supply a small fraction of our transportation fuel. A dedicated band of pioneers and agrifarming industrial corporations are promoting fuels made from everything from corn and sugar to vegetable oil. The serious question is how we advance their use. Their use is limited by the need for corn and soy for food and the scarcity of additional land for agriculture.

I worry about destroying more habitat, and thereby killing wildlife, in order to drive our big cars. To the extent we are using waste products of the growing cycle of forests, agriculture, and the food we eat—fine. But let's not count on biofuels for more than 30 percent of the replacement for

The National Biodiesel Board reports that America's biodiesel industry may add up to $24 billion to the United States economy by 2015. Source: DOE/NREL

oil. The lesson of Brazil, where biofuels from sugar cane are replacing oil, is instructive as to what can be done with vision and a substantial policy. But it is not an exact model for the U.S. to follow.

We can and should advance the use of ethanol and biofuels up to the 30 percent level. But America has an option that dwarfs the prudent use of biofuels and even dwarfs our existing consumption of oil. That option is the sun and the wind converted to electricity or hydrogen.

Electric Vehicles

The electric car was born as a result of a rule by the California Air Resources Board (CARB) in 1990 requiring zero-emission cars. General Motors, Toyota, and others actually designed and built a small number of electric cars, which were leased to consumers. Charging stations were built all over Los Angeles, Sacramento, and other California cities. The people that leased the cars loved them and there was a long waiting list of people wanting to lease more of them.

It is true that battery development lagged and the range of most of these vehicles was less than about one hundred miles. Even so, they clearly could serve a sizeable market as a town car. But then in 2002, CARB buckled to industry pressure and let the auto industry off the hook. They rescinded the rule that required more and more electrics each year.

Then General Motors actually killed their own baby. They recalled every single one of their electric cars and, believe it or not, physically smashed them into pieces of junk. If you don't believe me, see the film *Who Killed the Electric Car?*, which has dramatic footage of the killing fields on which GM demolished these cars.

In the summer of 2006, the electric vehicle (EV) rose from the dead. Tesla Motors, an auto company independent of the giants that dominate the American market, unveiled a slick new electric sports car. It purports to have a 250-mile range powered by lithium ion batteries and a top speed of 130 mph. True, it does come with a hefty price tag—nearly $100,000. But, the first run of one hundred sold out in three weeks. The company promises to produce more affordable, mainstream electric cars. Perhaps the all-electric car is not dead after all!

The electric car has two major advantages over the plug-in hybrid. One is that the renewable electricity that powers the motor can be used directly and much more efficiently than any fuel in an internal combustion (IC) engine or even a fuel cell. The other major advantage over a hybrid is that the all-electric car doesn't require a backup IC engine. One drive system rather than two is inherently cheaper.

All-electric cars need not dominate the market to be a success. No one-car model serves everyone's needs anymore. Most families have more than one car. For trips around town and to work, driving an electric car with a 200-mile range may be near perfect. It is a choice Americans deserve to have available.

Battery development goes forward and the lithium battery looks very promising. It appears to be the key to an all-electric car with a 300-mile range. The Chinese are also pursuing its development. And it is quite possible that the all-electric car—with a long enough range—will be available with a "Made in China" label, but little Tesla Motors suggests that the vision and business sense of the Americans may still be alive and well, even if it seems missing in Detroit.

In any event, the electric car is still very much alive in the electric drive system under the hood of hybrids, which utilizes the technology developed for California's electric car program. In the hybrid, the range problem of the all-electric is overcome by the small IC engine, which runs on gasoline and serves as a range booster. But with the ability to plug into electricity, hybrids would do much more of their driving on electricity and less on gasoline, and would thus achieve the equivalent of an 80- to 100-mpg car. And as the electric grid becomes fueled increasingly by renewables, it's possible for all our energy to really become renewable.

As we make the transition to an all-renewable energy supply, electricity made from renewables can play the key role. The renewable electricity to power plug-in hybrids can replace a quantity of imported oil each year as they become mass-produced. And perhaps all-electric cars may join them. At some point, all our cars may run on renewable hydrogen. But that will take time because first the hydrogen highway (i.e., hydrogen filling stations) must be built over a large part of the nation.

> In October 2006, I rode a maglev train in Shanghai, China, from downtown to the airport. It reached speeds of over 200 mph but the ride was smooth and comfortable. Maglev is not just a "far out" idea. It is a reality in China.

The Train (and Bus) Keeps on Rollin'

Of course, electric vehicles also come in much larger sizes—namely railroad locomotives and mass transit systems in urban centers. Building electric trains to connect to major cities could reduce the role of gas-guzzling trucks and short-distance airline traffic, and the savings in oil and overall energy would be significant.

The electrification of the railroads can take place within the next decade or two at the most. And there are exciting new technologies such as maglev (magnetic levitation) trains that move without friction,

The magnetic levitation train transports passengers from Shanghai's Pudong airport to downtown at speeds over 250 miles per hour. Source: Railway Technical Research Institute

powered by electricity. When the price of oil is over seventy dollars a barrel, electrification becomes an attractive alternative to petroleum-fueled railroads. Yes, it will require major investments, but they will be profitable investments. This important step won't happen if it is not part of a focused federal program that helps a reluctant railroad industry transition from oil. Maglev trains are being developed in Germany, Japan, and China as you read, and the U.S. is falling dramatically behind.

We Americans love our mobility—our desire to go our own way—so much that we clog our roads so we can't go anywhere for hours. By clinging to our personal mobility we've become immobile. If there were a rapid means of getting chauffeured to work in a large vehicle—such as a train or bus—then a great many people would stop driving to work in their own gas-guzzling minivans, SUVs, Hummers, or sedans. We would save energy and save time for everyone.

Renewable Hydrogen
We will discuss the current myths and neglected possibilities of hydrogen in the next chapter. For now, it is sufficient to say only two things.

First, hydrogen, solar, and wind are the most plentiful things on Earth. It is a fact beyond dispute that the technology exists today to use solar and wind electricity to split water and free up hydrogen in quantities that would displace all our gasoline consumption.

Second, the IC engine loves hydrogen, and when it burns hydrogen the effluent is water and tiny amounts of oxides of nitrogen that can be contained. Renewable hydrogen is carbon free and homegrown. It will, of course, take time to build the hydrogen highways that California governor Schwarzenegger and New York governor Pataki advocate. Yet cars that utilize hydrogen for their IC engine, including plug-in hybrids, can now begin to be produced for business and government fleets. And as soon as the infrastructure is built they can be mass-produced. The fundamental solution to our troubles needs to begin now. Improved efficiency, plug-in hybrids, and biofuels can gain our transportation independence from oil. They are one of the most important things America can do to meet the greatest threats to our security—terrorism and global warming.

HEATING BUILDINGS AND INDUSTRIAL PROCESSES

America uses a lot of energy to keep warm. Natural gas has, for the most part, replaced coal in our homes and factories. Natural gas is also used extensively in industry as a raw ingredient in fertilizer and for a wide variety of manufacturing processes. But there is still a sizeable market for home heating oil, propane, and other petroleum products (about 30 percent of our total oil use).

Most of our natural gas is produced in the U.S. or imported from Canada and Mexico. Its continued use is vital to transition to renewables since it is our cleanest source for fossil fuels. What is needed, as previously stated, is to shift some of its use from boiler fuel for electric generation to replace oil for home heating and transportation fuel, especially for trucks, buses, and railway locomotives.

We also need to avoid the slippery slope of large-scale importation of natural gas. Instead, a stronger conservation program emphasizing the incentives to persuade homeowners to install new highly efficient furnaces could cut natural gas usage by 20 percent and more. Greater use of ground-source electric heat pumps that bring solar energy into the building could displace some of the gas used for heating. Solar hot water would also help, and municipal solid waste can be converted to biogas to replace natural gas.

These measures and other efficiency options could easily obviate the need for importing sizeable volumes of natural gas from overseas.

While natural gas can be a useful transition fuel for the next twenty to thirty years, it does emit carbon, although much less per unit of energy than coal or oil. And the natural gas resource is depleting. Since 1970, we have burned more natural gas each year than we have discovered. The remaining potential sources are in offshore areas near our coastal zone or places where the natural beauty would be disturbed by the construction that accompanies drilling.

We need to start developing the renewable alternative to natural gas now. And that alternative is renewable hydrogen; that is, hydrogen made from solar, wind, or other renewables (see chapter 9).

A serious development program is needed to determine what combination of centralized and decentralized hydrogen is best. Central station hydrogen at the source of the wind farm and the sun complex in the desert would require a new pipeline system similar to the one built to deliver natural gas. The decentralized option could be as local as one's home where water and electricity are uniformly available. It would also require a "home kit" to make, store, and utilize the hydrogen.

CONCLUSION

The resources are available for electricity to meet all of our growing needs quite reliably with renewables and natural gas used efficiently. The peak loads in the future can be managed with modern technology, automatically reducing peaks by providing customers the proper incentives. We don't need new nuclear or coal facilities.

The technology and resources are equally available for kicking the oil habit with plug-in hybrids that run mostly on electricity and flex-fuel cars that use biofuels. And in ten to twenty years, we can have hydrogen-fueled cars and all-electric vehicles.

The rest of our energy needs can be supplied by natural gas and the use of efficient, decentralized heat and power systems that turn waste heat into useable energy.

The technology and resources are here. All we need is the leadership of public officials, people who can say no to the oil, coal, and nuclear lobbies.

* * *

1 U. S. EIA, "U.S. Primary Consumption by Source and Sector" (2004). http://www.eia.doe.gov/emeu/aer/pdf/pecss_diagram.pdf.

2 U. S. EIA, "Basic Electricity Statistics" (2004). http://www.eia.doe.gov/neic/quickfacts/quickelectric.html.

3 "Up in Smoke," US PIRG Education Fund, (July 1999).

4 U.S. EPA, "National Totals of SO_2, Nox, CO_2, and Heat Input for Coal Fired and Non-Coal Fired Title IV Affected Units for 1996–2001." http://www.epa.gov/airmarkets/emissions/score01/table1.pdf (2001).

5 From personal conversation with Greg Hanssen of EDrive Systems (May 13, 2006).

6 Set America Free, "A Blueprint for U.S. Energy Security," http://www.setamericafree.org/. If, by 2025, all cars on the road were hybrids, and half were plug-in hybrids, then U.S. oil consumption would be slashed from 20 million barrels per day to eight.

6
DOES RENEWABLE ENERGY REALLY COST MORE?

{THE ANSWER IS NO!} ✳✳✳

THE OIL, COAL, AND NUCLEAR FOLKS have for thirty years dismissed solar and wind power as too expensive for ordinary Americans. They've targeted renewables as a "show-off" symbol for environmental elites. In the meantime, the price of oil, our electric bills, and their "hidden" costs have crept steadily upward. Whether it is electricity rates, costs for gasoline, medical bills for pollution-related illnesses,[1] or the cost of our national defense budget to safeguard our international oil supply, guess who pays for it—no one else but the American people.

But now that the price of gasoline has jumped up so far and so fast, price is the last thing the oil folks want to talk about.

But that's exactly what needs our attention. The price. If we look at what each source really costs the American people, renewable energy today and certainly tomorrow is our lowest cost source.

Renewables are a better financial bet for the consumer than oil, coal, or nuclear power for the following reasons:

* The total cost to the American consumer is lower over the life of their energy-using equipment.
* The direct cost of the renewable energy is fixed when it is built. There are no fuel costs for solar and wind, and it is thus virtually inflation-proof.
* Renewables are converted to electricity, the price of which is regulated to reflect costs plus a reasonable profit. This is in contrast to the unregulated price of oil and fossil fuels and the unknown price of new nuclear power.

* Renewable costs are going down while the price of oil and gas is going up.
* The savings in cost of renewables over coal, oil, and nuclear power are virtually incalculable. These indirect costs are health benefits, savings in our defense budget, and the overall benefits to the environment.

THE ESCALATING PRICE OF OIL

Let's be clear that the price of gasoline has little to do with what it actually costs to produce it. Saudi Arabia produces much of its oil for one dollar a barrel and has no problem selling it for sixty or seventy dollars. American companies are earning similar windfall profits on U.S. production to the tune of billions of dollars. The price has no relation to cost—it is a result of speculators bidding the price up and fear of shortages caused by the combination of terrorism and runaway increases in demand.

There is no competition among oil producers. What exists is a well-established cartel called OPEC that is keeping the world on its toes with artificially short rations, which results in high prices for you and windfall profits for them. OPEC's job is relatively easy these days. It is getting help from Mother Nature because additional oil production is becoming harder as it faces political and environmental obstacles. It is getting help from speculators who fear political embargos or terrorist acts on the oil fields. And OPEC is getting help from the new consumers in China and India, where demand

The Arab oil embargo broke out in 1973, and the Ford Foundation study was the only show in town that was not biased. The oil-producing nations of the Middle East had cut off oil to the United States to raise prices and as retaliation for our support of Israel. I found myself on Capitol Hill dozens of times testifying before Congress about energy. I briefed members of Congress and national columnists alike. Our study organization became a makeshift think tank on the scene in Washington, D.C., that everyone wanted to talk to in order to learn about this topic.

In the middle of all that, I made a speech to the Consumer Federation of America in which I said that this energy crisis may be a smoke screen under which the oil industry was picking the pockets of the American people to the tune of billions of dollars by charging more for gasoline. Walter Cronkite ran some of it on the CBS Evening News.

for gasoline is growing so fast as to outstrip new discoveries. The shortages are becoming real and OPEC is fully equipped to keep it that way.

THE COST OF RENEWABLES

In contrast, the price of solar, wind, geothermal, and biomass electricity sold by a utility can be controlled to reflect its actual cost, which is, in fact, on a downward trend. Today, electricity from wind, biomass, and geothermal can be generated at or near the cost of natural gas—in the six- to ten-cents-per-kWh range. Coal is lower priced, but new coal-fired plants with good controls will not cost consumers much less than renewables directly and will cost

THE PRICE OF GASOLINE HAS LITTLE TO DO WITH WHAT IT ACTUALLY COSTS TO PRODUCE IT

much more indirectly. And we have no valid idea what a new nuclear plant in America will cost, except we know it won't be cheap, and the indirect costs will be awesome and forever.

Here's the crucial difference—once the infrastructure is built, the cost of renewables is largely fixed. The fuel, which is most of the cost with oil or coal, is free. As long as the sun rises and the wind keeps blowing, the fuel costs remain the same—zero.

The initial cost of renewables has gone down over the years and, as anyone who took Economics 101 will know, costs will decline with increased demand. So, the costs of renewable power will keep going down as more plants are built and technological innovation allows for more natural "fuel" to be collected and turned into usable energy more efficiently.

Fixed Costs of Renewables

There is another basic reason why renewables are a better bet for the consumer. Their costs are pretty well fixed at birth over the long life of the solar panel or windmill. Long-term contracts can assure that the price remains stable and even goes down as adjusted for inflation, which the renewables pretty much avoid because their costs are fixed. This is a crucial distinction for consumers. What you see now, in terms of price, is what you get for now and the future. As the saying goes, there are few guarantees in life—that the sun will rise and the wind will keep blowing are two of them.

Solar Costs

Solar panels can be used directly to power homes, buildings, and even plug-in hybrid cars. More fundamentally, solar power can be owned by the customer! You can own your own power plant. The costs can't go up—you

THERE ARE FEW GUARANTEES IN LIFE—THAT THE SUN WILL RISE AND THE WIND WILL KEEP BLOWING ARE TWO OF THEM

own it—it's paid for and the fuel is free! There are no moving parts and virtually no maintenance. Sounds like a much better deal than your gas station can offer you!

Solar panels can also be built and operated by electric utility companies that are still largely regulated. This provides a reasonable guarantee that the price will reflect costs and a reasonable profit and that consumers will not be gouged.

Today the direct cost of rooftop solar power is high, about twenty centers/kWh, but it will drop rapidly with scale and the new thin-film breakthrough (see chapter 8). Thin-film technology promises to create solar power in your backyard as low as six cents/kWh. With that, you can charge your plug-in hybrid for less than one dollar a gallon equivalent. You could even make hydrogen at a cost competitive with the future price of gasoline.

If one looks at the cost of concentrated solar power (CSP—Big Solar in the desert) with fixed operating costs, the inflation-proof, zero fuel cost of the sun is a winner. Big Solar promises to be very competitive over the life of the energy plant. We can eliminate the pain at the pump, stop global warming, and save money. That's a potent combination.

Wind Costs

Wind power plants reveal dramatically how the oil, coal, and nuclear lobbies have totally misled the American people. The direct cost of wind power is now as low as natural gas and on par with the life-cycle cost of a new coal-fired plant. And wind, like solar, has zero fuel cost. And, of course, wind power doesn't carry with it the health bills, global warming dangers, and nuclear war threats of what we are using today.

Wind power also reveals the trends. Its costs have tumbled as volume has increased, in contrast to the escalating costs of the poisons we are using. It is no wonder that wind power is now favored in France, Germany, and even Texas!

Biomass Costs

For years, the cost for ethanol was a bit more than gasoline. In May 2006 the price of ethanol from corn was $2.75 to $2.95 a gallon, right on par with the cost of gasoline. In farm states, like Iowa, the price of gasoline blended with ethanol, E10, or E85 was even cheaper than gasoline. In April 2006, regular gas in Iowa sold for $2.71, while E10 and E85 sold for $2.65 and $2.33, respectively.[2] Cellulosic ethanol requires some improvements to the conversion process to bring down costs substantially. This will be discussed in the chapter on technologies (chapter 8). Once the more efficient process is fully mature, it is expected that the price will drop further.

Government Incentives

A renewable power plant (solar or wind) requires little or no labor and fuel to operate. Almost all of its costs are what's required to build it in the first place. That means its total costs are largely determined by how it is financed. A plant financed with tax-free debt by a public power agency at 5 percent interest can cost less than half that of a plant financed in large part by equity that expects to earn 10 to 20 percent on the investment. Today there is a crazy quilt of tax credits that are temporary in nature but useful until volume production is achieved.

For the long haul, the best government incentive would be to make the interest on loans for renewables tax free for all renewable power plants and plants used for conversion to hydrogen.

Fueling Our Cars with Renewables

With 5 percent interest money, the going rate for tax-free municipal bonds, and existing incentives, wind power can be built and transmitted to our cities for less than eight cents/kWh, which, when used in a plug-in hybrid car, is one-sixth the price of an equivalent amount of gasoline today.[3] And if you figure in the greater efficiency of the electric motor over the IC engine, electricity is equivalent to less than one dollar per gallon of gas. Solar-powered electricity at most would be the equivalent of two-dollar-a-gallon gas.[4]

Electricity, roughly speaking, could deliver most of the energy needed to run your plug-in hybrid car. The back-up IC engine could be fueled by the growing production of ethanol and other forms of biofuel. Of course, it will take many years before all our cars and buses are plug-in hybrids. But electricity, biofuels, and hydrogen can replace more gasoline cars steadily every year from now on. The electricity will be much cheaper and cleaner than gasoline and will not be tied to the world market for oil.

There is no doubt that the combination of renewable electricity, biofuels, and renewable hydrogen, together with more efficient cars, will dramatically reduce consumers' cost of driving.

New Coal or Nuclear Plants Will Cost Consumers More Than Renewables

Existing coal and nuclear plants built decades ago still have lower direct costs than new renewable plants. But that is not a meaningful comparison because it doesn't reflect future direct costs or all of the real costs.

History and experience tell us that the price of coal is greatly influenced by natural gas prices. There is a lag because coal for power plants is sold under long-term contracts. But coal prices for new plants would approach the equivalent price of competing fuels. Renewables costs are going down and the lines are already crossing.

As for nuclear plants, we haven't built a new one in the U.S. in over twenty years, in large part because of the costs.[5] No industry has a worse record of cost overruns than the nuclear power industry, which requires major government subsidies to operate. It is a pure act of faith and misinformation by the nuclear advocates, who share a cultlike belief in their product, to suggest that a new nuclear plant can be cheaper than wind power or even concentrated solar, much less geothermal or municipal waste.

Indirect Costs

If we examine new power plants, we must look at all of their costs. Burning coal creates poisons that contaminate the air, create smog, and bring on global warming. Nuclear plants expose the U.S. to massive doses of radiation and require major subsidies from the federal government, greater than those required by other energy sources, in the form of accident insurance and the security cost of protecting the plants against terrorism.

In poll after poll the American people have said that they are willing to pay more in their electric bills for renewable power to reduce environmental impacts. This "more" really is the people's understanding that if they pay a little more in their electric bill now, over time they, their children, and their grandchildren will pay less in their health-care bill, live a little longer, and leave a better Earth for generations to come.

THE NEED FOR REGULATION OF UTILITIES

One thing we do know—competition does not exist among electric companies or oil companies. These are oligarchies that sell commodities vital to the functioning of our society and, as such, they can charge whatever they want because they have guaranteed customers no matter what. If there are no government controls, the consumer gets ripped off. Greed is directly proportional to grasp. And price has little or no relation to cost.

The untold story is that the cost to an oil producer in Saudi Arabia or even Texas does not matter; it is the price they charge that counts and hurts. Electricity can deliver energy that will run your car far cheaper than oil, and the price of electricity can be kept under control through a long-standing policy of regulating the price of electricity on a cost basis. The price of oil shoots up when a country like Iran rattles its sword and speculators get in a bidding contest to avoid shortages. It is much easier for oil producers to pump more slowly if holding back helps them to hold us up. Why run the risk of jeopardizing the steady flow of sky-high profits?

That last line of defense for consumers—the regulation of utilities—is under attack. We must be aware of the recent attempts to deregulate the electric power industry.

From 2000 to 2001, I served as senior advisor to California governor Gray Davis. I was appointed to try to end the massive rip-off of Californians by the Enrons of the world. I saw firsthand the pain at the electric meter. The lesson, which has yet to be fully appreciated, is that if you remove price controls over electricity, which people cannot store or do without, the companies selling it can create a shortage and take you to the cleaners.

Remember this. The California electricity crisis revealed that power plants could "get sick" to add to shortages and jack up prices. During the

IT IS MUCH EASIER FOR OIL PRODUCERS TO PUMP MORE SLOWLY IF HOLDING BACK HELPS THEM TO HOLD US UP

crisis, power plant operators would cut their production or go offline entirely during the times of highest demand to drive up the price of electricity to many, many times its typical rate. The result—a whole lot of money was made and distributed to a very small number of people.

Executives for utilities that are regulated follow a rule of thumb—at all costs they avoid raising rates by double-digit amounts at any one time. The reason is obvious. Consumers can't easily adjust to large increases in the cost of an item they can't do without. That's why Americans get angry at the obscene run-up of the price of gasoline, home heating oil, and natural gas, all of which are unregulated. By contrast, electricity prices have increased, but under regulation the increase has been at a modest pace.

Consumers prize certainty and stability in what they pay for electricity and gasoline, items they must keep buying. They are the lifeblood of this high-energy civilization we have created for ourselves. That's a central reason renewables are preferable for consumer protection.

We must continue to have regulation on our electricity in order to avoid what happened in California. Over the long haul, it is a foregone conclusion that renewable electricity at a regulated price will be cheaper for the consumer than unregulated oil or unregulated natural gas.

ENSURING EFFICIENCY

Getting the price of fuel under control by shifting to renewables is only half the job of consumer protection. We must marry renewables with efficiency. And here consumers can save big money.

When you buy a car for $15,000 and finance it with payments of $250 per month, you are also committing yourself to a gasoline bill of $180 per month if you drive 1,200 miles a month at 20 mpg with gas at three dollars per gallon. If instead you buy a car that gets 40 mpg, you cut your gas bill in half, to just $90 per month. You save $90 a month.

It doesn't take a MBA from Harvard to figure that one sure way to cut your gas bill is to buy a car with better mileage. The same is true for air conditioners, furnaces, refrigerators, and the like.

The federal government and regulators can help with standards and incentives, but consumers can really help themselves by recognizing that energy—yes, even renewable energy—is priced so high that the fuel that feeds your car or appliance over its life may cost about as much as the item itself. Whether you are high income or low income, the way to save money without giving up any convenience is to buy the most efficient model. Even if it costs a bit more, that extra cost will pay monetary dividends to you.

CONCLUSION

The surprising truth is that new investments in efficiency and renewable resources will cost consumers less money than the out-of-control market price of oil, the escalating cost of coal, and the subsidized and uncertain forever costs of nuclear plants. Once a renewable energy source is built, its costs are fixed and there are NO fuel costs.

So efficiency and renewables are cheaper even on the misleading pricing system we use. If we consider—as we must—the health costs of air pollution, the proliferation and radiation risks of nuclear, and the health and global warming costs of coal, it is a no-brainer.

Renewables are the best bet for the consumer.

* * *

1   Asthma is the most frequently cited reason for children's visits to the nurses' office in California schools, according to the American Lung Association.

2   Libby Quaid, "Ethanol Dazzles Wall Street, White House," *Associated Press* (June 3, 2006).

3   Hybrid batteries achieve about four miles per kWh. The average mpg for vehicles, according to the Department of Transportation, is twenty-four. So, six kWh is about equal to one gallon of gasoline. Using three-dollar-a-gallon gasoline and eight cents/kWh electricity, the electricity is forty-eight cents/gallon equivalent, or about six times less in cost than gasoline. Note that plug-in hybrids also use a gasoline engine backup, so the combined cost is typically estimated at one-dollar-a-gallon gasoline equivalent.

4   The cost of solar electric power varies greatly depending on the cost and type of the system, which often varies itself based on what sorts of incentives are available, interconnection fees, and other costs and benefits that are separate from the system itself. That said, the delivered cost of PV power is between fifteen and twenty cents/kWh at present. This figure may decrease dramatically with the introduction of new nonsilicon, thin-film panels.

5   TVA's Watts Bar Nuclear Plant began construction in 1973. Unit 1 went online in 1996. Unit 2 never went online. See http://www.tva.gov/sites/wattsbarnuc.htm.

NUCLEAR WASTE STORAGE SITES

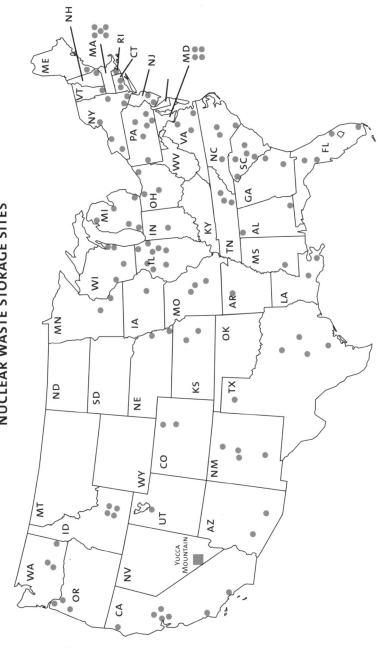

● SITES STORING SPENT NUCLEAR FUEL, HIGH-LEVEL RADIOACTIVE WASTE, AND/OR SURPLUS PLUTONIUM DESTINED FOR GEOLOGIC DISPOSITION

SYMBOLS DO NOT REFLECT PRECISE LOCATIONS

YUCCA MOUNTAIN

February 1, 2007
Source: U.S. DOE

KNOWN OIL FIELDS IN THE UNITED STATES

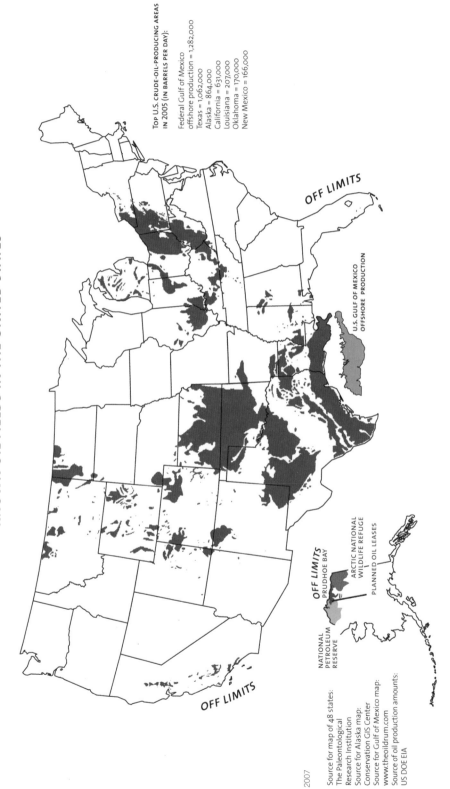

TOP U.S. CRUDE-OIL-PRODUCING AREAS
IN 2005 (IN BARRELS PER DAY):

Federal Gulf of Mexico
offshore production = 1,282,000
Texas = 1,062,000
Alaska = 864,000
California = 631,000
Louisiana = 207,000
Oklahoma = 170,000
New Mexico = 166,000

OFF LIMITS

U.S. GULF OF MEXICO
OFFSHORE PRODUCTION

OFF LIMITS

OFF LIMITS

OFF LIMITS
PRUDHOE BAY

NATIONAL
PETROLEUM
RESERVE

ARCTIC NATIONAL
WILDLIFE REFUGE

PLANNED OIL LEASES

2007

Source for map of 48 states:
The Paleontological
Research Institution
Source for Alaska map:
Conservation GIS Center
Source for Gulf of Mexico map:
www.theoildrum.com
Source of oil production amounts:
US DOE EIA

COAL FIELDS IN THE COTERNIMOUS UNITED STATES

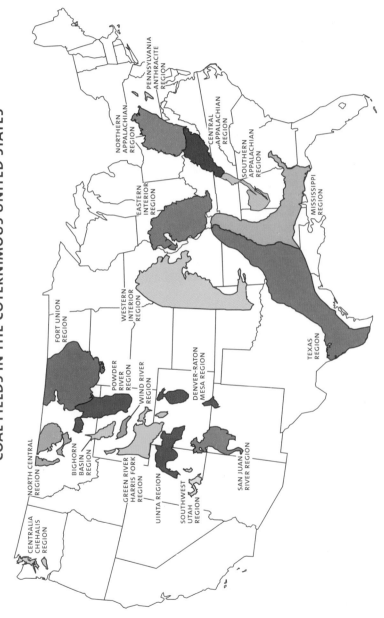

PENNSYLVANIA ANTHRACITE REGION

NORTHERN APPALACHIAN REGION

CENTRAL APPALACHIAN REGION

SOUTHERN APPALACHIAN REGION

EASTERN INTERIOR REGION

MISSISSIPPI REGION

WESTERN INTERIOR REGION

FORT UNION REGION

POWDER RIVER REGION

WIND RIVER REGION

DENVER-RATON MESA REGION

TEXAS REGION

NORTH CENTRAL REGION

BIGHORN BASIN REGION

GREEN RIVER HARRIS FORK REGION

UINTA REGION

SOUTHWEST UTAH REGION

SAN JUAN RIVER REGION

CENTRALIA CHEHALIS REGION

SOLAR RESOURCE

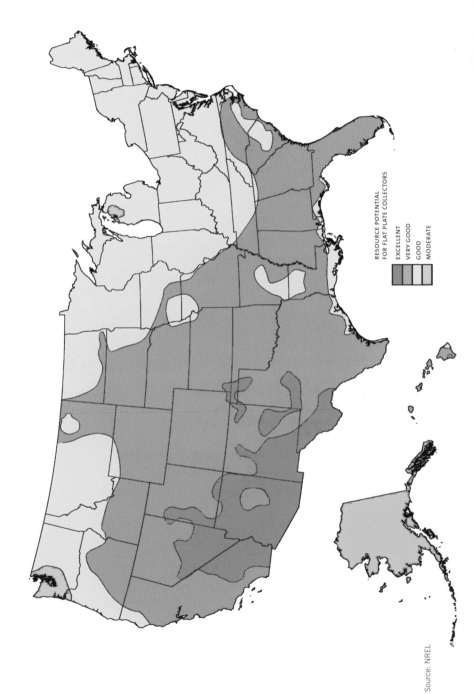

RESOURCE POTENTIAL
FOR FLAT PLATE COLLECTORS

EXCELLENT
VERY GOOD
GOOD
MODERATE

Source: NREL

UNITED STATES ANNUAL AVERAGE WIND POWER

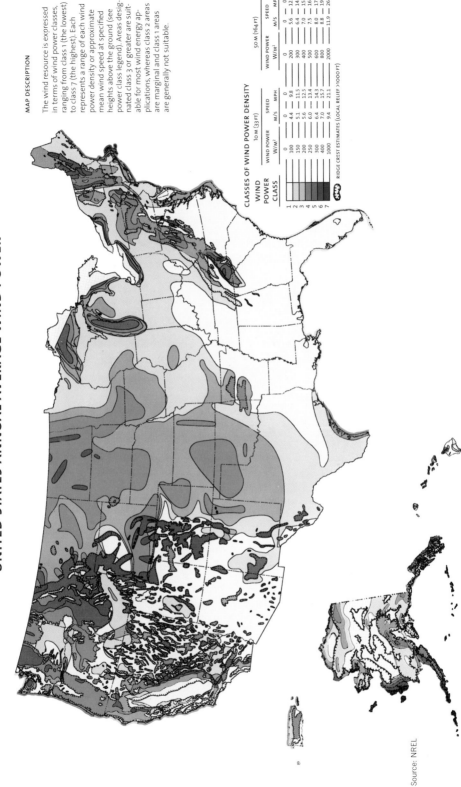

MAP DESCRIPTION

The wind resource is expressed in terms of wind power classes, ranging from class 1 (the lowest) to class 7 (the highest). Each represents a range of each wind power density or approximate mean wind speed at specified heights above the ground (see power class legend). Areas designated class 3 or greater are suitable for most wind energy applications, whereas class 2 areas are marginal and class 1 areas are generally not suitable.

CLASSES OF WIND POWER DENSITY

WIND POWER CLASS	10 M (33 FT)			50 M (164 FT)		
	WIND POWER W/m²	SPEED M/S	SPEED MPH	WIND POWER W/m²	SPEED M/S	SPEED MPH
1	0	0	0	0	0	0
	100	4.4	9.8	200	5.6	12.5
2	150	5.1	11.5	300	6.4	14.3
3	200	5.6	12.5	400	7.0	15.7
4	250	6.0	13.4	500	7.5	16.8
5	300	6.4	14.3	600	8.0	17.9
6	400	7.0	15.7	800	8.8	19.7
7	1000	9.4	21.1	2000	11.9	26.6

RIDGE CREST ESTIMATES (LOCAL RELIEF >1000 FT)

Source: NREL

BIOMASS RESOURCES AVAILABLE IN THE UNITED STATES

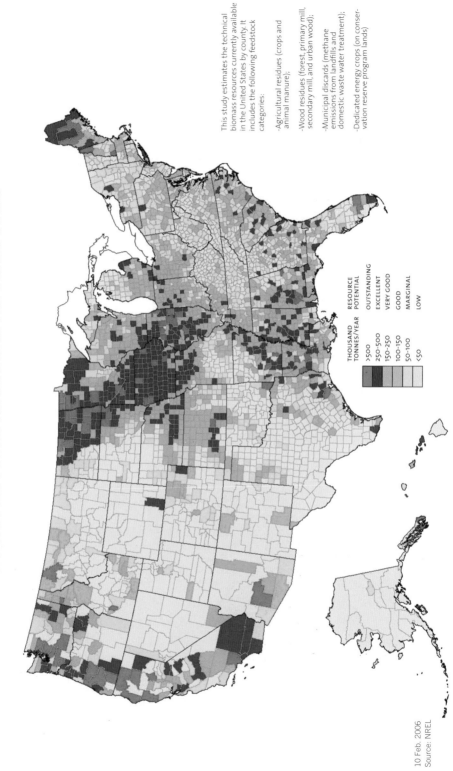

This study estimates the technical biomass resources currently available in the United States by county. It includes the following feedstock categories:

- Agricultural residues (crops and animal manure);

- Wood residues (forest, primary mill, secondary mill, and urban wood);

- Municipal discards (methane emissions from landfills and domestic waste water treatment);

- Dedicated energy crops (on conservation reserve program lands)

THOUSAND TONNES/YEAR	RESOURCE POTENTIAL
>500	OUTSTANDING
250-500	EXCELLENT
150-250	VERY GOOD
100-150	GOOD
50-100	MARGINAL
<50	LOW

10 Feb. 2006
Source: NREL

GEOTHERMAL RESOURCE

Data Source:
Southern Methodist University
  Geothermal Laboratory
Alaska Department of
  Natural Resources
Hawaii Dept. of Business,
  Economic Development
  and Tourism

RESOURCE POTENTIAL

EXCELLENT

GOOD

Source: NREL

HYDROGEN POTENTIAL FROM RENEWABLE RESOURCES
Total kg of hydrogen per county normalized by county area

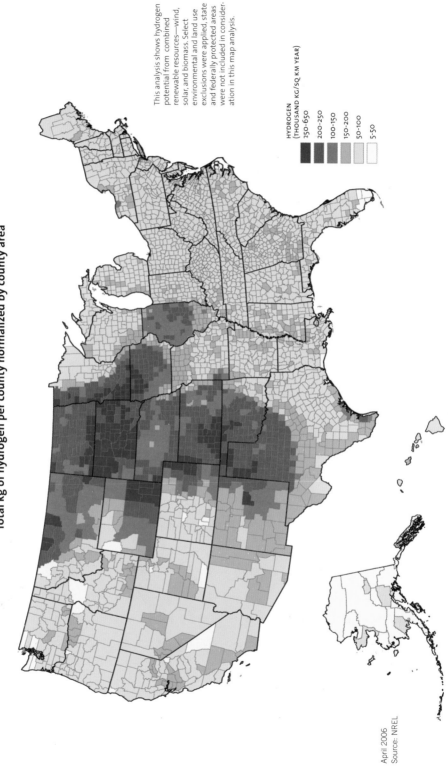

This analysis shows hydrogen potential from combined renewable resources—wind, solar, and biomass. Select environmental and land use exclusions were applied, state and federally protected areas were not included in consideration in this map analysis.

HYDROGEN
(THOUSAND KG/SQ KM YEAR)

250-650
200-250
100-150
150-200
50-100
5-50

April 2006
Source: NREL

7 ENERGY EFFICIENCY

{THE CHEAPEST AND
CLEANEST ENERGY} ✳✳✳

THE CHEAPEST, CLEANEST, AND MOST RELIABLE source of energy is the energy we avoid using. The energy we save through more efficient cars, refrigerators, or air conditioners occurs automatically, year in and year out, over the life of the equipment.

Energy efficiency measures and their costs vary widely, from simple and cheap methods like screwing in an energy-efficient lightbulb, to more expensive methods like installing a heat pump in a home or buying a new hybrid car. For devices that run on electricity, the cost per kWh saved may be as low as one cent or as high as eight cents per kilowatt hour. But these costs are still well below the retail cost of electricity, without counting the savings of environmental and health costs of not using the electricity.

 There are other energy saving opportunities that are pure savings, with no extra costs at all. Take the example of white roofs. It costs almost the same amount to construct and install a white roof as it does a black roof on a building. But the energy bill savings can be enormous over the life of the building because white roofs reflect the heat and cut down air conditioning costs dramatically.[1]

Buying a fuel-efficient car is a bargain in that the savings in the cost of gasoline are sizeable, and better fuel economy doesn't necessarily mean a higher-priced car.

Unfortunately, energy efficiency is confused with "doing without"—"freezing in the dark," some people call it. Voluntary action by citizens to "do without" is an entirely different concept than being energy efficient and it depends on individual preferences and values. People do respond in an acute crisis to appeals to change their habits and to monetary

It has taken a long time for Americans to recognize energy savings as a big deal. I can recall a large meeting in 1969, when Richard Nixon was president, with the electric utility executives in the office of Secretary of Interior Rogers Morton. I dared to suggest that we should start conserving electricity and was called a socialist by industry leaders who then claimed the use of electricity and economic growth were the equivalent of Siamese twins.

incentives to turn off the lights and turn up the thermostat on the hottest days of summer. But we call that "conservation" and it's quite different from "efficiency," even though the two words are often used interchangeably.

Efficiency is building energy-using equipment to perform the same service with less energy. It is as American as apple pie. Every business tries to cut its costs. Greater efficiency has enabled America to steadily improve its standard of living. Thankfully, it is no longer considered a threat to our lifestyle but a means of balancing a very unbalanced national energy budget.

I have often thought we should create an organization called "Conservatives for Conservation" because it is a very conservative idea.

In the 1960s, the idea of saving energy was indeed considered anti-American. When I was the executive assistant to the chairman of the old Federal Power Commission in the early 1960s, I remember the reaction of my boss Joseph Swidler to the staff's projection of U.S. electric demand for 1980. He said, "Folks, this is lower than what the Russians are projecting. We're not going to let Russia beat us. Go back and give me a higher projection that shows the U.S. as a winner." And they did.

We actually thought that the more electricity we used, the better off we were. Electricity was connected to "living better electrically," the industry slogan. Electricity usage was universally accepted as our best barometer of progress.

Ironically, it was considered a revolutionary idea to imply that we could achieve the same progress—air conditioning, refrigeration, attractive cars—with less energy and thus save money and preserve the environment.

However, as late as 2001, Vice President Dick Cheney said that conservation was simply "a sign of personal virtue . . . not a sufficient basis for a sound, comprehensive energy policy." Despite all the evidence to the contrary, some people still believe that if we do more drilling, stripping, and burning, we can live happily ever after. They see efficiency, solar, and wind as a threat. Thank the Lord for that threat. We have finally learned that increased efficiency promotes economic growth and waste is just what we call it—a waste. The shameful failure to improve the gas mileage of cars for the last decade vividly demonstrates where we have stood in recent years. And consumers are paying the price for much of that neglect as gas prices shoot up and they are stuck with SUVs and other gas-guzzling cars.

STATES TAKE THE INITIATIVE

A few states have taken efficiency seriously and have recognized its importance. At the time of this writing, greater efficiency is a central part of the energy policy of California, New York, and Oregon. California has nearly the lowest per capita consumption of electricity of any state in the nation, and it has stayed level over the years, whereas consumption has steadily gone up for the rest of the nation.[2]

In California, Oregon, and New York, they get it. The proof is that the utility commissions in these states reward efficiency investments as much as they reward power plants, so utilities don't lose money while their customers are saving energy and money. The utilities in these states have incentives to encourage their customers to use less. Groups like the Natural Resources Defense Council and others helped put this policy in place with their advocacy and expertise. We need this policy to spread nationwide.

I am proud that the Ford Foundation study I chaired in 1974 demonstrated conclusively the huge opportunity greater efficiency presented for avoiding energy shortages and reducing pollution. But this stance hasn't been easy. Before the study was approved, I appeared before the entire Ford Foundation board, which included Robert McNamara and Henry Ford II, in their glass building in New York City. Mr. Ford accused me of prejudging the study by favoring efficiency over more drilling for oil and gas. I told him that I had an open mind but not an empty one. I suggested we all just take a look at the building we were in, where the temperature was kept 20 degrees cooler than the outside in summer and 30 degrees warmer in winter with only a single pane of glass as shelter. Surely we could all agree that greater efficiency has to be a focus of the study. Everyone then seemed embarrassed by the question and the study was approved.

ZERO-GROWTH ENERGY

We continue to base policy on projections showing that the consumption of energy is going to keep growing in the years ahead. This will be true if we fail to implement policies based on known facts that it would be cheaper, cleaner, and quicker to make the investments in cars with better mileage, more efficient appliances and furnaces, and better insulated buildings to assure a near-zero energy growth future.

We are not starting from scratch. The awareness of efficiency opportunities and a variety of laws and regulations to implement them have advanced significantly in the past forty years. The Truth in Labeling Act provides customers with facts labeled on each item about how much they can save. There are laws to require better mileage and more efficient appliances. State and local governments provide monetary incentives for efficiency as well as standards for new buildings.

These laws provide a good foundation. What's needed next for efficiency is to "raise the bar" and strengthen the requirements and policies to achieve zero growth for energy. This will allow us to maximize economic growth and create a safer planet. America has done it before (1973 to 1985), and we can do it again.

As we consider the transition away from the poisons we currently rely on to an all-renewable world, efficiency plays a key role. All the projections of future energy needs project growth, growth, growth. We can achieve efficiencies of 2 to 3 percent per year for at least the next decade to satisfy the growth that is on the way, and maybe even shave a little off the top over time.[3]

> AS WE CONSIDER THE TRANSITION AWAY FROM THE POISONS WE CURRENTLY RELY ON TO AN ALL-RENEWABLE WORLD, EFFICIENCY PLAYS A KEY ROLE

In fact, from 1973 to 1985, the United States economy grew over 20 percent in the GNP with near-zero growth in energy use.[4] We did it by passing a law in 1975 that required automakers to build cars with better gas mileage. And many other laws and regulations mandated buildings to be better insulated and utilities to make investments in efficiency.

Consider these figures if brave, patriotic leadership is taken by government and the business community: we can get 40 to 80 mpg in our cars

rather than today's 24 mpg; we can cut lighting loads in half as old fix-
tures wear out; we can reduce usage for air conditioning and heating by
25 percent; we can decrease today's energy usage by 2 to 3 percent per year
but also provide the energy for 2
to 3 percent growth if needed. The
knowledge and insistence from consumers for more efficient products,
coupled with strong government
programs, are all we need to make a
secure energy future happen.

People focus on the rates—cents
per kilowatt, dollars per gallon—but
they really pay a bill that reflects the
rate multiplied by the amount they
use. Efficiency measures reduce the
bill just the same as a rate reduction. They save money, cut back on
air pollution and oil dependency,
and, in the case of gasoline, they
reduce the amount of money going
overseas that funds terrorists and
nuclear proliferation.

In 2007 the California Public
Utilities Commission's top priority
for investments is energy efficiency.
According to CPUC president Mike
Peevey, that means that the cost-

When I took over as general manager of
the Sacramento Municipal Utility District
(SMUD) in 1990, I set the goal of zero growth in
electricity for the 1990s, even though the population and the economy were projected to grow at a
healthy pace. It was not just a goal on paper. We
initiated efficiency programs calculated to make
it happen.

In one program we paid people to trade in their
old refrigerators for a very efficient new one. We
destroyed thousands of these electricity wast-
ers and shipped the bad chemicals inside them
to Dupont. Another program was to plant a million trees near the homes in Sacramento to provide shade and thus cut down on air conditioning
usage. It all worked. People would stop me on the
street and give me a big hug and say, "Thanks for
cutting the electric rates." We didn't cut the rates
at all; we cut the people's usage and their bills
were lower.

effective investment in efficiency comes before new power plants or
transmission lines are installed. There is a $2 billion efficiency investment
underway by California utilities, to be spent over a three-year period—from
2006 through 2008.

Refrigerators, air conditioners, furnaces, and motors become more
efficient with each model year. Technology is also available today for new
types of lighting such as light-emitting diodes (LEDs) and compact fluorescent lights (CFLs) that use less than half the electricity per unit of light
as the most efficient lighting in general use today. LEDs last approximately
ten years and they contain a semiconductor dish that, when zapped with
electricity, emits lights in any color one chooses. CFLs have improved greatly
over the years and now provide as much light as incandescent bulbs and

can last up to ten years. Because of their efficiency, LEDs are likely to revo-
lutionize the lighting business.

Cars present the most dramatic example of increased efficiency. Before
1975, cars averaged twelve miles per gallon. The 1975 law got them up to
around twenty miles per gallon, but consumers can buy hybrids today that
get 40 mpg or more with the same range and conveniences. Tomorrow's
plug-in hybrids will get the equivalent of 80 to 100 mpg.

CONCLUSION

Without getting bogged down in an energy-efficient cookbook, the reader
must understand that each of us has the power to help get the U.S. off
oil, coal, and nuclear power. When we buy a car, a home, or any appliance,
we can look at the label to read all the facts and choose the most efficient
product available. And we can urge government to continue to tighten
standards so that manufacturers of everything from refrigerators to cars
build more efficient products. They are a very long way from approaching
the levels of efficiency that technology can produce, but we can influence
corporate business practices by demanding greater energy efficiency in
the products they manufacture.

Energy efficiency is thus a very large and growing source of energy. The
energy saved causes no pollution and never has to be used, and it is relatively cheap to produce. It is an important member of the renewable family,
and indeed we must think of renewable energy and efficiency as a team.
After all, renewable energy is too precious to waste. Coupled with energy
efficiency, it will actually reduce America's energy bill, medical costs, and
harmful pollution.

***

1   Reflective white rooftops can be up to 70 degrees F cooler than conven-
    tional black rooftops in the sun. Lawrence Berkeley National Laboratory,
    Environmental Energy Technologies Division, Heat Island Group, http://
    eetd.lbl.gov/HeatIsland/CoolRoofs/ (April 2000).
2   California ranks forty-eighth in per capita electricity consumption,
    behind only New York and Rhode Island. U.S. DOE EIA, "State Energy

Data 2002: Comparison," http://www.eia.doe.gov/emeu/states/sep
_sum/html/pdf/rank_use_per_cap.pdf.

3 According to the demand projections in the U.S. EIA's Annual Electricity
   Outlook 2006 With Projections to 2030, our electricity demand will
   grow by between 1 and just over 2 percent per year.

4 According to the U.S. EIA, the increase in total energy consumption
   between 1973 (75.708 quadrillion BTU) and 1985 (76.469 quadrillion
   BTU) was only about 1 percent.

THE TECHNOLOGY
IS AVAILABLE

THE GOOD NEWS IS that the technology is commercially available today to convert the superabundance of renewable energy into electricity and other usable forms to power our high-energy lives.

Fortunately, there has been steady progress over the past thirty years in developing the technology to harness the powers of the sun, the wind, and biomass, including municipal waste. Let's examine that progress and the current state of the art for each source.

SOLAR

It is ironic but true that President John F. Kennedy's initiative to go to the moon resulted in developing the photovoltaic (PV) cells that may save our way of life here on Earth. The PV cells were developed out of necessity because the space mission required a power source up in the sky and the source—the sun—was quite obvious.

Government funding for solar energy on Earth started with President Carter and created product improvements and a steadily reduced cost of PV power. In the meantime, the price of electricity from the grid has steadily increased to the point that today a PV home installation is becoming competitive over the life of the home, especially if installed in a new building and if the cost is built into the mortgage payment.

The PV cell, which today utilizes the waste products of silicon from the telecommunications industry, converts the sun's rays into electricity with no moving parts. It can now be manufactured in the form of a roofing material to cut costs. But the solar industry is about to grow beyond the limited supply of the useful form of silicon, which is the waste product of another industry.

Thin-film Technology

The solar revolution is now at the manufacturing stage as described earlier. Research and development of nonsilicon, thin-film solar technology is bearing fruit. These thin films are flexible, and so can be used as coatings for windows, roofing tiles, and awnings, and possibly also on cars to feed the batteries of electric vehicles (EV) or hybrid vehicles. Before it dropped its thin-film production business, British Petroleum (BP) installed it on awnings in some of their gas stations to power pumps. Given the high and rising global demand for solar installations, and the shortage of affordable silicon supply, the time for thin films is at hand. Production of thin film is expected to grow by as much as 70 percent in 2007.[1]

Quite exciting are new ultra-thin panels developed independently in South Africa, Germany, and California, made of a unique alloy that is

THIN FILMS HAVE WITHSTOOD OVER A DECADE OF TESTING TO PROVE THEIR EFFICIENCY AND DURABILITY

dramatically cheaper than silicon-based panels. They can generate enough electricity to meet all the electrical needs of a home, and more.

The thin-film technology is not a "Johnny come lately." Several thin-film companies have been working for twenty-five years to improve and streamline the manufacturing process and develop cheaper panels that are not made of silicon. Thin films have withstood over a decade of testing to prove their efficiency and durability. They are literally paper-thin. The most promising type is made of copper, indium, gallium, and selenium sulfide (CIGSSe).

As often happens with major scientific advances, bright people in different parts of the world come to similar conclusions almost at the same time. Thus, within months of each other, breakthroughs took place in South Africa and California in 2006 that took thin film out of the laboratory and into the manufacturing plants. Right now plants are being built that will manufacture a total of at least 500,000 kW of thin film per year,[2] adding 30 percent to the world's solar supply.[3]

The fact that investors with deep pockets are involved and $100 million is being invested is ample evidence that this solar technology is not just a "Dave Freeman dream." This is hard-nosed venture capital talking.[4]

Experts have said for some time that solar would need to reach two dollars a watt to be truly cost competitive. The buzz in 2007 is that the new South African process and the Nanosolar plant in Palo Alto, California, will drive costs down to that level in a few years. The revolution is really on.

The solar industry of today is quite small by comparison to the giants of oil, nuclear power, and coal, and they have yet to achieve the economies of scale. And even in the Sunbelt the retail marketing efforts of the solar industry varies from scant to nonexistent. But their day is coming. Giants such as General Electric and British Petroleum are entering the field and large electric generating companies such as AES are feeling their way into renewables. A solar revolution is on, and it will grow just like computers did in the late '70s.

Today's market penetration of solar—which is far less than 1 percent of our electrical needs—is not due to lack of technology but due to the lack of marketing and promotion, and an absence of any widespread effort to commercialize Big Solar in the U.S. The small companies now in business still have a research orientation and are happy with becoming profitable from the relatively small number of concerned and interested citizens who seek them out.

Big Solar

Our vision of solar power needs to be dramatically enlarged. Solar power expansion need not take place like a guerilla war, one house at a time. We can have Big Solar, with installations of many, many thousands of megawatts and more. We need only to place solar power plants where there is lots of space and lots of sun. And I don't mean in the sky, but rather on the roofs of commercial buildings and the terra firma of the desert sands in the Southwest and the South. And the technology to do so is ready to be put to use.

The most promising concepts for Big Solar, which have been built in pilot size, are called concentrated solar power (CSP). There are a number of different concepts. One approach relies on a PV cell, a cell actually used in space that has an efficiency of 39 percent (not the rooftop version that has an efficiency of 10 to 15 percent). While this cell costs more, it is placed near a field of cheap mirrors that directs five hundred times

Solar dish/engine systems are a type of "solar power plant." These systems track the sun's rays and concentrate the heat to produce electricity. Source: DOE/NREL

more heat onto the high-efficiency PV. If you've ever used a magnifying glass to burn holes in leaves or paper you get the idea. Essential to this process is an invention to remove the extra heat so the cell won't burn up. As a result, the cost of the power produced is much lower than rooftop PV—and it can soon be competitive with today's cost of electricity from natural gas. In addition, the longer hours and additional days of uninterrupted sun in the desert figures in the lower cost per kWh.

There are a number of variations on the Big Solar theme, which include parabolic troughs, solar towers, Stirling dish engines, and concentrated photovoltaics (CPV). We need a federally funded demonstration project that, unlike nuclear power plants, can be built in a year or two. We don't start from scratch. The Big Solar technologies have passed feasibility tests. They work. They need to be scaled up to answer the questions about cost and performance at a commercial scale. With a sense of urgency and a mere billion or two dollars of federal funding, Big Solar will become the power plant of choice.

Big Solar technology requires no new inventions. It simply requires an energy policy that recognizes the potential of the sun and commercializes the technology that has emerged through patient, poorly funded research. Big Solar technology needs to be at the center of energy policy now, not something we'll do tomorrow.

It is important to know that the technology to convert this solar electricity to hydrogen is also well known and usable. It is called electrolysis. It simply uses the electric current to split water (H_2O) into hydrogen (H_2) and oxygen (O_2). We will discuss the myths, concerns, and advantages of hydrogen in chapter 9.

VEHICLES: PLUG-IN HYBRIDS

Hybrid electric vehicles (HEVs) currently make up about 1 percent of vehicles sold on the U.S. market. There are four types—micro, mild, full, and plug-in (PHEV). Micro, or "start-stop hybrids," get about 10 percent better fuel economy than a comparable conventional vehicle. Mild hybrids, such as the Honda Civic and Accord hybrid models, are about 20 to 25 percent more fuel efficient. Full hybrids, like the Toyota Prius, get up to 40 to 45 percent better fuel economy.[5]

Plug-in hybrids will be the gold standard for fuel efficiency, and they should be equipped with a flex-fuel internal engine so they consume little or no oil at all. These vehicles use no gasoline when within battery range or if the flex-fuel IC engine runs on biofuels. They are also called GO Hybrids (gas-optional hybrids).

I hope the development of plug-in flex-fuel hybrids is a priority item for the auto industry. This presents a huge opportunity, much more valuable than marketing gimmicks of one hundred dollars in "free" gas or guaranteed one year of gasoline for $1.99 per gallon that some automakers were pushing. The best sources of information are not the auto companies, but rather concerned citizens who have formed Plug-In America and the experts at the South Coast Air Quality Management District who have actually added a plug-in feature to the Prius and have shown that in ordinary driving they do, in fact, get eighty miles to the gallon. These folks have taken the initiative to revolutionize the automobile. They have developed, and are promoting, plug-in hybrid vehicles far ahead of the multibillion dollar auto industry.

Freedom of movement is a defining characteristic of Americans. Americans own roughly 200 million motor vehicles, a number that grows every year.[6] And the American people are going to keep on buying cars every year. So, if we are really going to cut the consumption of oil, we need cars that provide the mobility and style that Americans cherish, can be quickly built, are affordable, and use little or no oil. That car is the plug-in hybrid.

A misconception, probably left over from the short-distance range of the all-electric cars, is that plug-in hybrids are less powerful than all-gasoline cars. Not true. Not true at all.

The horsepower of any hybrid is actually higher than its conventional counterpart. And the electric motor gives you as fast a rubber-screeching take-off as an internal combustion engine. If in doubt, try driving one.

"THE 'PERFECT' IS THE ENEMY OF THE GOOD." TODAY THE PLUG-IN HYBRID ISN'T PERFECT, BUT IT'S AS GOOD AN ANSWER AS WE HAVE FOR AN EARLY START ON ENDING OIL ADDICTION, GLOBAL WARMING, AND URBAN AIR POLLUTION

To be sure, the plug-in hybrid can dramatically reduce oil dependency. But some environmentalists will ask, "Since renewables are still such a small portion of our electric power supply, aren't you increasing global-warming-causing carbon emissions by replacing electricity from a dirty central station power plant (especially coal) for gasoline?"

The answer is NO! The additional electricity for the plug-ins should and will come largely from natural gas and future renewables, which are cleaner and emit less carbon than oil. Coal and nuclear plants currently operate around-the-clock anyway. The additional electricity to charge batteries, which initially will be small in number, will be fueled mostly by natural gas. As the plug-ins grow, so will the supply of renewable electricity. Even if we use the average emissions from power plants, the CO_2 is lower in a plug-in hybrid than today's Toyota Prius.[7] Don't forget the solar revolution that is underway. The thin-film arrays can provide the reasonably priced solar power to charge the batteries of the plug-ins while providing shade for parking lots.

As to air pollution in general, power plants are easier to control than cars. People who live in urban areas will benefit from any reduction in the pollution where they live and breathe.

Perhaps the best answer is that "the 'perfect' is the enemy of the good." Today the plug-in hybrid isn't perfect, but it's as good an answer as we have for an early start on ending oil addiction, global warming, and urban air pollution.

There are several variations of the plug-in hybrid, including plug-in hybrids that have been developed with all-electric ranges of twenty up to sixty miles. Here are the pertinent facts.

To achieve a sixty-mile all-electric range, the charging time is four hours with a 220-volt connection for a compact car, and eight hours for a full-size SUV. It would take twice as long with an ordinary 110-volt plug-in. An HEV 20 (hybrid electric vehicle with a twenty-mile range) would require only half the time.

Lots of this charging could be done at night when there is plenty of spare electricity—nearly half of America's electric system is idle at night. In fact, the existing system could power tens of millions of PHEVs if they were all powered at night.[8] Yet, through net metering, the new cheap solar panels would help to meet the air conditioning load during the day and thus, in effect, supply the extra green power to run the hybrid cars.

The basic difference between an HEV 20 and an HEV 60 is that the 60 requires three times as much battery power and would cost about $4,000 more than an HEV 20. But the extra fuel savings would return the extra investment, on average, in about five years.[9]

About 80 percent of U.S. vehicles travel less than sixty miles each day, so with a sixty-mile plug-in hybrid, they could use no oil at all. Seventy-eight percent of Americans live within twenty miles of their job,[10] yet about half the total miles traveled are on the nation's highways.[11] On longer trips, the plug-in hybrids could still go beyond sixty miles running on their gas tank, which could be filled with E85 or biofuels.

If everyone drove an HEV 60, it would cut gasoline consumption by over 70 percent. If everyone drove an HEV 60 with a flex-fuel engine, gasoline consumption could be cut 80 to 90 percent.

The sixty-mile plug-in not only saves gas, but it saves the consumer money. Simply put, in the average car, gasoline costs fourteen and a half cents per mile. Electricity costs two cents per mile. A person driving 12,000 miles a year at twenty-four miles to the gallon buys 500 gallons of gasoline. At three dollars a gallon, that's $1,500. If an HEV 60 ran on electricity 75 percent of the time, the fuel bill for the year would be less than $1,000. It could cut your gas bill by about a third. For people who drive a lot, like taxi drivers, real estate agents, and fleet vehicle operators, an HEV 60 would save so much money as to be a no-brainer.

With all these advantages, why aren't plug-ins being offered for sale by automakers? That's a good question. It's taking a long time for the SUV-loving auto industry to wake up to reality. But let's be clear, the problems aren't technical even though there is some engineering yet to be done. Judging from the latest reports, one or more of the major auto companies will be offering plug-ins in a year or two.

With mass production of plug-ins by an auto company, we are talking about extra initial costs of $5,000 to $10,000, which would be recovered in fuel savings over the life of the car. Since most consumers react to the "first costs" (which are costs upfront), I propose a tax credit to pay for the extra cost of the plug-in so we can jump-start our nearest-term option for cutting back on oil imports and pollution (see chapter 12). Since cars are mostly financed by auto companies, the credits could go directly to the car company so the consumer would pay no more for the plug-in up front.

The American people are ready to buy the sixty-mile-range plug-ins. The basic technology (electric drive system and advanced batteries) and the infrastructure (regular outlets in regular homes) exist today. We don't need any brand new inventions or massive breakthroughs to bring PHEVs on the road today. The steps in front of us are to improve the batteries (longer life and lighter) and the battery engine control systems, and that work is underway.

What we really need is the dedication of Detroit to bring these cars and batteries to market. In 2004, the Public Policy Institute of California (PPIC) did a survey of citizen attitudes towards a myriad of environmental issues, one of which was so-called "alternative vehicles" and "alternative fuels." The study found that 63 percent of Californians would seriously consider purchasing a hybrid vehicle, 47 percent would do so even if it were more expensive than a conventional alternative, and 67 percent believed that hybrid vehicle owners should be rewarded with advantages like carpool lane access.[12]

Austin Energy (of Austin, Texas) has built a national coalition, called Plug-In Partners, of nonprofit organizations, state and local governments, utilities, and businesses to start grassroots campaigns in fifty to seventy-five cities to boost the market for PHEVs. At the time of this writing, the movement was gaining steam, and a dozen local governments, one hundred or so electric utilities, and a number of businesses and other groups had joined the Partners. One of the objectives of the Partners is for utilities to provide funding to support the purchase of the first round of PHEVs.

The city of Austin is setting aside $1 million for rebates for PHEVs once they come available and circulating a petition among its citizens to pressure automakers to make PHEVs. Los Angeles is vying to take the lead over Austin. The race "to the top" is on!

WIND

The technology to utilize wind power has an ancient origin. Without going too far back into history, the modern wind turbines had their trial by error from the 1970s until about 1995. In America, they generated electricity only during a few hours a day when the speed was just right. They were not very reliable. They were small and they cost too much. They were pretty much a failure.

A second generation of wind turbines is now on the market. It is a big winner. The machines have variable-speed turbines, they generate 2 MW (2,000 kW) or more each, are lower in cost, reliable, and huge—the biggest blades are eighty meters.[13] Turbines designed for offshore projects in the Gulf of Mexico are purported to be able to generate 3 MW (3,000 kW) each.[14] The formula is simple—the longer the blade, the more wind energy it can harness and the more electricity it can produce. And the marketing of wind power is strong compared to solar. In fact, General Electric, one of a number of manufacturers, advertises its wind turbines on TV.

The exciting fact is the electricity from the latest models of wind turbines is priced near the price of energy from natural gas. And just as with solar power, there is no fuel cost, so the total cost of the electricity is the capital cost and some maintenance.

Wind turbines are a huge source of electricity in Europe, with some 40.5 million kW in operation in Germany, the Netherlands, and the rest of Europe.[15] The technology is proven and has come of age. Wind power is now recognized from Texas to California as an economic source of energy. The obvious drawback to wind is that it is not continuous. However, wind energy in off-peak times can be stored in many ways—including in the form of hydrogen—and then used to produce electricity in a generator during peak times when electricity is so much more valuable.

To cash in on this resource, the utility industry will need to build a considerable upgrade to its transmission system. They know how to do this, but there needs to be a national policy to assure that it happens.

BIOMASS

Before the environmental awareness of the 1970s, wood-burning stoves were often a source of local air pollution in the U.S. In addition, attempts at relatively primitive technologies for converting municipal solid waste to energy generated a lot more opposition from nearby residents than they did useful energy. And the science of converting agricultural by-products like corn and sugar to fuel for our cars had not yet made it to the market.

There are many different biomass fuels, and there are also a number of different ways to process those fuels to create energy—either electricity or liquid fuels. Here are three basic methods:

1. Combustion. This is the process by which biomass fuel is burned and is used for electricity production.
2. Gasification. Biomass is heated to form a flammable gas called synthetic gas, or syngas, which can be used to feed a generator to make electricity, or can be converted into a number of fuels—ethanol, methanol, or hydrogen—for transportation. In terms of environmental impact, the air pollution from a biorefinery is similar to that of a natural gas plant and is controllable with existing pollution control technologies. This is also the case for water pollution.
3. Fermentation. This is the simplest way to make ethanol. But the only sources that can be made into ethanol this way are sugar, sugar beets, and corn. If you've ever made grain alcohol, either for fun or in science class, you know this particular experiment.

The past thirty years have seen a steady march of progress on these fronts. Biomass is now the largest source of renewable electricity in the U.S., making up 3 percent of the total U.S. energy supply.[16] The major potential for biomass is in its conversion to transportation fuels, particularly ethanol, for use in what are called flex-fuel engines.

As for municipal waste, interestingly, 103 plants burning 15 percent of the nation's trash are operating and generating about 20 million kWh of electricity throughout the United States in a number of states, including New York, Massachusetts, Florida, and California.[17] These plants are not only cleaner than the 1970s models, but there are new technologies that are technically feasible and environmentally acceptable for converting large quantities of municipal waste to energy.

While the volume of biomass is small compared to the sun and the wind, it clearly could replace the nuclear power now online (98 million kW from 105 plants nationwide) and much more. And there are promising new technologies. The plasma torch generates arcs of energy as hot as the sun to melt or vaporize inorganic materials, including toxic wastes, into gases H_2 and CO, which can then be run through a turbine to generate electricity. The technology is in use in Japan, where there is very little land available for landfills. European countries such as France are using it for similar purposes, and the U.S. military uses it to dispose of toxic wastes from old ships. [18]

The technological improvements that are being developed now focus on improving the efficiency of the conversion process to get more "bang for the buck" per ton of biomass. With existing technology, you can get about fifty gallons ethanol per ton of biomass for cellulosic sources. [19] Corn is double that. There is an effort underway to develop

RENEWABLE ENERGY IS NOT RENEWABLE ENERGY IF PRODUCED USING COAL!

a conversion process that combines gasification and biological processing, and would purportedly more than double the conversion of cellulosic sources. [20] There is also research and development underway to increase the productivity of biomass crops to yield more tons per acre.

Also, a better method for transporting and blending ethanol with gasoline is needed. Right now, ethanol cannot travel through pipelines with gasoline because it is contaminated by picking up water and debris in the pipeline along the way. Today, ethanol is transported in trucks to be blended with gasoline. This will, of course, require some better strategies and technological breakthroughs if we are to move to E85, E95, or biobutanol as a widespread option.

There is also some controversy about the pollution generated by ethanol plants, because some plants use coal as a cheap fuel source to power their operations. While advances in pollution control technologies take care of some of the emissions, the use of coal is a deal breaker. Simply put, renewable energy is not renewable energy if produced using coal!

Right now only four of the one hundred ethanol plants in the U.S. run on coal. However, about 190 new plants are currently under construction or are planned and the U.S. EPA has been looking to relax federal Clean Air Act standards to allow for coal powering of ethanol plants. [21] That would make ethanol a fraud as a clean form of energy. The public should demand that the U.S. EPA not continue to be a party to this deception. The public needs to know the dirty secret about "clean ethanol" made with dirty coal.

Fortunately, cellulosic ethanol is more conducive to conversion with a process that does not use fossil fuels.

Also, straight wood-burning stoves and power plants now can be equipped with effective pollution-control devices so that wood constitutes a large renewable resource of homegrown energy, estimated at 368 million dry tons a year.[22] Thus wood, one of our oldest sources of energy, has the technology today to clean up its act and grow as a sizeable member of the renewable family (404,800 million kWh/year,[23] or about 11 percent of total electricity, or 18.4 billion gallons ethanol equivalent to 13.8 billion gallons gasoline, or nearly 10 percent of current petroleum use).[24]

Yet it is the energy from other growing plants—sugar, corn, and wastes from the food chain—that is a new prominent option to replace oil. The organic molecules of biomass can be processed to make a number of different fuels—ethanol, methanol, hydrogen, biodiesel, biogas, and synthetic fuel. The technology is not an obstacle. We know how to make ethanol from corn and sugar. We know how to make biofuels with a varying percentage of diesel or 100 percent biofuel. Here the resource base itself is the constraint because it must be shared with the food chain.

Advances in vehicle efficiency substantially improve the chances for ethanol to play a significant role in replacing oil. For example, the National Commission on Energy Policy found that only 30 million acres of switchgrass crops (for which land is available) could produce enough cellulosic ethanol to fuel half of our passenger vehicles if our fuel economy were to reach 40 miles per gallon. Bear in mind that 40 mpg is still below the fuel economies of Europe and Japan today.

CONCLUSION

For now, biomass can be a large and growing source of energy. But biomass alone cannot fuel the world's thirst for oil at current levels of consumption. We need to do both—produce and drive plug-in hybrids with flex-fuel engines in a serious way, and ramp up ethanol production, to really cut down our oil consumption. But most important of all, we must move the electric power industry along from fossil fuels and nuclear to solar, wind, and biofuels. And we can.

* * *

1   Michael Kanellos, "Solar Panel Shortage to Continue through 2006," CNET News.com (April 10, 2006).
2   Nanosolar of Palo Alto, CA, is planning a 430,000 kW facility, and there are large plants planned in Germany that would reportedly produce 500,000 panels per year. The panels are about 60 watts each. Source

Willem Steenkamp, "SA Solar Research Eclipses Rest of the World," IOL. www.iol.co.za (February 11, 2006).

3   Total solar photovoltaics installed worldwide in 2005 was 1.46 million kW, according to Solarbuzz.

4   Michael Kanellos, "With Hefty Funding, Solar Start-up Takes on Big Guns," CNET News.com (June 21, 2006).

5   U.S. EPA and U.S. DOE. www.fueleconomy.gov (November 3, 2006).

6   U.S. Bureau of Transportation Statistics (September 2006).

7   The average, conventional, nonhybrid vehicle emits about 11,000 to 12,000 pounds of CO_2. A Prius, which gets the best gas mileage of all the hybrids—about 50 mpg, double that of the average conventional car of similar size—cuts that in half to about 6,000 pounds CO_2. The average emissions factor for electricity in the United States is about 1.3 lbs/kWh. So, using the estimate of 2,000 to 3,000 kWh/year for a plug-in hybrid, cut the CO_2 in half again, to between 2,600 and 3,900 pounds CO_2. Calculation taken and adapted from an e-mail from Joseph Romm to Felix Kramer from "Gas-Optional and Green" blog, http://www.world-changing.com/archives/002891.html (June 14, 2005).

8   50,000 MW excess generating capacity in the United States currently is unused at night, roughly between the hours of 10 p.m. to 6 a.m.

9   An HEV 60 would consume between 3,000 and 4,500 kWh/year to travel 9,000 to 13,000 miles/year. At eight cents/kWh, this equals $240 to $360/year electricity. At the national average fuel economy of twenty-four miles/gallon, that same mileage would require 375 to 550 gallons of gasoline. At three dollars a gallon, 9,000 to 13,000 miles of driving costs about $1,125 to $1,650.

10 "Plug in Hybrids," *Consumer Reports* (May 2005).

11 General and commonly used estimation that, of total miles traveled in the U.S., about 45 percent of these are highway, and 55 percent are off-highway.

12 "Special Survey on Californians and the Environment," PPIC Statewide Survey 2004, Public Policy Institute of California (San Francisco CA: July 2004).

13 American Wind Energy Association (AWEA) (2005).

14 "Gulf Wind: Harnessing Offshore Wind off the coast of Texas," *REFocus*, Elsevier Ltd., (January/February 2006).

15 European Wind Energy Association (2005).

16 About 10,000 MW of installed capacity nationwide—7,000 MW forest and agricultural residue, 2,500 MW municipal solid waste, and 500 MW

fall into the "other" category, which includes landfill gas U.S. DOE EIA (August 2005).

17 U.S. DOE EIA (2004).

18 Kimberly Link-Wills, "Plasma Power," *Georgia Tech Alumni Magazine* (2002).

19 The conversion factor is 117 gallons ethanol per dry ton biomass, and conversion technologies are at about 43 percent to create ethanol, leaving a conversion factor of about fifty gallons ethanol/dry ton cellulosic biomass.

20 Nathaniel Greene, "Growing Energy" (December 2004).

21 Amanda Griscom Little, "Warts and Ethanol," *Grist Magazine* (26 May 2006) and Mark Clayton, "Carbon Cloud over a Green Fuel," *Christian Science Monitor* (23 March 2006).

22 U.S. DOE and USDA, "Biomass as Feedstock," (April 2005).

23 Assumed that one dry ton of wood waste is equivalent to 1,100 kWh/ year at a 65 percent plant capacity factor and 35 percent plant conversion efficiency.

24 Using the conversion technologies with an efficiency of about 43 percent, you can get about fifty gallons ethanol/dry ton cellulosic biomass.

HYDROGEN—
MYTHS AND REALITY

{MAKING IT WORK WITH
RENEWABLE ENERGY } ✳✳✳

WE ARE INTERESTED IN HYDROGEN because it is a form of energy that, if produced using renewable sources, truly can be called clean. When it is burned, hydrogen recombines with oxygen in the air to form water (H_2O) vapor. There is no carbon released and it has, at most, 1 percent of the pollution of burning fossil fuels and none of the dangers of nuclear power. Imagine if the only emission from tailpipes was a faint mist of benign vapor; consider what it would be like if filling stations did not reek of gasoline. And, unlike petroleum, hydrogen is the most plentiful element on earth as well as in the universe. It makes up about 75 percent of all matter.

That's the good news—hydrogen is superabundant and relatively clean and safe.

The bad news is that there are no hydrogen wells—it doesn't exist all by itself in nature. So hydrogen is not a source of energy. It is a form of energy created only by separating the hydrogen molecules from other sources— water and all fossil fuels— and it takes a lot of energy to separate it.

MAKING HYDROGEN

Today hydrogen is used in the manufacturing industry and the space program, and 48 percent is produced by steam-heating natural gas.[1] Hydrogen also exists in coal and oil, but in a less concentrated form than in natural gas. Coal and oil are used to generate about 18 percent and 30 percent, respectively, of the hydrogen produced today.[2] The problem is that any process to extract hydrogen from fossil fuels releases the carbon in the fuel and requires lots of energy to achieve the separation.

Thus, making hydrogen from fossil fuels or nuclear electricity with the goal of producing clean energy and reducing pollution or petroleum dependence is like a dog chasing its tail. Taking this route, we would use even more fossil and nuclear fuel sources and actually add to the emissions of carbon, particulates, and nuclear danger.

Furthermore, even though natural gas is the cleanest of the fossil fuels, if we used it for the production of hydrogen, it would cause a faster depletion of natural gas, given the energy lost in the conversion process. Natural gas is in short and finite supply, and we will realistically need to rely on it as we transition to an all-renewable electricity supply. It is not the huge new source of hydrogen that the world needs.

So, with hydrogen from coal and nuclear power really being the same poison by another name, and natural gas being too scarce and valuable, we now turn our attention to water, our superabundant source of hydrogen. Electricity used to split water to free up hydrogen must be generated by a renewable source. Otherwise, hydrogen becomes a hyped-up solution for those same dangerous energy sources that we must cease using.

MAKING HYDROGEN FROM FOSSIL FUELS OR NUCLEAR ELECTRICITY WITH THE GOAL OF PRODUCING CLEAN ENERGY AND REDUCING POLLUTION OR PETROLEUM DEPENDENCE IS LIKE A DOG CHASING ITS TAIL

The huge source of hydrogen on our planet is water, which must be considered *the* source if hydrogen is to be our long-term energy supply. Today's technology requires electricity, or electrolysis, to free up the hydrogen.

In electrolysis, electricity from renewable sources is passed through water. The electricity is used as a catalyst to break down the water molecules into their elements, oxygen (O_2) and hydrogen (H_2). It is proven technology and it works reliably, but it is not a mass-produced product and is too expensive to be used to make industrial hydrogen. Today, only about 4 percent of hydrogen is made by electrolysis.[3]

Research is underway to use thermal conversion to remove hydrogen molecules from water molecules using heat, a couple thousand degrees Celsius, and zero electricity. Concentrating solar collectors are able to generate enough heat to support a very efficient conversion process, and the National Renewable Energy Laboratory found that hydrogen could be generated from thermal conversion using concentrating solar collectors at a rate of 51 percent efficiency.[4]

Another approach is gasification of biomass. In the gasification process, the biomass fuel source (basically any organic molecule), is heated to form a flammable gas.

But we need not wait for "something better" to get started with hydrogen by electrolysis, which simply needs economies of scale to become competitive with the price of gasoline.

FUEL-CELL TECHNOLOGY

The auto companies have fallen in love with a device called the fuel cell, and they proclaim that hydrogen-powered fuel-cell cars are the wave of the future. But neither the auto companies nor the federal government funding the research has taken any position on how the hydrogen is produced. They both fail to make a clear distinction between good and bad hydrogen. They ignore the impact on global warming of coal-based electricity, the dangers of nuclear, or that natural gas resources could not possibly support a large-scale hydrogen market without serious depletion.

President Bush declared his dedication to pursuing a hydrogen future. He unveiled his Hydrogen Fuel Initiative in his 2003 State of the Union address:

> To be economically competitive with the present fossil fuel economy, the cost of fuel cells must be lowered by a factor of 10 or more and the cost of producing hydrogen must be lowered by a factor of 4. . . .
>
> Performance and reliability of hydrogen technology for transportation and other uses must be improved dramatically. . . .
>
> We can envision the hydrogen economy as a linked network of chemical processes that produces hydrogen through fossil fuel reforming, biomass conversion, and electrolytic, biophotolytic, or thermochemical splitting of water; [this] stores hydrogen chemically or physically; and converts the stored hydrogen to electrical energy and heat at the point of use.

In proposing research on hydrogen, President Bush did not make the fundamental distinction between renewable hydrogen and fossil or nuclear hydrogen. He even made coal and nuclear power part of his pitch: "To change how we power our homes and offices, we will invest more in zero-emission coal-fired plants, revolutionary solar and wind technologies, and clean, safe nuclear energy."

The president's statement explains why most environmental leaders have taken a very negative and skeptical attitude toward any strong initiative to develop hydrogen as a form of energy. They fear, as I do, that this new, impassioned call for a hydrogen future may be no more than coal or nuclear power with a pretty name. I said it before and I will say it again: there is no such thing as "zero-emission" coal or "safe" nuclear power.

I fear that the president's endorsement of hydrogen could be reflective of the effort of the nuclear diehards to adopt hydrogen as their reason for staging a comeback. Regardless of what clothes the nuclear power industry chooses to wear—whether it's a "zero-emission" electricity source, or a safe source of hydrogen—the danger of meltdowns, everlasting radioactive wastes, and proliferation of atomic bombs doesn't go away if nuclear power is used to make hydrogen. The sun and the wind can supply hydrogen without these dangers.

Hydrogen could be a form of renewable electricity that could put the renewables in the gas tank to replace imported oil. That would be a very good thing.

The clean power crowd must get behind and support the use of renewable resources for hydrogen with the same fervency they have used to attack the making of hydrogen from coal and nuclear power. Mainstream environmental organizations, community groups, and lobbyists who have generally attacked the president's hydrogen initiative must offer their own alternative, and that alternative should be renewable hydrogen. I feel compelled to advance the "good hydrogen" option because we need all possible choices to get off oil.

THE HYDROGEN OPTIONS: INTERNAL COMBUSTION AND FUEL CELLS

Hydrogen cars are not a reality today even though the technology exists. To be sure, there are demonstration models of $1 million fuel-cell cars. A few hybrids have been converted to hydrogen by funding from the South

Coast Air Quality Management District in California, and Ford has built and shown its Model U hydrogen hybrid SUV, a concept car. But there are no hydrogen cars available to the general public.

In 2003, Ford unveiled its Model U, an SUV that was a hydrogen hybrid, a car with an internal combustion engine that runs on hydrogen and an electric motor. It has a 300-mile range and is a carbon-free, pollution-free modern successor to the Model T.

We tried to persuade Ford to start making the Model U. The Ford engineers assured me if they could mass-produce the hydrogen IC cars at 100,000 per year, the sales price could be about the same as gasoline cars. And they could start with fleet sales, where the hydrogen filling stations could be installed and hydrogen produced at the fleet parking lots. But even though the Ford engineers had made tremendous progress on IC hydrogen equipment, the company did not show any initiative to mass-produce or market hydrogen IC cars.

The technology is available to start the "hydrogen highway" that the governors of both California and New York have proclaimed they wish to build. But until one or more major auto companies are given sufficient incentives or requirements to go into the business, it's not going to happen in any meaningful way.

> In 2003, when I left California state government, I joined with my partners Ari Swiller and Cole Frates and formed the Hydrogen Car Company. We had a strategic partnership with Stuart Energy Company that manufactured electrolyzers to free up hydrogen from water. Our idea was to retrofit standard cars by adjusting the engine and installing a hydrogen tank to replace the gas tank. This equipment is commercially available. In fact, the Ford Motor Company was willing to sell us engines already designed to run on hydrogen.
>
> We faced two insurmountable obstacles. First, there were few if any hydrogen service stations. Right now there are still not very many, about ten so far in California. The number is growing very slowly. This is the old "chicken and egg" problem. Which comes first, the car or the hydrogen service station?
>
> Second, personal hydrogen systems, while technically feasible, cost more than the car to which we were doing the conversion. And it was hard to take a new car, retrofit it at high cost without mass production, and then find a buyer for the resulting high price.

The fuel cell is another piece of excellent technology that is a by-product of the space program. In contrast to the hydrogen hybrid car with its internal combustion engine, the fuel cell is a device that chemically converts hydrogen into electricity more efficiently than an internal combustion engine and without even the 1 percent pollution inherent in burning hydrogen.[5]

A fuel cell operates in the reverse of what happens in electrolysis. Hydrogen gas (H_2) is injected into the fuel cell. The electrons are then stripped from the hydrogen molecules and run through a circuit to generate electricity that runs the car. The remaining protons are drawn through a membrane and combine with oxygen to produce water vapor and heat. So, while electrolysis uses electricity to split water and create hydrogen molecules, the fuel cell breaks down hydrogen molecules to create electricity, water, and heat. Like a solar panel, the fuel cell produces electricity without any moving parts.

MOST EXPERTS SAY THAT THE HYDROGEN FUEL CELL COULD BE A PART OF THE TRANSPORTATION MIX IN THE NEXT TWENTY TO THIRTY YEARS. WE CAN'T COUNT ON IT MUCH SOONER

The auto industry speaks of the hydrogen fuel cell almost as one word. But hydrogen can also be used in an internal combustion engine, and that technology is available now. They and President Bush portray the hydrogen fuel cell as a research project, which it certainly still is, and are content to speak of it as something that our kids or grandkids might use. They do not act with any sense of urgency to get off oil.

I am quite familiar with fuel cell technology. In my service in the White House from 1968 through 1971, I saw to it that the Office of Coal Research gave priority to funds that advanced fuel-cell technology.

I believe the fuel cell is an excellent device for making electricity, and the utilities I managed in California each purchased an experimental fuel cell. But after all these years, the fuel cells are not yet competitive to generate electricity, and the fuel-cell car is a much tougher challenge.

As I stated earlier, fuel-cell cars today cost $1 million each and are not going to be available in mass production for many years to come. Even the automakers say they are years away. I like to joke that the fuel-cell car has been fifteen years away for the last fifteen years. It's the power plant of tomorrow, and it may always be. Most experts say that the hydrogen fuel cell could be a part of the transportation mix in the next twenty to thirty years. We can't count on it much sooner.

My fear is that the ballyhoo and hype about the hydrogen fuel-cell car has now become a diversion from moving ahead with hydrogen internal combustion cars. In a sense, it is a rabbit in a dog race. We are the dogs chasing a fuel-cell rabbit. It keeps us occupied but we never reach it. Considering the urgency of our problems, the fact that there may be a better, more efficient, hydrogen generator tomorrow is no reason not to pursue hydrogen now. We don't need to wait for the fuel cell.

Hydrogen is an ideal form of energy that needs to be pursued for uses to replace fossil fuels today. There are three major roles for utilizing hydrogen, without waiting for the fuel cell:

1. Fueling internal combustion engine motor vehicles in large numbers within a decade;
2. Fueling the internal combustion engine portion of a hybrid car to make it zero-oil and zero-carbon;
3. Powering aircraft. Hydrogen is a much lighter fuel than petroleum and could power aircraft. Hydrogen would enable today's jets to fly nonstop around the world, albeit with fatter airplanes.

Hydrogen should also be developed for uses beyond transportation:

* It could be used to store intermittent solar and wind power and then used to generate electricity in peaking plants with no pollution.
* It could be used in hydrogen fuel cells to generate electricity.
* It could become one of the substitutes for natural gas for home heating and cooking. It is not too early to be designing the furnaces and stoves that would accommodate hydrogen fuel as well as address the safety concerns.
* It could meet most industrial uses for energy.

Concerns are raised about the safety of hydrogen, and these concerns must be taken seriously. No form of energy is absolutely safe. Gasoline is highly flammable and kills hundreds of people every year. People tend to think that high combustibility is also true for hydrogen. Strangely, the 1937 fireball disaster of the hydrogen-fueled Zeppelin *Hindenburg* is still referred to. But, contrary to popular belief, it was the outer material of the airship that caused the fire, not the hydrogen.[6] The truth is that hydrogen is lighter than air and simply evaporates into the air if released.

Another fear is that if hydrogen is kept under pressure, as it would be with today's technology, it might explode. Safety is built into the hydrogen technology from the beginning. Hydrogen fuel tanks are designed to make an explosion nearly impossible. These tanks have been extensively tested and certified by reliable authorities.

A principal reason that renewable hydrogen hasn't caught on is its perceived cost. But the gap between hydrogen from renewable electricity as compared to making it from natural gas has closed dramatically.

The price of wind power has been cut in half from ten to about five cents per kilowatt-hour over the last three decades, while the price of natural gas has doubled.[7] Experts from the Universities of California at Davis and Berkeley predict that wind-generated hydrogen will be three dollars per kg in the future, down from its current price of seven to eleven dollars per kg. For reference, one kilogram of hydrogen is equivalent to one gallon of gasoline. This same team also estimates that it is possible for solar-generated hydrogen to decline in price from the current ten to thirty dollars per kg to a more economical three to four dollars per kg, and for utility grid-generated hydrogen to decline from six to seven dollars per kilogram now to four dollars in the future, all competitive with today's cost of gasoline.[8]

The next step is delivering hydrogen to the customer. Hydrogen can be produced at the wind farm or solar plant and piped to market. Or it can be made anyplace there is water and electricity, which means virtually anywhere.

THE NEXT STEP IS DELIVERING HYDROGEN TO THE CUSTOMER. HYDROGEN CAN BE PRODUCED AT THE WIND FARM OR SOLAR PLANT AND PIPED TO MARKET. OR IT CAN BE MADE ANYPLACE THERE IS WATER AND ELECTRICITY, WHICH MEANS VIRTUALLY ANYWHERE

Vital to any real progress in making hydrogen cars available to the public is a network of hydrogen "service stations," which California governor Arnold Schwarzenegger refers to as the Hydrogen Highway. Critics have dismissed hydrogen by saying that the infrastructure will cost many billions of dollars. But energy is the most capital-intensive industry in the nation. We need to do a more thorough job of evaluating costs, including the costs to society, national security, public health, and the environment, than simply proclaiming that "it will require a huge investment." The federal interstate highway system was a tremendous investment, as was the network of 200,000 petroleum fueling stations we enjoy today.[9] Hydrogen service stations may well be the twenty-first-century version of that great visionary undertaking by the federal government in the 1950s. But where are the Dwight Eisenhowers and the Al Gore Seniors of today to lead that effort?

Automakers won't really mass-produce hydrogen cars until the "hydrogen highways," or fuel distribution networks and filling stations, are built, and these seem to be waiting for the cars to come. All this is an excuse, not a reason. Both should be built on a coordinated schedule, with a few stations and a few vehicles in a few locales and then grow from there. Municipalities like the city of Santa Monica in Southern California have the right idea. They installed their first hydrogen fueling station in June 2006, and the city bought five Toyota Prius hydrogen ICE hybrids to start. They will add more over time.

Henry Ford built the Model T when there were no highways, few if any paved roads, and no gas stations; you could only purchase gasoline at a drugstore. Look at how much our country has changed in the last century to accommodate the 200 million vehicles on the road today.[10] We need to reignite the can-do American spirit, and we can.

A fundamental question about renewable hydrogen is, "How soon can we really count on it being available?" If we need solar, wind, or biomass-powered electricity to make hydrogen, surely we can use electricity to replace coal and nuclear power plants and in plug-in hybrids sooner and cheaper than converting it into hydrogen. There is short-term truth to this point. But electricity and biomass need another partner if we are to really get off oil for good, in the U.S. and around the world. It is going to take some time and that is all the more reason to get started today.

CONCLUSION

The rapid development and public acceptance of the hybrid car will provide a firm foundation for a great leap forward in getting off oil. It can be the vehicle for using renewable electricity and biofuels to replace oil.

Yet for the longer term, the hybrid needs a partner, and that partner is hydrogen. Renewable hydrogen can become a major player not just in hydrogen hybrids but also hydrogen internal combustion engines and later fuel cells, airplanes, and then as a replacement for natural gas. Hydrogen can play a huge role in getting us off oil.

We shall explore the incentives and government policies needed to make this dream come true in chapter 12. The technology is ready and waiting.

***

1 Timothy Lipman, "What Will Power the Hydrogen Economy? Present and Future Sources of Hydrogen," prepared for the Natural Resources Defense Council (July 12, 2004).

2 Ibid.

3 Ibid.

4 U.S. National Renewable Energy Laboratory (NREL), "Hydrogen Production and Delivery," http://www.nrel.gov/hydrogen/proj_production_delivery.html (November 20, 2006).

5 Hydrogen fuel cells are about two and a half to three times more efficient in fuel consumption than a gasoline-powered internal combustion engine. Hydrogen ICE conversions are only slightly more efficient, at about 38 percent efficiency, compared with an average 30 percent efficiency for a gasoline ICE.

6 Larry Elliot, "No! It Was Not the Hydrogen," *H2 Nation,* (November/December 2003).

7 U. S. National Renewable Energy Laboratory, "Wind in a Minute," (1999).

8 Daniel Kammen, "An Integrated Hydrogen Vision for California," University of California, Berkeley, Energy Resources Group (July 9, 2004).

9 As of June 1998 there are 187,097 retail locations selling motor fuel in the U.S. *Journal of Petroleum Marketing* (June 1998).

10 U.S. Bureau of Transportation Statistics (September 2006).

10

LESSONS FROM AROUND THE GLOBE

{OTHER NATIONS ARE
SHOWING THE WAY} ✳✳✳

THE UNITED STATES HAS A LOT TO LEARN from the rest of the world. Countries around the globe are becoming models of renewable energy innovation and marshalling the willpower to stay on a steady path toward success. Knowledge of these accomplishments by other nations can give a persuasive answer to the skeptics who say renewables can't be done. And it provides a test of whether American grassroots democracy can still produce results better than the centralized authority of China or South Africa.

America can afford to learn that patient persistence may be a characteristic we need to acquire. Let's examine a few places where it has paid off.

BRAZIL, SWEDEN, AND JAPAN

Brazil, Sweden, and Japan are all exemplary models of long-term dedication to renewable energy and alternative fuels. The commitment to reducing their reliance on oil did not necessarily come about to protect Mother Nature or "do the right thing." Nor did it come about as a result of an international treaty, such as the Kyoto Protocol. In fact, it was an international energy crisis, like the one we face today, that spurred action.

These countries diversified their energy supply in response to the energy crisis in the mid-1970s and, unlike the United States, stayed with the program for thirty long years. Nations and leaders have a choice when faced with huge problems, like shortages in energy, the lifeblood of modern societies. One option is to heed the omen, learn the lessons, and respond accordingly and logically. The flipside is to ignore the lesson, shove it under the proverbial rug, and forget about it. For an entire decade after the 1970s energy crisis hit, America followed the first path. After that, I am sorry to say, we succumbed to the market-driven policy of "do nothing, unless you feel the pain."

By 1979, under President Carter, there were major solar installations underway, a synthetic fuels corporation was formed to reduce oil imports, and more efficient cars and appliances were on the road and in homes.

As TVA chairman, I was present at Camp David when President Carter decided that oil imports had to be steadily reduced by government action. At Camp David, he agreed to reduce foreign oil, and he overruled his energy secretary on the basic issue of whether the federal government should take action to interfere with the market. Imported oil was then selling for fifteen dollars a barrel.

A few days later, President Carter gave a major speech to announce his decision, in which he said, "The generation-long growth in our dependence on foreign oil will be stopped dead in its tracks right now and then reversed as we move through the 1980s, for I am tonight setting the further goal of cutting our dependence on foreign oil by one-half by the end of the next decade—a saving of over 4.5 million barrels of imported oil per day."[1]

Unfortunately for our national energy policy, President Carter was replaced by a president (Ronald Reagan) who promptly stopped all government action to reduce oil imports and adopted the policy of giving market forces control, a fundamentally different response than the governments of Japan, Sweden, and Brazil.

UNITED STATES ENERGY POLICIES SINCE 1974

In my 1974 Ford Foundation report, I said, "If the indifference and neglect that helped create the energy gap continue, the United States could drift into a serious, long-lasting energy-environment crisis."[2]

And that's just what happened.

To quote the president of the Ford Foundation at the time, McGeorge Bundy, former National Security Advisor to presidents Kennedy and Johnson, "There is an energy crisis. It did not come and go in 1973–74. It will last a long time. Conservation [efficiency] is as important as supply. We do need an integrated national policy."[3] To be fair, we started down that path, but we lost our focus and lost our way.

The fundamental reason that Japan, Sweden, and Brazil stayed the course and the U.S. didn't is that the U.S. is the home of Big Oil, Big Coal,

and "Safe Nuclear Power." These financially and politically powerful enti-
ties have dominated American energy policy and they have opposed any
government action that would change their positioning in the American
energy world.

The "Big Poisons" have persuaded American politicians ironically to
worship the free market at the expense of the American way of life. The
marketplace is blind to national security, the environment, pubic health,
and social equity such as the economically disadvantaged getting stuck
with gas-guzzling cars and high prices at the gas pump. So, when the acute
shortages stopped, the American policy became benign neglect.

Television tells us constantly about the glory and moral high ground of
oil companies preserving nature and *researching* alternatives to go beyond
petroleum. The truth is that America has been persuaded to let the marketplace—that is, the energy industry—decide our fate. That has meant
little consideration for national security, the environment, or consumer
protection, and it has been reflected in the price of their products. Oil from
the Middle East is priced the same as oil from Texas. And cleaner energy
gets no better price than the toxic stuff.

Let me give you a personal example of the reach of the oil industry.

Because of the Ford Foundation report, I was one of Jimmy Carter's most influential
energy advisors when he was governor of Georgia. Yet as he campaigned for president, I was
curious that I was never invited into his inner circle. Finally, through a friend, Joe Brouder, I
was asked to come to Atlanta in September of 1976 to help with Carter's policy planning.

I arranged for a big meeting of energy leaders with the candidate. A week before the meeting, Frank Moore, Carter's financial advisor, asked me not to attend the meeting. I said, "Why
in hell not? It's my meeting!" Frank then said, "I know, Dave, but we were short of money during the Ohio primary and I accepted $80,000 from the oil people on the grounds that Freeman
would not be part of the Carter administration." Flabbergasted, I said, "Does Governor Carter
know about this, 'cause if he does, I'm out of here right now." Frank replied, "Oh, my gosh,
no! If he knew, I'd be fired!" So, for the good of our candidate, Frank and I agreed that his
promise to the oil people would be forgotten, but I didn't attend that one meeting. The next
time I saw Frank, he said, "I'm sure glad you're still around, Dave."

If it was worth $80,000 in 1976 dollars to get rid of me, just imagine what Big Oil spends
today to influence the federal, state, and local governments, the economists, and the public
at large through advertising.

ENERGY POLICIES OF OIL-PRODUCING NATIONS

It is worth noting that while America's government took little or no deci-sive action to develop energy policies for the betterment of the American people, oil-producing nations have taken an opposite course. First it was Saudi Arabia and other Persian Gulf states that nationalized their oil resources. Government ownership is the norm for Iran, Iraq, Saudi Arabia, and the Middle East. Venezuela and Bolivia have joined these coun-tries in exerting command over their oil reserves and kicking out any other interests.

During the 1973–74 embargo I recall that some officials threatened to embargo wheat to the oil producers who then were dependent on American wheat. Those Middle East oil-pro-ducing countries heard us. They are not dependent on imported wheat today, yet America is even more dependent on their imported oil.

WE HAVE AN OPPORTUNITY TO MASSIVELY INFLUENCE THE DEVELOPMENT OF NEW DESIGNS OF AUTOMOBILES AND OTHER CLEAN ENERGY TECHNOLOGIES. BUT FIRST WE NEED TO LEARN FROM OTHERS

It is time the American govern-ment started looking out for the interests of its people. We can look to the examples in the rest of the world for both technological inno-vation and the willingness and fore-sightedness to implement change and develop technologies that produce homegrown energy.

America has historically been a leader to which the rest of the world looks for new ideas and innovative technologies. Take the examples of computers, the Internet, and high-tech communications. In those fields, there was real competition, triggered in a vital sense by the government's antitrust action to break up the communications monopolies. In another sense, the Internet is so recent and far ranging that no version of the oil lobby could stand in its way.

Once Americans understand that renewable energy is, if anything, just as exciting and more fundamentally important than telecommunications, no lobby will be able to stand in its way.

The opportunities that are within our reach can be lumped into four cat-egories—policy steadfastness, technology innovation, large-scale renew-able development, and distributed-power technologies to make solar and hydrogen economical and feasible on a widespread basis. We have an opportunity to massively influence the development of new designs of automobiles and other clean-energy technologies. But first we need to learn from others.

There are a few vivid international examples of successful results that derived from steady, long-term policies and government implementation programs.

SWEDEN'S MULTIFACETED PLAN

Several countries are going for the green gold by putting strategies and targets in place to be 100 percent oil free. Sweden and Iceland are arguably the most famous examples, and Brazil is a unique and interesting look at renewable vehicle fuels.

Sweden provides a diverse example, one that is developmentally relevant to the United States. Sweden has embarked on a focused transition from fossil fuels to continue until their oil-free goals are achieved. They are well under way on a transition that is a paradigm shift for both electricity and transportation fuels.

Sweden has set the goal of being 100 percent oil free by 2020, and if it succeeds it will be the first country to be wholly energy independent. Their plan is a multifaceted array of approaches that will bring about steady, gradual change. It includes carbon taxes on energy sources, large-scale investment in renewable energy, research and development of new technology, incentives for efficient vehicles, biofuel heating initiatives, grants for climate research, and so on.[4]

In 1970, 77 percent of Sweden's energy supplies came from oil.[5] Over the past twenty-five years, biofuels have become a substantial portion of the country's energy supply, third to oil and nuclear power. About half of Swedish households are heated with biofuels and the manufacturing sector has made the transition to replacing some of its oil consumption with biofuels and electric power.[6]

Today, only about 32 percent of Sweden's energy comes from oil. The rest is a mixture of renewables and nuclear. And the renewables are mostly biofuels, wind, and hydroelectric.[7] Just as with biofuels over the last twenty-five years, the use of wind power is expected to increase sharply between now and 2020.[8]

It is interesting that two countries that really can't rely on solar because of northern latitude are still willing and able to pull off renewable policies, even without the benefit of the sun that the U.S. has in abundance. Embarrassing, actually.

ICELAND'S UNIQUE SITUATION

Iceland has set the goal of being completely oil free by 2050, and it is well over halfway there. The country already relies solely on its unique geothermal and hydroelectric resources to heat homes and generate electricity. Geothermal steam provides 86 percent of space and water heating in homes and 16 percent of the country's power. The remaining 83 percent of Iceland's electricity is provided by the huge hydropower potential provided by its glacial rivers.[9] This potential is so huge that Iceland has only harnessed a small fraction of its geothermal and hydro potential to power and heat the country.

Most countries do not have the simultaneous advantage of being both sparsely populated and heavily awash in geothermal and hydropower to take care of all their energy needs. But, as we demonstrated earlier in this

Geothermal hot spring in Iceland. Source: Blaine Harrington

book, nearly every nation and continent on the planet has sufficient solar, wind, and other renewable capabilities to provide 100 percent of their energy needs. It's just a matter of harnessing them.

Of course, electricity is one thing and transportation is another. It is in this area that the true transition has yet to happen in Iceland. But they have made a serious start. This small island nation is already a true leader in advancing renewable hydrogen, and some of the buses in Reykjavik, Iceland's capital, already run on hydrogen. Iceland is the home of the world's first hydrogen fueling station.[10] By 2050, 100 percent of all motor vehicles must run on hydrogen, according to their plan.[11]

Hydrogen fuel cell bus in Iceland's capital city, Reykjavik.
Source: EVWorld.com

BRAZIL AND ITS CARS

Brazil is the world's greatest manufacturer and exporter of sugarcane-based biofuels.[12] It provides nearly all of Europe's supply of ethanol and expects the industry to double within the next decade.[13]

Like Sweden, Brazil began focusing on biofuels with its "Pro-Alcohol" program in 1975, in response to the oil crisis, and, by the mid-eighties, over half of the nation's 800,000 cars could run on ethanol from sugarcane. This program stalled with the sugar price spike and cheap oil prices in the late 1980s,[14] but then took off again with the introduction of flex-fuel engines in 2003. These vehicles became popular quickly because they gave consumers the choice of using the cheapest fuel available.

Today, about 70 percent of vehicles sold in Brazil operate on flex-fuel engines,[15] a number that is expected to increase to 90 percent by the end of the decade, and about 48 percent of vehicles use pure ethanol.[16]

DEMAND-SIDE MANAGEMENT—
SOLAR AND EFFICIENCY—JAPAN

Japan is the home of the famous Kyoto Climate Treaty, ratified by 140 nations in 1997 with notable exceptions by the United States, Russia, and Australia. Japan is particularly unique in its energy policy because of its geography and almost total lack of fossil energy resources. Japan is thus extremely vulnerable to the volatility of energy supplies on the world market. As a result of having felt the pain in 1973, Japan decided to tackle its shortcomings by pouring its resources and brainpower into both efficiency and the one renewable resource it had, the sun.

The country's automakers responded to the energy crisis by producing smaller, lighter vehicles with much better fuel efficiency. These automakers also introduced smaller cars into the American market. In addition, the bulk of Japan's population lives in dense city centers with excellent mass-transit systems. Japan also shifted its economy to focus on less-energy-intensive industries. As a result, the volatility of energy prices is far less crippling in Japan than in the United States and elsewhere.

Since 1973, Japan's imports of oil have decreased, despite a doubling of its economy. The average fuel economy in Japan is 47 mpg, double that of the United States.[17] Japanese auto giants Toyota and Honda produce the most fuel-efficient hybrid vehicles on the road.

On the manufacturing side, Japan is a model of energy efficiency and sustainability. Paper mills, for example, use their own waste and other alternative energy for 38 percent of their energy. Japan's steel industry uses energy 20 percent more efficiently than the United States and 50 percent more so than China.[18]

Japan has adopted some energy conservation measures that would be difficult to duplicate elsewhere. Rigid and uncomfortable thermostat controls in winter and summer, for example, would be difficult to enforce in the absence of a strong centralized authority and the cultural unity to follow this mandate. However, some technologies such as "smart" escalators and subway ticket machines that switch off when not in use could be implemented without disruption of service.[19]

As for solar, Japan has been ahead of the pack for years. The small island nation is the undisputed world leader in solar energy development, accounting for 40 to 50 percent of the world market. Half of the world's top ten solar manufacturers are Japanese companies—Sharp, Kyocera, Kaneka, Sanyo, and Mitsubishi. Experts are predicting that in the next few years,

Japan will begin to flood the international market by massively exporting lower-cost solar technologies, thereby becoming the undisputed market leader.[20] Yet they may also face strong competition from new solar technology developed in South Africa and California, as we have discussed.

Japan has 300,000 kW of solar capacity, a full 20 percent of the world market,[21] nearly one-quarter of which was installed in 2004. The Japanese government has set the goal of multiplying its current capacity by several times, for 5 million kW of total solar capacity by 2010. Japan earned its leadership position through a combination of long-term guaranteed government investment and rebates, and other incentives for solar installation. The result has been rapid and massive solar development. It has been so successful in driving down the installed cost of solar that the Japanese solar market now sustains itself without the aid of government incentives.

CHANGING THE FACE OF DEVELOPMENT—CHINA

While Japan is a clear winner on solar and efficiency, perhaps more interesting and globally pertinent is the case of China.

China is developing at breakneck speed. Everywhere you turn in its major cities, and even in the countryside, there is mass demolition, construction, and reconstruction occurring twenty-four hours a day. The environment and air quality in China is suffering tremendously from its leapfrog into the industrial revolution; you can taste the soot in the air in Beijing and Chengdu and wipe it off your arms and face.

Never in world history has a country grown like China has in the past twenty-five years. The country's natural resource consumption has doubled. It consumes 40 percent of the world's cement, 30 percent of its steel, 30 percent of its coal, and 25 percent of its aluminum.[22] Its buildings are terribly inefficient and leak energy at a rate several times greater than other industrialized nations.[23] China's growth in energy consumption is expected to double by 2025, to 16 percent of the world market, rapidly approaching that of the U.S. at 22 percent.[24] And, as would be expected, China is faced with extreme potential power shortages.

Such a threat requires new sources of power generation and some new approaches to the use of energy.

It is certainly true that the bulk of China's industrialization has been fueled by coal and oil, and with nary an environmental control. However, important changes are occurring. China is rapidly developing its natural gas infrastructure to begin replacing its heavy reliance on coal (now 65 percent), the dirtiest of the fossil fuels, with the cleanest.[25]

In 2005, China surpassed Europe and the U.S. to win the distinction of the government making the largest investment in renewable energy. In that year, the Chinese government invested $6 billion in small hydro-electric, solar hot water, and wind power.[26] The country is among world leaders in wind energy potential.[27] China has set forth a renewable portfo-lio standard goal, similar to that adopted in California and Texas, that 5 per-cent of their energy will come from renewables by the close of this decade, 2010, and 10 percent by the close of the next, 2020. At the time of writing, China had installed 1.27 million kW of wind capacity, a small percentage of its goal of 30 million kW by 2020.[28]

And China's renewable goals exclude hydroelectric power, so the mas-sive Three Gorges Dam project will not count toward the renewable target. But it does, in fact, add 18 million kW of carbon-free renewable electricity.

IN 2005, CHINA SURPASSED EUROPE AND THE U.S. TO WIN THE DISTINCTION OF THE GOVERNMENT MAKING THE LARGEST INVESTMENT IN RENEWABLE ENERGY

The country's eleventh five-year plan for 2006 through 2010 calls for major and sweeping energy efficiency measures. It establishes aggressive green building standards and puts in place some interesting incentives for fuel-efficient automobiles. For the latter, China has initiated a Vehicle Tax Policy, which will levy a tax of up to 20 percent on vehicles with large, gas-guzzling engines to discourage their use over smaller, more efficient vehicles.[29] This is in addition to efficiency standards and performance that cuts in half America's per-car gasoline consumption.

With its nationwide efficiency measures and renewable portfolio stan-dard, Beijing is clearly way ahead of Washington, D.C. China, if it can pull it off, is certainly making far more of a commitment than the American government has historically been willing to make.

China is also making a serious effort to research and develop hybrid-electric, all-electric, and hydrogen vehicles. Toyota is opening a new production plant in China to produce its Prius,[30] arguably the best hybrid on the market in terms of fuel efficiency. If China displays the same aggressiveness in hydrogen vehicles and plug-in hybrids as it has in efficiency, the United States will be left in the dust. Instead of Japanese cars, we may soon be offered plug-ins and all-electrics made in China.

SOLAR AND WIND—GERMANY, SPAIN, PORTUGAL, ISRAEL, AND ETHIOPIA

European countries have been much more dedicated to wind development than the United States. As a result, the wind generation on the European continent far outstrips that of the United States, and almost the entire wind turbine manufacturing industry has moved to Europe. Though we pioneered the technology, we are now left behind because our government was passive about ensuring its use.

Germany

Let's take Germany first. Germany is not generally known as a sunny summer travel destination. Its only beaches, though beautiful and inviting, are in the northernmost point of the country. Germany is, however, a world leader in solar power investment, second only to Japan. The United States is third, but only because of state and local efforts, not the federal government.

The reason for German (and Japanese) leadership in solar development is really quite simple—it has massive government subsidies for solar energy in the form of rebates and special rates, and a commitment to continue this funding until increasing volume drives down the costs. It also has helped that a key legislator, Dr. Hermann Scheer, has exercised strong, persistent leadership to continue raising the bar.

Solar photovoltaic is a new technology that, like all products, requires massive increases in demand to drive down its cost. As the demand increases, the cost of solar systems will decline over time, alleviating the necessity of government rebates.

Under Dr. Scheer's leadership, Germany instituted the German Renewable Energy Sources Act, and its 100,000 Solar Roofs Program in 1999. These laws provided low-interest loans and net metering regulations that allowed customers to sell their surplus solar electricity back into the grid at a favorable price. Since then, the solar energy capacity in the country has increased more than ten-fold, from 69,000 kW in 1999 to 794,000 kW by 2004, with more in the works.[31] In addition, Germany has been rapidly developing its wind capacity over the past decade, accounting for half of all wind turbines built worldwide. It is developing its offshore wind resources as well.[32]

Spain and Portugal

Spain has emerged as another world leader in renewable installations. It is second to Germany in Europe for installed wind energy capacity.[33] The country is also investing in large-scale solar projects. In 2006, BP Solar and Spanish bank Santander entered into an agreement to build 278 solar plants across Spain for a total of 18,000 to 25,000 kW by 2008.[34] These new projects will provide enough renewable electricity to power 13,000 to 18,000 homes. After their installation, Spain's solar photovoltaic (PV) capacity will increase significantly from its current total of 37,000 kW.

Portugal announced in April 2006 its plans to construct and install a solar PV project large enough to power 8,000 homes, with the partnership of two American companies, Powerlight and General Electric.[35]

Israel

Israel, much like Japan, has none of its own energy resources apart from the sun. Sixty percent of the country is covered in the Negev desert—one of the best solar resources in the world, and the country is harnessing its solar fuel in a number of different ways. For starters, solar water heaters are a mandatory residential feature. Passive solar space heating is quite prevalent as well, and there are major new solar projects in the works.

The Israeli government announced plans for a 100,000 kW solar plant in 2006.[36]

Harnessing electric power from saline solar ponds and steam from solar concentrating technologies for industrial processes is also under way. And the list goes on and on.

Ethiopia

All of us cynics should take heart from a comment by former President Bill Clinton at a forum where he announced a major clean-energy initiative by his foundation, the Clinton Global Initiative. President Clinton related a recent visit he had with President Girma of Ethiopia. Clinton commented on Brazil's success with ethanol from sugarcane, and President Girma said that his country is capable of growing sugarcane and making ethanol. Then he added, perhaps all of Africa can grow sugarcane and will no longer need oil. African nations will then be able to keep their money in their own countries and at the same time help prevent global warming. It will be interesting to see the direction that Ethiopia takes in moving toward renewables.

With a vision like that, there is still much hope and promise for all the people living on this planet of ours.

CONCLUSION

With the right vision and leadership, other nations have moved ahead in the path to a secure energy future. The U.S. has much to learn from others but even more to give to others if we, too, choose the right road and put enough effort into the struggle to arrive at a secure energy future one year at a time until we get there.

It's time for the United States to join the renewable energy race in earnest. There is plenty of room left to be a leader. Big Solar is not yet a reality. Neither is a plug-in hybrid car, an all-electric car, or a hydrogen-driven car— all American inventions waiting to be transformed into problem-solving realities.

The development of renewable energy is of international significance, not at all unlike the arms race. The difference is that it can result in saving our civilization, not destroying it. This is a race in which every nation that helps everyone else becomes a winner. Surely the largest consumer of energy on earth needs to be a major player. The world is waiting.

✳✳✳

1   Jimmy Carter, "The Crisis of Confidence," (July 15, 1979).

2   Freeman, 1974.

3   "A Time to Choose: America's Energy Future," Energy Policy Project of the Ford Foundation (1974).

4   John Laumer, "Sweden Raises The Renewable Energy Bar"(January 24, 2006), www.treehugger.com /files/2006/01/sweden_raises_t.php.

5   Larry West, "Sweden Aims to be World's First Oil-Free Nation," http://environment.about.com/od/renewableenergy/a/oilfreesweden.htm (February 2006).

6   Karin Ericsson and Lars. J. Nilsson, "International Biofuel Trade—A Study of the Swedish Import," Division of Environmental and Energy Systems Studies, Lund Institute of Technology (2004).

7   Ibid.

8   Karen Mattias, "Sweden, a Leader in Renewable Energy, Aims to End Oil Dependency by 2020," *Associated Press* (February 2, 2006).

9   Ingvar B. Fridleifsson, "Geothermal Energy for the Benefit of the People," United Nations University—Geothermal Training Programme (2003).

10 Alister Doyle, "Iceland's Hydrogen Buses Zip to Oil-Free Economy," *Reuters* (January 10, 2005).

11 Mike Lee, "Iceland the First Country to Try Abandoning Gasoline," *ABC News* (January 18, 2005).

12 The United States runs a very close second to Brazil as the largest producer of ethanol in the world. In 2005, Brazil produced 16.5 billion liters from sugar and the United States produced 16.23 billion liters, 90 percent of which was from corn crops.

13 David Luhnow and Geraldo Samor, "As Brazil Fills Up on Ethanol, it Weans off Energy Imports," *Wall Street Journal* (January 9, 2006).

14 Larry Rother, "With Big Boost from Sugar Cane, Brazil is Satisfying its Fuel Needs," *New York Times* (April 10, 2006).

15 Ibid.

16 Alan Clendenning, "Brazil Leading Effort to Boost Ethanol Use," *Associated Press* (March 10, 2006).

17 "Let's Get Serious About Alternatives to Oil," *Wall Street Journal* (18 April 2005).

18 Anthony Fabiola, "Turn off the Heat—How Japan made Energy Saving an Art Form," *The Guardian* (February 17, 2006).

19 Ibid.

20 Oliver Ristau, "The Photovoltaic Market in Japan: Unquestioned Leadership of World Market," *The Solarserver* (Sept. 15, 2001), http://www.solarserver.de/solarmagazin/artikelseptember2001-e.html.

21 "Marketbuzz 2006," *Solarbuzz* (March 15, 2006).

22 "A Rising China and the Flourishing China–Australia Relationship," The Embassy of the People's Republic of China in Australia (11 July 2005), http://au.china-embassy.org/eng/zggk/t203070.ht.

23 Zijun Li, "China Aims to Build Energy-Efficient Society in Next Five Years," *Worldwatch Institute* (October 20, 2005).

24 Andrezej Zwaniecki, "U.S–China Cooperation Could Advance Mutual, Global Energy Goals" (April 2005), http://usinfo.state.gov/eap/Archive/2005/Apr/04-622583.html.

25 U.S. EIA, "Country Analysis Briefs" (August 2006).

26 "China is World's Leading Investor in Renewable Energy," *Xinhua News Agency* (May 17, 2006).

27 Yingling Liu, "Made in China, or Made by China? Chinese Wind Turbines Struggle to Enter Own Market," *Worldwatch Institute* (May 19, 2006), http://www.worldwatch.org/features/chinawatch/stories/20060519-2.

28 Ibid.

29 Zijun Li, "China Aims to Build Energy-Efficient Society."

30 "Toyota Takes Green Car to China," *BBC News* (Sept. 15 2004).

31 International Energy Agency, http://www.oja-services.nl/iea-pvps/isr/22.htm (October 12, 2005).

32 Waytt King and L. Hunter Lovins, "Boom, Bust and Efficiency, " *Fueling the Future* (Toronto, Ontario: House of Anansi Press, 2003), 195.

33 Ibid.

34 Giles Tremlett, "BP Joins Bank in Record Solar-Power Project," *The Guardian* (April 22, 2006).

35 "Portugal Starts Huge Solar Plant," *BBC News* (June 7, 2006).

36 "Israel's Experience in Sustainable Energy," United Nations Environmental Program (January 2006).

11
AN ALL-RENEWABLE LOS ANGELES

{A MODEL FOR THE WORLD}   ✳✳✳

LOS ANGELES MAYOR ANTONIO VILLARAIGOSA has placed great emphasis on his dream of making Los Angeles the greenest city in the world. This chapter is a modest effort to test the thesis of this book using L.A. as an example. We can safely assume that if Los Angeles can kick its oil habit, so can Shanghai, Mexico City, and Jakarta. If L.A. continues to guzzle gasoline as if there were an endless supply, it's going to be impossible to persuade other cities to make progress.

I chose L.A. because I live there, I know the utility situation there the best, and I know the vision of the mayor. I hope that all readers would think of their cities as they read this, and analyze point by point how changes could take place where they live.

Los Angeles has a very large asset that can play a tremendous role in getting the city off oil, coal, and nuclear power—L.A. owns its own electric power company, the L.A. Department of Water and Power (LADWP), which I managed from 1997 to 2001. The major road to progress lies in substituting green electricity for petroleum to power motor vehicles and in replacing coal and nuclear power plants in Los Angeles's electric system with solar, wind, biomass, geothermal power, and investments in efficiency and distributed power.

Mayor Villaraigosa has made a start by setting an ambitious goal for Los Angeles to achieve 20 percent renewables by 2010. The important point is that the 20 percent goal must be viewed as a beginning, not an end. L.A. lies in close proximity to significant wind resources in the nearby Tehachapi Mountains, sizeable geothermal power in the Imperial Irrigation District to the south, mountains of municipal waste begging to be converted to usable energy, and superabundant solar power in the metropolitan area and the nearby Mohave Desert. In addition, there are major opportunities to use this renewable energy more efficiently.

Los Angeles is uniquely situated to lead a steady march away from coal, oil, and nuclear power. It is blessed with access to renewable resources and it also has the leadership in its city government to provide green electricity to "keep the lights on" and power hybrid cars, trucks, and buses; expand

LOS ANGELES IS UNIQUELY SITUATED TO LEAD A STEADY MARCH AWAY FROM COAL, OIL, AND NUCLEAR POWER

mass transit; and provide power to the city-owned Port of Los Angeles for ships at the dock and transport containers away from the port. It can also substitute renewable electricity at the city-owned Los Angeles airport (LAX) to tow the airplanes on the ground and power the buses and trains that serve the airport. Over time Los Angeles can convert its renewable electricity to hydrogen (the LADWP also owns the city's water) that will replace natural gas, fuel airplanes, and become an alternative fuel for motor vehicles.

To make all this happen, Los Angeles must enlarge its vision to match that of its mayor. It must be more than just another city with excuses. Greening its electricity supply must be its highest priority.

There is a very legitimate question as to whether Los Angeles can acquire the renewable energy soon enough and in large enough quantities to meet a steadily expanding market for electricity. Can it actually grow from 20 percent green in 2010 to 40 percent in 2020, 60 percent in 2040, etc? The answer is YES. But only if there is the public pressure and political will to carry out the ambitious plans. Ironically, the costs to the consumer over time will be lower, not higher, compared to the dirty and dangerous alternatives.

Let's get some facts on the table as to what is available to Los Angeles.

WIND POWER

There are at least 3 million kW of good wind potential in the Tehachapi Mountains.[1] The California Energy Commission estimates a total wind potential of at least 4.5 million kW in Southern California.[2] This is enough to power about 1.4 million homes.[3]

Los Angeles owns extensive electricity transmission resources to the northwest, which can be expanded over time. They could help transmit to Los Angeles the enormous wind power of the upper Midwest. This resource potential is economically available in huge quantities, as much as 10 million kW, which is more than the LADWP's total generation system of 7 million kW. Such a quantity would still be only a small fraction of the wind potential in that region, estimated at more than 500 million kW.[4] These resources could be developed over time as needed.

GEOTHERMAL

Los Angeles lies between major geothermal resources within relatively short transmission distance to the south and the north.

The Imperial Irrigation District is a treasure trove of geothermal power just waiting to be harnessed. A conservative number is 1.5 to 2 million kW,[5] with more being uncovered at the Salton Sea. The Department of Water and Power is participating in building an additional transmission line to the area and already owns a small steam field. The geothermal potential is enough power to light more than one million homes.[6]

SOLAR—WATCH YOUR ELECTRIC METER SPIN BACKWARDS

The sun shining on Los Angeles itself is a significant source of power. Solar is financially attractive to consumers if it is properly valued by the utility.

It is a tragedy that the rate structure and metering policies in Los Angeles at present discourage the expansion of solar power. But with proper incentives, solar panels could be a commonplace sight on every block in Los Angeles.

Imagine the smiles on the faces of consumers as they watch in amazement as their electric meters run backwards when surplus energy from their solar panels is sold back to their electric utility. This is all possible if we allow rates to increase with volume (L.A.'s are flat). Solar would gradually displace the highest-cost power and thus be more economically attractive for the consumer. The money made available each year by Los Angeles for subsidies under its current program can fund only about 3,000 kW per year—700 to 800 homes—a trivial amount for a city of over a million buildings.

With two actions—a revised rate structure and larger funding for subsidies—rooftop solar would be attractive to L.A. consumers. A modest investment of $30 million per year, about the level of the state of California's program, could easily result in 100,000 kW of solar in L.A. by 2017. But that alone would not be real leadership.

If L.A.'s utility gave solar a serious priority, it would become the nation's first solar utility and decide to make solar rooftops a city-owned source and integrate it into its power system. With a large order, Los Angeles could take advantage of the breakthrough in solar costs from thin-film technology described in chapter 8 and bring green manufacturing jobs to L.A. Installing 500,000 to 1,000,000 kW in Los Angeles by 2017 is within the realm of possibility. Groups such as the Apollo Alliance (a group of labor unions and allies), local electrician unions, and community advocates are promoting this kind of economic development.[7] It would require a focused major effort, but it is doable for a city that wants to be "dark green." With such an effort, L.A. would become "Solar City." Imagine flying into LAX and seeing a vast array of solar collectors shading and electrifying the entire city!

The Wasteland of the Desert is the Goldmine of Our Future Energy Needs
An even greater solar potential for Los Angeles lies in the Mojave Desert, less than 200 miles east of L.A. In the Mojave, the sun is hot and there are vast stretches of empty space. In fact, it would only take about eighty square miles of concentrated solar power in the desert to replace all the electricity consumed by L.A.'s customers. (See Mohave Map, page 147.)

Once a program is underway (in three years), Los Angeles could start completing one 500,000 kW plant every other year. This is doable because solar plants, unlike coal or nuclear plants, are essentially prefabricated and can easily be assembled in less than a year. Los Angeles could become dark green with that huge input of solar firmed up by their gas-fired power plants.

> AN EVEN GREATER SOLAR POTENTIAL FOR LOS ANGELES LIES IN THE MOJAVE DESERT, LESS THAN 200 MILES EAST OF L.A. IN THE MOJAVE, THE SUN IS HOT AND THERE ARE VAST STRETCHES OF EMPTY SPACE

This Big Solar technology is ready to take off with a three-year commercialization effort. After the first plant is built, the cost for a city-owned plant financed by lower cost municipal bonds is projected to produce energy competitive with natural gas over the lifecycle of the plant. But Big Solar needs someone to "break the ice" so to speak, to be a leader, to take the risk by being first to build a commercial-sized plant.

Interestingly, the Southern California Edison Company has just such a Big Solar project under way, although it is moving at a snail's pace. Los Angeles needs to grab the lead in making Big Solar a reality if it is to leave a legacy for our children and their children.

Mojave Desert

BIOMASS

There are huge forest residues in Southern California, and all along the West Coast. I don't mean forests that have been clear-cut, but just the remains of natural decay that fuels massive forest fire. The forests would benefit from a controlled burn in a power plant rather than an uncontrolled, raging forest fires. Over the next twenty years, I believe that L.A. could obtain 1 or 2 million kW from a number of these biomass plants. These costs would be economical compared to natural gas, and L.A.'s utility owns its own transmission all the way to the Northwest. But to do so will require a sustained, focused procurement program that locates plants near concentrations of forest residue.

MUNICIPAL WASTE—YOUR GARBAGE COULD BE A TREASURE

If there ever were a win-win situation it would be taking the municipal waste that no one wants to live near and converting it—with advanced technology—to electricity, biogas, or hydrogen. Advanced technology—such as the plasma torch—is fundamentally different from the toxic-waste-to-energy plants in the 1970s. They are as clean as natural gas power plants, and competitive with them, and building them would help solve the serious waste-disposal problem for Los Angeles.

Once a demonstration plant has been built and put into operation, plants could be built at the pace of 50,000 kW per year or more, so that in fifteen years' time (allowing five years for start-up) L.A. could have 500,000 kW of municipal waste power, or 750,000 kW within twenty years, enough power to keep the lights on for 450,000 homes.

As an alternative, pyrolysis technology—a process in which organic materials are heated rapidly in an anaerobic environment—can convert the waste to hydrogen that could power cars or power plants.

TOTAL RENEWABLE RESOURCES FOR LOS ANGELES

A ten-year action program of steadily selling off the LADWP's coal and nuclear plants and bringing on the renewables could convert the LADWP into the greenest large utility in the nation by 2020. The system would then consist of over 40 percent renewables and the rest hydroelectric and natural gas in terms of capacity. In terms of energy, it would be over 50 percent renewables!

The numbers make a more eloquent case than any amount of rhetoric. L.A.'s utility has available potential of 13 million kW of wind power, 5 million kW of solar, 2.5 to 3 million kW of geothermal, 2 million kW of biomass, and 750,000 kW of municipal waste for a total of 23.25 million kW, and 5 million kW of usable hydro and natural gas. That totals 28.5 million kW of new capacity potentially to replace 2.2 million kW of coal and nuclear and supply 5 million kW of growth for electric transportation.

LOS ANGELES'S ABILITY TO GO GREEN IS NOT LIMITED BY TECHNOLOGY OR RESOURCES

Thus we see that abundant renewable energy is available to Los Angeles to meet all of its needs. In fact, there are four times the renewable resources needed to meet a 60 percent renewable goal in thirty-three years. No logical person can say it can't be done. It can be done, but it will require committed, knowledgeable management and a concerted, focused effort.

The phasing out of the LADWP's coal resource can be done one year at a time because the utility's largest coal source is a contract for the output of the plant. This source can be sold gradually, and not before the replacement renewables are online. There is no need to jeopardize reliability or buy power that Los Angeles doesn't need, but it does require decisive leadership to put polluting fuel in the city's past.

In terms of nuclear holdings, the LADWP owns 366,000 kW of the Palo Verde nuclear plant. This investment should be sold before the plant's next large capital investment is needed to replace worn-out equipment. All of the sales of coal and nuclear supplies can be coordinated with introducing the renewables so the transition is seamless.

Los Angeles's ability to go green is not limited by technology or resources. The only limit is the ability of its utility to implement the vision of Mayor Villaraigosa.

Energy Efficiency—Neighborhood by Neighborhood, Block by Block, Kitchen by Kitchen

Too often we rely on slick TV ads to promote energy conservation. The problem is that these ads quickly lose their effect once they go off the air. Yes, we need effective communication, but to really change the dynamic, our efforts must be neighborhood by neighborhood.

Of course, Los Angeles will continue to grow in both numbers of people and potential use of electricity. Even so, an aggressive efficiency program would offset normal growth in the consumption of electricity and assure that the major additions to L.A. utility's power supply loads would be to power motor vehicles and fuel electric transportation. Growth in population could be offset largely by growth in efficiency. The LADWP did stress energy efficiency from 1997 to 2000 when I was general manager.

Los Angeles has recently encountered higher loads than expected, which is in large part the result of the utility virtually eliminating its efficiency programs from 2001 to 2005. That changed with a new board of directors appointed by Mayor Villaraigosa in 2005, but conservation programs can be further strengthened considerably. L.A. should have a goal of a 4 percent gain in efficiency per year that would offset growth and reduce existing loads by 20 percent in ten years. To achieve that result, L.A. would need to encourage solar installation on homes and businesses and finance big-ticket items for its customers such as highly efficient lighting, air conditioning, and other electrical equipment. L.A. could also apply the

When I was general manager of the LADWP, we invested in a program named "Just Do It." We sent a team to poor neighborhoods and, without any charges or loans, took action on the spot, like replacing broken windows, caulking huge cracks in doors, and cleaning refrigerator coils, which saved low-income customers about 15 percent in their electric usage and bills. And we provided monetary incentives to all consumers for purchasing the most efficient appliances and lighting. The utility even paid for highly efficient traffic lights.

20/20 program that was crucial to ending the state's energy crisis in 2001, a 20 percent rebate for all customers who reduce their load 20 percent or more over the previous year.

The goal of a 4 percent per year reduction can be achieved if there is a will to become more efficient and encouragement for decentralized, customer-owned additions to the power supply for the city.

Decentralized Power—Customer-Owned Power Plants

The green revolution is advanced by utilities encouraging their customers to invest in efficiency, solar power, fuel cells, and other smaller power plants that utilize cleaner fuels and enhance the reliability of the power supply. Yet the natural tendency of most utilities is to sell more of their product—electricity—and not encourage their customers to unplug, even in part.

L.A.'s city-owned utility is in a unique position to serve as a leader in encouraging decentralized plants in the city as an important element of going green. Instead, today its policies actively and deliberately discourage such projects.

The city blackouts affecting 80,000 customers in the summer of 2006 due to failing transformers and other distribution equipment dramatically underscores why power generated at the source is more reliable. Yet the LADWP's rate structure and service rules discourage customers from installing solar panels and businesses from installing small plants that generate heat as well as power for adjacent industries.

The actions that need to happen in L.A. are as follows:

* Encourage customers, through rate structures, to invest in efficiency or build their own power sources.
* Eliminate backup charges that require the decentralized power customer to pay for capacity it doesn't use.
* Standardize agreements to cover the connection between the decentralized system and the grid.

Such actions would make the solar potential previously mentioned a firmer reality. In addition, fuel cells and small natural gas plants could easily add 100,000 kW per year, more than enough to meet annual growth.

Distributed generation can be fueled by hydrogen in conventional generating plants and fuel cells. The hydrogen could be made from municipal waste and landfill methane. Such a policy, if actively encouraged and implemented, would help assure that the LADWP's green power focus would also be reliable. It would be a significant step in making L.A. the greenest city of all.

One Dollar-a-Gallon Gasoline—That Creates No Pollution

Imagine telling people in Los Angeles that they could buy one-dollar-a-gallon gas and when they use that gas they will create no pollution. As unbelievable as this notion sounds, it can become a reality in the near future, but only if we have the fortitude to take aggressive steps to provide green power and plug-in hybrid cars.

The exciting prospect for Los Angeles is that electricity from solar, wind, and biomass used in a plug-in hybrid can displace most of the gasoline needed to run motor vehicles, which emit most of the pollution in L.A. County.[8] Imagine Los Angeles with air that actually meets health standards. It would all be possible because L.A.'s electricity would be priced to the car owner at the equivalent of less than one-dollar-a-gallon gasoline. And the electricity could increasingly be generated from clean renewables.

> **IMAGINE LOS ANGELES WITH AIR THAT ACTUALLY MEETS HEALTH STANDARDS**

I am not suggesting that the L.A.-owned utility go into the automobile business. On the contrary, I am suggesting they expand the business they are already in—selling electricity—and sell green electricity directly and in the form of hydrogen to replace imported oil.

The marketing of electricity for plug-in hybrids presents a marvelous opportunity for the L.A.-owned utility to significantly enlarge its business over time. If thirty years from now, the motor vehicles in L.A. were mostly plug-in hybrids with a sixty-mile range in electric mode, it would require about 2,500 KWh per vehicle per year. For 2 million cars a total of 5.0 billion kWh would be needed. That would add 23 percent to today's electric use.

The good news is that all the electricity needed for hybrid cars can be generated mostly at night and during off-peak hours during the day; thus they would not require additional capacity, just off-peak energy. But in thirty years the LADWP would be selling 23 percent more kilowatt-hours of green power. To be sure it will require natural gas plants to run at night, but solar and wind can free up the natural gas during the heavy-use portion of the day.

The interesting fact is that this "new business" for the LADWP could result in lower prices than would otherwise be the case, both for regular users of electricity and for motorists currently stuck with high-priced gasoline. That is true because the utility investment in electric power would be used more of the time (about 70 percent rather than 40 percent), so the cost per unit of capacity will be lower than it would be without the new business. And the fuel costs for wind and solar are zero.

So L.A. can go green—and sell that green power to run hybrid plug-in cars. This would set the stage for renewables to play a major role in kicking the oil habit in Los Angeles. It would require an aggressive and proactive array of programs along with a citywide set of actions that Mayor Villaraigosa could lead with enthusiasm and skill.

Plug-In Hybrids

Los Angeles could jump into the lead in the plug-in hybrid revolution with these actions:

* Offer an off-peak rate of ten cents a kilowatt-hour that would be the equivalent of less than one-dollar-a-gallon gasoline and still be cost effective for the utility.
* Offer to install an inexpensive 220-volt plug for anyone buying a plug-in hybrid so he or she could charge the car battery with speed while sleeping or at work.
* Provide similar plug-in facilities at all existing electric-car parking places and throughout the city.
* Make a large order for plug-in hybrids for city-owned fleet purchases, local businesses, and perhaps surrounding interested fleet owners.
* Enlist Hollywood celebrities to order plug-in hybrids and promote them.
* Exempt plug-in hybrids from city sales tax. Lobby to exempt plug-in hybrids from state tax.
* Amend California's zero-emission vehicle law to make plug-in hybrids "zero-emission" cars and require a steady increase of new cars sold in California to be plug-in hybrids .
* Give discounts to plug-in hybrids at city-owned parking lots.
* Give preference to plug-in hybrids in the car pool lane.
* Enact sizeable city tax incentives to the first car company that sells 100,000 plug-in hybrids in Los Angeles.

The plug-in hybrid appears to be the best bet for early and steady reduction of gasoline consumption by substituting green electricity. But real success will be met when we diversify our renewable solutions.

Alternatives to Gasoline Made from Crops and Waste

The plug-in hybrid has an internal combustion engine that normally runs on gasoline. But it can run on any of the homegrown alternatives such as ethanol, biodiesel, or even vegetable oil. L.A. should encourage such use so that the plug-in hybrid uses virtually no oil. L.A. should encourage the manufacturers of plug-in hybrids and all cars to be flex-fuel; that is, cars that can run on biofuels or gasoline. The goal should be for biofuels to displace 10 to 15 percent of the gasoline burned in cars in Los Angeles within ten years, and even more in the future.

The only problem with relying on biofuels for a larger share is that, as previously stated, we will soon be raising the price of corn and soy until we are literally taking food off the table to fill the gas tank. So we need to maximize the use of renewable electricity.

Electric Cars

Los Angeles, with its city-owned utility, can help bring back the all-electric car. To my knowledge, the electric car is the first piece of technology in America that was destroyed because it was successful. An all-electric car can be a worthy competitor to the plug-in hybrid. One hundred percent electricity is better than any hybrid in consumer costs because it eliminates the internal combustion engine altogether and runs entirely on one-dollar-a-gallon electricity rather than higher-priced gasoline.

Almost all of the people who drove the electric cars a few years ago are still angry with General Motors and Toyota for recalling their vehicles. As the movie *Who Killed the Electric Car?* reveals, the electric car gained passionate endorsements from the people who drove them. And that was when gasoline was just two dollars a gallon. Just think what the market would be today if L.A. placed itself on the waiting list for buying electric cars, invited others to sign up, and enticed a car company to fulfill the orders.

Millions of Trees

Mayor Villaraigosa has already launched a program to plant a million trees in L.A. And no pun intended, it is an essential feature of his green vision for the city. Trees serve a number of functions in addition to beauty and shade. Properly placed, they replace or reduce the need for air conditioning. Trees can be an integral part of the L.A. utility's energy conservation program. The utility could offer tree-planting services and also assure water and maintenance of the trees. Similar programs at schools will enable the trees to be a learning experience for the kids.

Trees also absorb some of the carbon emitted by burning fossil fuels and thus help in the efforts to reduce the climate changes caused by global warming. Planting a million trees would be a small step toward making L.A.'s giant fleet of cars carbon neutral, but not nearly as great as substituting plug-in hybrids for gas-guzzlers.

Since the mayor has already taken the lead on this issue, it would be useful to connect it to the people who drive cars and operate the power plants, ships, airplanes, and fleets of trucks in L.A. There is a direct connection. More and more concerned citizens wish to become carbon neutral. For homeowners, there is the double benefit of reducing the energy for air conditioning and absorbing some carbon. You would need to plant, or pay others to plant, one acre of trees to neutralize your car's carbon for the year. There aren't enough acres in L.A. to affect the emissions of 2 million cars. But every bit helps.

A well-publicized program to promote widespread participation in the Million Trees L.A. initiative could be a wonderful example for other cities to follow.

The Port of L.A. is one of the largest container ports in the world and the largest cruise ship port in the western United States. It is a huge source of petroleum-based pollution in the region, accounting for 12 percent of diesel particulate matter, 9 percent of nitrogen oxide pollution, and 45 percent of sulfur oxides pollution.

Greening Los Angeles Port

The role for green electricity in Los Angeles can and should go beyond today's uses of electricity, and extend past cars and mass transit. I refer to the Port of L.A. and the L.A. Airport (LAX), both huge sources of petroleum pollution. Let's discuss the Port of L.A. first, since I have responsibility there as Mayor Villaraigosa's appointee as president of the Harbor Commission.

Historically, Los Angeles Port has been one of the biggest sources of pollution in the entire region. We are in the process of turning this around. Soon, all the ships will be powered by electricity or its equivalent when they are tied up at the dock, and all the huge cranes that move the containers from the ships to the docks will operate on electricity, so this program is already well under way. But the dock power won't be green unless it's made from renewable resources. And that's what Los Angeles must do if we really mean to be green.

The port can over time require all the on-dock equipment that now uses petroleum to be powered by green electricity. Today no one makes such equipment, but with a cooperative effort we can persuade manufacturers that for the short distances involved, electricity will be cleaner and cheaper than petroleum, and the electric vehicles need not be more expensive.

From Dock to Destination

The major opportunity for greening the port operations is in the transportation of the huge volume of containers from the port to final destinations within 200 miles. These 16,000-plus trucks are now moved entirely by petroleum, and the surrounding communities suffer from high asthma rates and respiratory illnesses. In addition, the railroads that move the containers to all ports of the U.S. need to be electrified. Over a thirty-year period, they all need to be converted to electricity or renewable hydrogen.

The port has a Clean Air Action Program under way. Under that program, there are opportunities to advance the use of renewable hydrogen at the port, first mixed with petroleum to reduce pollution since the hydrogen molecules are very active and help clean the entire mix. Over time, hydrogen in IC engines or fuel cells can enable the port to meet air quality health standards.

To supplement and replace the trucks, we can build a twenty-first-century version of a railroad. One option is called maglev—a fast-moving elevated concept powered by electricity, which already exists in Germany and China. The train is actually levitated above the track and moves with great speed and no friction by electric power. As a result, it holds promise of a long life and low maintenance costs.

Another option is a version of a monorail that moves containers on the equivalent of a fast conveyor belt. This system can replace trucks in 50 percent of the containers that end up at California destinations. For very short trips an all-electric truck may be feasible.

These are gigantic projects, but as petroleum prices rise, renewable electricity, with its stable prices, can help attract private capital to fund these projects and help America kick the oil habit. L.A. can lead the way and green manufacturing, installation, and operating jobs can be part of the equation.

The Port of L.A. can and will over time substitute electricity from L.A.'s city-owned utility for much of the petroleum pollution at the port. But this will be progress only if the electricity is green. It all ties together. It can, and it will. As we get it done we will be making the mayor's vision of the Port of L.A. being the greenest in the world a reality.

Greening Los Angeles Airport

The L.A. Airport (LAX) is another huge source of petroleum pollution. We can't yet fly airplanes on electricity, but we can eliminate most of the use of petroleum on the ground. This is no small matter. A single jet arriving at an airport releases as much of the toxic air contaminant NOx as a gas-powered automobile driven over 26,000 miles.[9] It is a major source of pollution in L.A.

LAX can become electrified in several ways:

* The old, inefficient power plants on site near the central terminal area can be shut down. LAX can get all its electricity from L.A.'s utility and it can be all-green.
* All airplanes must be required to shut off their jets after they land and be towed by electric tugs.
* All the trucks on site and vans and buses servicing the airport should be converted to electric or at least plug-in hybrids or flex-fuel, which can use a mixture of biofuels and gasoline.
* Solar panels can be installed on parking lots, rooftops, the sides of buildings, and vacant land.

Plug-in hybrids, biofuels, and all-electric vehicles are the best bet for reducing oil consumption in L.A. But we need all the options available; we need to make renewable hydrogen a commercially available alternative as well.

In the future, airplanes will be powered by hydrogen and L.A. can encourage that transition.

Clean Hydrogen to Replace Dirty Oil

Los Angeles could be the place where the "chicken and egg" problem with hydrogen is overcome. L.A. is already home to seven hydrogen filling stations, with another three in the works.[10] Ford, and perhaps others, might be persuaded to respond to an order from the popular mayor of L.A. to purchase the first fleet of hydrogen IC vehicles in the world. Making such an offer would be a major act of leadership and would invite similar initiatives nationwide.

Ford cannot deny that five years ago it showed off its Model U, a hydrogen-fueled hybrid SUV with a range of 300 miles. It offers for sale IC motors designed to run on hydrogen. Surely it should respond favorably to an offer to lead its rivals in the new world of hydrogen.

We do not need to wait for the fuel cell. And Los Angeles can take the lead to move hydrogen usage forward.

Fleets would be an important start. Once people see that hydrogen-fueled internal-combustion-engine vehicles are feasible, hydrogen service stations can be built at fleet locations throughout the city so ordinary people can become hydrogen car customers. As time goes by and fuel cells are perfected, in the next decade hydrogen can become a serious competitor to plug-in hybrids, flex-fuel cars, and all-electric.

In the long run, I predict that hydrogen from renewable electricity will be a major factor in our energy supply. It will displace petroleum as the fuel for air travel. It will displace natural gas as supplies continue to deplete. But for now, hydrogen is made primarily from natural gas and we need renewable hydrogen.

> WE DO NOT NEED TO WAIT FOR THE FUEL CELL. AND LOS ANGELES CAN TAKE THE LEAD TO MOVE HYDROGEN USAGE FORWARD

The cheapest source of renewable hydrogen is methane that seeps out of landfills and could be converted to hydrogen. Methane, if released into the atmosphere, is one of the worst greenhouse gases. Los Angeles should get the hydrogen revolution started with hydrogen from methane from its municipal waste.

Big Hydrogen, like Big Solar, requires a Big Daddy, and in L.A. that has got to be the LADWP. After all, to make hydrogen you need water and electricity, and the LADWP sells both.

CONCLUSION

The Romans used the expression *carpe diem*, or "seize the day," to express their worldview that is necessary to take decisive action in times of crisis. Today is our time of crisis and it is our time to seize the day. And by seizing the day, Los Angeles can show the world that it is possible to turn a huge polluted metropolis into an ecopolis. And if it does, others will follow.

It is clear that L.A. has the resources and technology, and a city government led by visionaries to provide all the ingredients for a green revolution to take place. But the implementation and success of the vision depends on the priority the city and its people give to the hard work needed to make it happen. Public education is essential so that the people know what is doable. It is my hope that this book, and this chapter in particular, can help serve that purpose.

✳✳✳

1   California Energy Commission, "Renewable Resources Development Report," (2003), Appendix C.
2   Dora Yen-Nakafuji, "California Wind Resources," California Energy Commission Staff White Paper CEC-500-2005-071-D (April 2005).
3   Assuming a 35 percent capacity factor, and 10,000 kWh per house per year. This figure does not take into consideration the intermittent nature of the resource. Without storage, you would not be able to power your home entirely with wind.
4   Matt Schueger, "Midwest Wind Power Development," Wind on the Wires Presentation (February 11, 2004). The upper Midwest states referred to here are Illinois, Iowa, Minnesota, Nebraska, North and South Dakota, and Wisconsin.
5   "Integrated Energy Policy Report 2005." California Energy Commission (November 2005).
6   Assuming at least a 70 percent capacity factor and 10,000 kWh per house per year.
7   Apollo Alliance, http://www.apolloalliance.org (August 2006).
8   California Air Resources Board, 2005 Estimated Annual Average Emissions, Los Angeles County, http://www.arb.ca.gov/app/emsinv/emseic1_query.php.
9   Jennifer Stenzel and Jonathan Trutt, "Flying Off Course: Environmental Impacts of America's Airports," Natural Resources Defense Council (October 1996).
10 California Fuel Cell Partnership, http://www.cafcp.org/fuel-vehl_map.html (2005).

12 A NATIONAL RENEWABLE ENERGY POLICY

{WHAT CONGRESS NEEDS TO DO}   ✳✳✳

SINCE THE DAYS OF RICHARD NIXON, U.S. presidents have sent energy policy messages to Congress. The one theme that united all these ill-fated efforts was the notion of independence—most particularly, independence from imported oil. But the harsh truth is that the general public has not

> I was working for the Federal Power Commission when President Kennedy was killed. It wasn't until a few days after Kennedy's death that it hit me that we now had a Texan as president. We had already had confrontations with members of Congress over regulating the price of natural gas and now we were facing an oil and gas man in the White House! By the day of the funeral, I figured that our work was history. It would soon turn out that I was wrong.
>
> In many ways, President Lyndon B. Johnson felt his job was to prove he was a consumer's man. He was no longer a U.S. senator from Texas, his position before becoming Kennedy's vice president in 1961. His constituency was now the entire nation.
>
> Lyndon Johnson became our strongest supporter in beginning to reshape the nation's energy policy. Under President Johnson, the Federal Energy Commission continued the work begun under President Kennedy. We kept cutting the price of natural gas and President Johnson put out news releases bragging about our work.
>
> We asserted the authority of the federal government over electric utilities engaging in interstate commerce. In cases where electricity passed across state lines, the Commission said the federal government could fix the price at the wholesale level. That was a big deal. Private companies had been selling electricity to cities and co-ops, but there was no place where the price could be regulated. It was a monopoly. We had President Johnson's strong support for our consumer protection activities.

had a sustained interest in energy independence. Consumer attention is like a bolt of lightning. It can strike with intensity during an oil embargo or seasonal blackouts, but then the fury fades and people became preoccupied with their everyday lives. It's then that the oil, coal, and nuclear lobbies quietly control the energy policies.

The Nixon era was euphoric about the promise of the nuclear breeder, but it failed to become a commercial reality, and the cost overruns in light-water reactors were so devastating that utilities stopped buying them. It wasn't Jane Fonda or Ralph Nader who shut down the nuclear option. It was the financial vice presidents of the American utility industry.

At a cocktail party in early January 1969, I met President Nixon's science advisor, Lee DuBridge, who was the first person Nixon appointed at the beginning of the new administration. He had been president of the California Institute of Technology, Cal-Tech, in Pasadena.

I walked up to him and told him I was delighted to have the chance to meet him. "I was here under Lyndon Johnson, and I'm one of the guys who's leaving," I added.

"No, you're not," he answered. "I've already discussed this with President Nixon and we want to continue the studies you have under way on energy. You're the guy in charge of energy policy in the government and we believe that's an important activity."

"But I'm a lifelong Democrat," I replied.

"I don't care," DuBridge replied. "It's not a political job."

So I stayed on.

I was there at the center of the action of the environmental revolution in 1970 and 1971. I drafted the first message on energy policy ever delivered by a U.S. president, a message that Richard Nixon sent to Congress in 1971.

I helped put together the Environmental Policy Act, which created the nation's first Environmental Policy Council. We pushed through the first clean water and clean air acts. I worked with John Erhlichman and Doug Costel in creating the U.S. Environmental Protection Agency (EPA), the federal agency whose job is to protect the environment. We wanted an independent agency that didn't have a conflict to enforce the environmental laws.

All the basic environmental laws that exist in the nation today were enacted in 1971 under President Nixon. We sent presidential message after presidential message to Congress that would be considered radical today. Those new agencies and laws became the focus of environmental protection. And they have largely been successful in preserving much of America's most precious natural resources and environmental treasures, and in substantially reducing air and water pollution.

President Carter succeeded in establishing a strong start for making efficient use of renewables our national policy, and funding was made available to advance solar technology and the rest. But this renewable thrust came to a dead end in the early 1980s. The price of oil went down and America went to sleep. The Reagan administration was content to let the market decide our energy policy so that the effort directed toward efficiency and renewables halted. It was more than just symbolic when President Reagan removed the solar panels on the roof of the White House that President Carter had put up there. He literally killed the program.

> President Carter gave energy his highest priority attention during his first ninety days in office. I was part of the staff under Jim Schlessinger that completed the president's energy plan. I recall working all night to finish it in time. At the White House ceremony in the Rose Garden when the president revealed his program, he began by saying, "If you see these guys squinting at the sun, it's because they haven't seen any daylight for ninety days." It was a high point for energy policy.

This nation has been dozing on energy policy through the 1980s and ever since. But it wasn't because some of us didn't continue to sound the alarm. On October 13, 1982—some twenty-five years ago, when I was a managing director of the TVA—I spoke at a conference on coal and nuclear power at the University of Illinois. I said the following:

> That brings me to the crux of my argument here today. If we are to attack our continued energy dependence with the seriousness it deserves, we must mount a truly comprehensive conservation strategy. That will mean making the investments in energy research and development and in retooling our industrial bases that are required to put our energy system and our economy on a sound and sustainable footing. It will take billions of dollars—and I realize dollars by the billions are considered to be in short supply in the national budget today. But unless we make these investments in a more energy-efficient system based on renewable energy and a less energy-intensive pattern of growth, we will spend even more billions—and send most of it overseas. We will continue to exhaust our strength and our resources in the effort to drain this nation and the world of oil and gas and to exploit coal and nuclear in unwise ways.

Author with President Bill Clinton.

But the Reagan administration and the business leaders didn't listen and America kept guzzling. Energy was not a priority for President George H. W. Bush. In the 1990s President Clinton did obtain more funding for efficiency and renewables and advanced our progress. President Clinton was a knowledgeable and articulate proponent of efficiency and renewables. He tried to enact a tax that would encourage the efficient use of energy, but a Congress overly influenced by the energy industry defeated it. After that, energy policy was not President Clinton's top priority.

Until the price of oil hit three dollars a gallon, President George W. Bush's policies reflected his Texas oil background. He gave the subject some lip service but seemed oblivious to the nation's oil dependency and did nothing about it. His vice president disparaged conservation and his Congress gave the oil industry and nuclear power big tax breaks.

The price of oil in 2006 did something that we energy policy types had failed to do for the past thirty years with all our foot stomping and hand wringing. It forced the American people to become interested in alternatives. As a result, it is possible that America will stay interested long enough to hammer out policies to deploy the renewable sources and use them efficiently with today's technology.

As Thomas L. Friedman pointed out in October 2006, the American people are ahead of their government on this issue. "Focus groups around the country show that 'reducing dependence on foreign oil' is voters' top national security priority."[1]

Let me be clear: research alone is not the answer. To be sure, research is important to maintain the march of technological progress, but it is often used as an excuse for not promoting the use of commercial products made with known technology. And, yes, product improvement (as distinguished from research for new projects) is an essential part of business, but improvements only take place in earnest once a product goes into commercial use and there is sufficient cash flow and competition incentives to fund it.

When we consider how cameras, computers, cell phones, and even razor blades have evolved, what's revealed is that real progress for machinery (as opposed to, say, pharmaceuticals) occurs after the research and development process ends and commercial sales begin.

We need to begin massively building wind turbines, solar power systems, and modern, relatively clean-burning plants to convert municipal wastes to useful energy. And we need to use clean, homegrown resources efficiently.

The time is at hand to enact a national energy policy that will be a combination of requirements and incentives to make it happen. The policy must be comprehensive, realistic, and long-term so that progress is made each year with the commitment for going all the way.

President George W. Bush has argued that business needs to be certain that his tax breaks will remain in effect far into the future so operating decisions can be based on them. That same argument is even more valid for energy policy. It is vital that the oil-producing nations know that America is serious, that we will reduce our need for oil every year for a long, long time, and any further trouble will only accelerate the pace.

Other nations, especially developing countries, must hear that America has turned the corner on global warming—that carbon emissions from the U.S. will get smaller and smaller—so they will have reason to follow our lead.

The duration of our policy commitment is perhaps more important than the exact pace of change. In the past the U.S. has enacted a laundry list of energy measures—some useful, but most of them subsidies to the existing sources. In no way did these measures add up to a policy with strength or purpose.

I think it fair to say that if our purpose is to protect our security, environment, and public health at an affordable price, in the past we've gone for the capillaries and not the jugular. It is time that we enact the laws that will turn energy policy toward the best interests of the American people.

A comprehensive policy must include the following:

* A movement of our electric power production steadily toward more and more renewable sources
* A 20 percent federal tax credit to electricity and natural gas utilities that gives highest priority to the efficient use of the energy they supply
* A ban on new coal-fired or nuclear power plants
* Retirement of existing coal-fired and nuclear plants within the next thirty years
* A government-funded program to demonstrate Big Solar and convert it to hydrogen in demonstration projects of 500 MW or larger
* Federal fuel economy standards that move from 24 to 48 miles per gallon over the next twenty-four years, one mpg per year
* Large enough tax credits for both purchasers and manufacturers of plug-in hybrid and flex-fuel automobiles to assure that they become the standard fixture of all motor vehicles within ten years
* Extra tax incentives if the car is all-electric or zero-oil
* An excess-profits tax on oil sufficient to fund the tax credits
* A tax on natural gas used for boiler fuel in excess of 20 percent of the capacity of any power plant unit
* A policy nationwide to remove obstacles and to encourage decentralized electric power production

Remember the story of the hummingbird that saw the jungle on fire. He flew to the river, put a few drops of water in his beak, carried them back, and put them on the fire. The squirrel said, "You foolish bird, that's not going to put out the fire." The hummingbird replied, "Well, I did my part. What are you doing?" It is time for each of us to do his or her part.

* A twenty- to thirty-year plan to build and complete the hydrogen infrastructure needed for use in motor vehicles and aircraft, and begin to replace natural gas.

These policies need to be supplemented by a massive educational campaign to let consumers know what can be available to them and that the
ultimate act of patriotism is to support an energy-independent America.
We need to enlist all of America—business, labor, the faith-based community, civic groups, and students—to purchase energy-efficient products
and support renewables. Active consumer participation can be measured
by purchases of motor vehicles, appliances, and the rest.

When consumers demand that their next car is a plug-in hybrid, they
can be just as effective as government regulations or tax credits. In fact,
without consumers eagerly wanting to buy the more efficient, renewable-
powered machines, it will continue to be business as usual.

Consumers must resist the negative thought, or excuse, of "What difference will little ol' me make?" The answer is that as a consumer you have
tremendous influence on the manufacturer, and don't discount the satisfied feeling of knowing that you've done your part.

LAWS THAT ARE NEEDED

These policy measures may appear to be a wish list, but let's examine
them more carefully. They are the strong medicine necessary to cure a
long-term addiction to oil, coal, and nuclear power.

The main sources of energy that are of concern are oil for transportation and coal and nuclear for electricity.

First we must revise federal laws to require steadily higher requirements for overall motor vehicle fuel efficiency. The 24 mpg standard of
today must go to 48 mpg over a twenty-four-year period, an increase of one
mpg a year. This is doable if we recognize the simultaneous rapid growth
in plug-in hybrids, which would get the equivalent of 60 to 100 miles per
gallon of gasoline. The standards should credit zero-gasoline vehicles as
the equivalent of 100 mpg in meeting the overall requirement to give the
manufacturers added incentive and flexibility. We can exceed the one mpg
per year increase in efficiency, but this is the minimum that needs to be
required by law.

I am aware of the resistance in the past fifteen years by automakers and their allies to "raising the bar" for auto efficiency. But I am also aware that it wasn't always that way. In 1975, the Democratic Congress under President Gerald Ford enacted the basic law that steadily raised gas mileage from 12 mpg to 24.

I believe the timing is good for a giant leap forward. In 1975, as now, the country was focused on the danger of imported oil because citizens were trapped in line waiting to get gas during the oil embargo a year earlier. Senator Fritz Hollings of South Carolina held the hearings on the bill in 1974 and brushed aside, with a smile, the auto industry's pleas that they would increase mileage voluntarily. The industry really didn't fight the bill and even their employee union, the United Auto Workers (UAW), supported the legislation. Senator Ted Kennedy added the efficiency bill as an amendment to legislation President Ford wanted the next year, it passed Congress, and the Republican president from Michigan signed it into law.

> One interesting incident occurred during the lobbying for the passage of the 1975 efficiency bill. Robert Redford personally called on members of Congress and he had a strong impact on the nearly all-male membership. They loved to drop his name to their women friends, and he also knew more about the subject than they. At one critical point, a committee chairman in the House, Lud Ashley, threatened to oppose the bill. We staffers told him if he did, Redford would be in his district at reelection time telling his constituents about his behavior. He quickly came back onboard.
>
> I later told Robert Redford what we'd done and asked him if he'd really follow through on what we said. Bob laughed approvingly but, with a twinkle in his eyes, he replied, "You'll never know, will you, Dave?"

Minimum fuel economy standards are essential, but not enough to slash gasoline consumption. We need to see plug-in hybrids mass-produced for all models of cars. To do that we need tax credits. First we need a consumer credit of $5,000 to $10,000 a car to offset the extra cost of a plug-in. An additional tax credit of $2,000 to $5,000 should help consumers choose cars that use no oil at all. Also to give the manufacturers incentives to mass-produce these cars, any manufacturer that sells 200,000 of such vehicles in any year would get a huge tax break, provided the money would go to their employee pension or health benefit fund, if underfunded.

The tax credits for plug-in hybrids justifiably should be funded by an excess-profits tax on oil. These tax credits are needed to jump-start the market and should end five years after they are enacted.

The steadily increasing average mileage requirement, combined with tax credits for plug-in hybrids and cars without oil, will move us steadily to slash gasoline consumption.

Congress has already enacted serious incentives for ethanol. The public is aware of the option and its use will grow. It is important that the auto industry makes huge numbers of flex-fuel cars so cautious consumers who want to run on biofuels can have a gasoline fallback. This is a choice in addition to the plug-in hybrids. But biofuels can also substitute for gasoline in the plug-in hybrid to make a near-zero-gasoline car.

I must admit that my review of energy policy while writing this book has changed my view of the timetable for ushering in the hydrogen economy. Previously I had felt great urgency about using renewable hydrogen as the substitute for gasoline. I was reacting to the death of the electric car and felt (as I still do) that biomass in all its forms could not sustain our needs, even with more efficient cars.

But the development of hybrids, their popularity, and most importantly the real possibility of early adoption of plug-in hybrids make them a more practical early giant step forward. The hybrid is a model auto companies are already building, and all we need to do is add the simple plug-in feature and a few more batteries. Surely we can get that idea going strong in this decade.

I am also influenced by personal experience with trying to kick-start a "hydrogen now" initiative. We ran into a brick wall in 2003 because an all-hydrogen car requires the infrastructure to make, store, and deliver the hydrogen to the consumer. And despite the brave initiatives brought forth

Every civic organization, business, or sensible American citizen should join in demanding that automakers start offering plug-in hybrids for sale. Let's not waste the gasoline to drive to Detroit. Let's have a "'sign-up for a plug-in" campaign culminate on July 4, 2008, and make it a real Independence Day, independence from our dependency on imported oil. People should sign up with offers to buy plug-in hybrids for their next car. Let's have a goal of a million people sign up. This would be a true act of patriotism.

A million Americans offering to buy plug-ins should impress our lawmakers in Washington, D.C., and automakers in Japan and Korea as well as Detroit. This campaign can be the equivalent of a popular uprising that persuades the auto industry that substituting electricity for gasoline is the smartest thing they can do to sell more cars. Clearly the less a consumer pays in fuel, the more money he or she will have to buy cars.

by the governors of New York and California, after three years their hydrogen highway is still mostly talk. It needs to be built, but the country can't wait for that to happen before it takes bold moves to get off oil.

The plug-in hybrid can run directly on the off-peak electricity supplied more and more from the sun, the wind, and the rest of the renewable family. And let's be honest about the electric system. Today it is largely powered by fossil fuels. But our electricity supply can and will get greener and greener with each passing year, and electricity even from the existing grid will get us off imported oil and dramatically reduce local air pollution.

This takes us to the policies needed to steadily move our electricity supply from the pale green of today to really dark green.

MARKETPLACE VS. FEDERAL REGULATION

The policies that I believe are essential require the federal government to take serious direct action. I realize my policy suggestions for both getting off oil and on to renewable electricity go against the grain of the last thirty years when both political parties put their trust in the invisible hand of Adam Smith. The unwritten guiding principle seems to have been that the market can do no wrong and the government can do nothing right.

It is time for the American people to have their say. In the field of energy, we consumers have no choice but to buy electricity, heat, and gasoline. We have been "taken to the cleaners" by market forces, and the only protection has been that state utility commission regulations have kept electricity prices reasonable, except when California let the market take over from 2000 to 2001.

Let's face it. Progress on behalf of consumers in the field of energy and the environment has been made primarily by the force of law. Voluntary action is a joke. It has taken laws to:

* Get seat belts and then air bags into cars
* Mandate better gas mileage for cars
* Control pollution from power plants, industry, and cars
* Build electric cars that developed the electric motor technology for hybrids
* Obtain federal funding to develop solar, wind power, and, of course, nuclear

In contrast, where we have placed energy policy in the hands of the marketplace the consumer is suffering. Examples are:

* The price of gasoline
* The price of natural gas
* The price of electricity under deregulation
* The price of home heating oil

And the higher prices have not resulted in the market making a transition toward renewables. The oil people are happy to keep selling us gasoline at higher and higher prices. If we want alternatives, the people must act individually and through their governments.

In the marketplace, major investments are made only if the investors see a return on their investment that is attractive. They use a discounted cash-flow analysis to determine if a dollar invested today will earn enough over time. And if the payoff is long-term it must be high enough to cover the years until it pays off. Benefits to national security don't count, so the harsh truth is that on a discounted cash-flow basis this country isn't worth saving!

For that reason, when America sees a threat to our national security, the nation, through its government, takes action. When we foresaw the threat of Asian flu, the government took action. When America decided to build an interstate highway system, it took federal action to build it. When President Kennedy challenged us to go to the moon, the government did it. When America needed to win World War II, we quickly learned how to unleash atomic power.

Let us not treat the clear and present danger of oil dependency, global warming, and nuclear radiation dangers like we did Hurricane Katrina, resulting in a feeble and ineffective effort to repair our battered country after the damage was done.

What needs to be done with respect to electricity are four things:

1. Use it more efficiently.
2. Stop building new fossil-fueled and nuclear power plants.
3. Start building solar, wind, and other renewables big time.
4. Encourage decentralized power plants.

It is critical that we apply a more realistic, common-sense way of thinking about our energy policy. We must treat it as a crucial part of our defense policy.

A primary duty of government according to the U.S. Constitution is to "provide for a common defense." There can be no more awesome threats to this country than those posed by the weakening of our power in the world due to dependency on imported oil, threats of physical destruction of our land and people by the impacts of global warming, and the threat of nuclear destruction.

We received one wake-up call with the oil embargo in 1973. It's now more than three decades later and high-priced gasoline is again awakening us from our slumber. To give an old saying a new twist: "If we get hit once, shame on them; if we don't mount a defense, shame on us."

GETTING UTILITY COMPANIES TO CHANGE

This book sets forth a firm and clear set of marching orders for the electric utility industry that has grown and thrived under regulation all of its life. This industry is not a hotbed of innovation, and I make this statement knowingly.

Generally speaking, folks who run utility companies want to do tomorrow what they did yesterday. They are good at resistant behavior, but their organizations, like troops in an army, can and will take orders. And if we need change, as we do, then orders must be issued.

Historically the regulation of utilities has been at the state level. Retail rates and local service can and should remain a state responsibility. But national and indeed international interest requires that the utilities move rapidly from "dirty to clean" and that they take on much of the load of powering our cars. That is clearly a national, indeed a national defense, responsibility. And it requires federal law.

THERE CAN BE NO MORE AWESOME THREATS TO THIS COUNTRY THAN THOSE POSED BY THE WEAKENING OF OUR POWER IN THE WORLD DUE TO DEPENDENCY ON IMPORTED OIL, THREATS OF PHYSICAL DESTRUCTION OF OUR LAND AND PEOPLE BY THE IMPACTS OF GLOBAL WARMING, AND THE THREAT OF NUCLEAR DESTRUCTION

Energy efficiency must move to the highest place in investment priority for utilities, and that requires governmental action. Investments in efficiency must be tailored to the varying uses in different parts of the nation. In the South and Southwest it's air conditioning. In Vermont it is heating. But every state does react pretty much the same to one thing—money from Uncle Sam.

Therefore we need to enlist every utility in what California is already doing and make efficiency investments their number one priority. I suggest the federal government provide each utility, publicly and privately owned, a refundable tax credit of 20 percent for every dollar invested in a state-approved efficiency program. Such an incentive will almost certainly ensure a vigorous response.

CONSUMER RESPONSIBILITIES

But just as important are the voluntary decisions by consumers when they buy a new refrigerator, air conditioner, house, or a car.

The notion "save energy, save money" needs to be taught in the schools, preached from the pulpits, spoken loud and clear by our political leaders, and then practiced by consumers.

In 1990 when I became the general manager of the Sacramento Municipal Utility District (SMUD) in Sacramento, California, I decided that we could meet the projected growth in the 1990s with improvements in efficiency. In other words, while the number of homes and appliances and factories would grow, and they did, we could insulate homes and replace existing appliances with new ones that saved enough electricity to power the growth. That's what happened and total consumption stayed level, but it took active programs, like rebates, to encourage consumers to purchase the most efficient electric-using equipment.

In a broader sense this is what the entire country did from 1973 until 1985; the economy grew, but overall energy consumption stayed the same, and we fueled the economic growth with the energy we saved through greater efficiencies.

But mind you, that happened by simply making the investments to use technologies that were already available, like cars with better mileage, more efficient appliances, thicker insulation, and fluorescent lights. There continue to be product improvements creating more efficient appliances, better lighting, and improved uses of electricity. If we initiated sufficient programs, incentives, and financing, electricity consumption in the U.S. could probably be cut to fuel decades of growth. In the meantime the march of progress for efficiency will continue. We have a long way to go before the laws of physics stop us.

Thus, efficiency gains can offset the expected growth in the current uses of electricity, but to power the plug-in hybrid car, electricity must now take on a huge new market—providing much of the power to drive our cars. That electricity must be generated more and more from renewable sources if we are to combat global warming as well as reduce oil imports.

As I stated earlier, there is plenty of spare capacity in today's electric power systems to power many millions of plug-in hybrids. But as we meet the new electric usage for transportation, we will need more renewable resources. It can be done but it won't be done unless the government, as a defense measure, provides the firm policy, the requirements, and then the incentives to make it happen.

The laws we need to enact are pretty straightforward. We have already addressed oil. Let's take the two other poisons that need to be replaced with renewables one at a time.

COAL

Coal contains more carbon per British thermal unit (BTU) of heat than any other fuel. Any new plant built today will operate for thirty to fifty years into the future. It is near suicidal to build a new coal-fired plant. Some will argue that coal is OK if the carbon is sequestered. But none of the coal plants being proposed include sequestration. It would probably kill their economics. The more fundamental problem is that no one can guarantee that sequestered carbon will stay underground indefinitely. The pressure on agencies will be to make such a claim, but none of us will be around when the carbon leaks out in the decades or centuries to come.

But sequestration of the CO_2 doesn't solve the basic problem that coal is dirty. It is not just the mercury and arsenic that are emitted; both land and lives are destroyed to mine it, and most troubling are the ultrafine particles in the air. The number of tiny particles emitted when burning a fuel is directly proportional to its carbon content, and coal is the worst.

We must once and for all ban the construction of new coal plants or additions to old ones. It is not a different action than the ban on natural gas for power plants that Congress enacted in 1978. It is just far more important for the health of our communities, our nation, and our planet.

ATOMIC POWER

The reason for banning new nuclear plants is, if anything, even more important. The federal government is now subsidizing and promoting new nuclear power plants. And it's sheer madness in an age of terror. How can the federal government reconcile its promotion of nuclear power with the ongoing terrorist threat? In reviewing the expansion of the spent fuel storage facility at Diablo Canyon Nuclear Plant in California, the Nuclear Regulatory Commission (NRC) said the possibility of a terrorist assault was so "speculative" that no environmental review of the possibility was needed. In a 3–0 decision the U.S. Court of Appeals cited the government expenditure of funds to combat terrorist attacks at nuclear plants since 9/11 and ruled that the NRC was wrong.[3] When it comes to nuclear power, the Bush administration gives safety lip service but then tries to ignore the threat as it promotes this radioactive menace.

The radiation, the wastes that last forever with no home, the huge subsidies, and all the rest are bad enough. But let's focus on the one life-or-death issue—the proliferation of atomic bombs. America has little credibility in stopping Iran and North Korea from pursuing the nuclear cycle as long as we are doing the very same thing.

It is time that the judgment of the market and the common sense of the American people be heard on this issue. The correct choice is clear—NO more nukes!

RENEWABLES

Stopping the poisoning of the planet is only half the job. The energy policy must be strong in making certain that renewables are available to meet the growing needs of electricity for today's uses and tomorrow's role in powering our motor vehicles and mass transit.

Wind

Wind power projects are advancing at a favorable rate of growth. They can and must be accelerated, but they have created an interesting source of hypocrisy in the energy field. Of course no one wants a visual impairment to their line of sight, but 99 percent of us have no choice but to see ugly signs, huge buildings, smoggy air, and litter every day. A wind farm doesn't pollute the air and it can be located so it can't be heard.

Wind power is essential to our national defense and we can't let "not in my line of sight" prevail over global warming, respiratory disease, and war in the Middle East. The needs of the nation must prevail over the self-centered views of any individuals or group. There needs to be an expedited process with deadlines for environmental review of wind projects, and no rejections should be allowed based on visual impairment alone.

Solar

The development of Big Solar needs a kick-start. Solar power cannot replace coal and nuclear a few panels at a time on the roofs of buildings, although decentralized solar does have a very useful role in moving us toward a greener electric system. Until solar power plants are the size of coal and nuclear they are not fulfilling their rightful role as a better answer than coal or nuclear.

We need to borrow a page from the nuclear promotion book. In the 1960s, when the federal government decided to promote nuclear power, they funded a series of large-scale demonstration projects. We need to do the same for Big Solar. A 500 MW solar complex could be completed in three years (sooner than a nuclear power plant) with existing technology for concentrated solar. Actually building the plant on an urgent basis would bring some reality into the energy debate. There is lots of federal land in the Sunbelt just waiting to be put to a higher and better use.

NATURAL GAS HAS LONG BEEN RECOGNIZED AS A CLEANER FORM OF ENERGY OF LIMITED SUPPLY

Natural Gas

Natural gas has been conspicuous by its absence from my energy policy discussion. The reason is that it is not a renewable resource, but it is by far the cleanest of the fossil fuels, containing one-half the carbon in oil and one-fourth the carbon in coal. And when burned, under controls, it emits far fewer pollutants. And since the most serious killers are the ultrafine particles, which are directly related to the carbon content, it is twice as clean as oil and four times as clean as coal.

Also natural gas, thus far, is produced almost entirely in the United States, Canada, and Mexico, all of which have a history of being reliable energy suppliers.

Natural gas is a raw material in making ammonia-nitrate fertilizer and other manufacturing processes. It is used mainly, however, for home heating and as a boiler fuel for a large number of electric power plants.

For decades America has been using more natural gas each year than we discover while drilling. There is growing pressure for the United States to begin importing more natural gas in liquid form (LNG), which would be transported in specially made tankers from overseas. Concerns arise as to the safety of these LNG terminals near population centers. And there are also legitimate concerns as to whether we are going down a slippery slope creating a natural gas import dependency before we even begin to kick our oil import habit. We should not do so.

ALL OF THIS NATURAL GAS CAPACITY WILL CONTINUE TO BE USEFUL, BUT WILL NEED TO BE OPERATED ONLY TO FIRM UP THE TIMES WHEN SOLAR AND WIND ARE NOT AVAILABLE

Regardless of how the LNG issues play out, natural gas must be used as a transition fuel for at least the next two decades. It does not pose the severe pollution problems caused by oil, coal, or nuclear power, and if we limit the use of LNG, it need not pose any foreign policy concerns. Its supply is limited, however, and it must be used more wisely to play its most useful role.

Natural gas has long been recognized as a cleaner form of energy of limited supply. The nation progressed from uncontrolled wood burning, to coal, and then to natural gas as the primary fuel for home heating. Each transition resulted in cleaner air. Natural gas also became the favorite way for the electric power industry to clean up, and most power plants built in the last twenty years run on natural gas.[4]

As stated earlier, all of this natural gas capacity will continue to be useful, but will need to be operated only to firm up the times when solar and wind are not available. We can add fuel cells and cogeneration plants fueled by natural gas or hydrogen with policies that encourage power customers to self-generate. Even so, the bulk of the energy can be replaced with wind power and solar. The gas plants, along with hydroelectric power that is stored behind dams, geothermal, and biomass can firm up the wind and solar plants to provide reliable electricity.

In order to free up the natural gas and provide a sharp incentive to substitute efficiency, wind, and solar, I propose a sizeable tax on natural gas used in excess of 20 percent of the total capacity to generate electricity of any power plant. This will give the electric utilities the incentive to acquire the renewables. Also, the law should require this tax be absorbed by the stockholders and not passed on to the ratepayers.

The basic idea here is to stretch out the life of our natural gas so that we have at least a thirty-year period to make the transition to hydrogen.

If the United States is to avoid getting into the natural gas import game then we must make an all-out effort to use our natural gas more wisely. That means we must put the following recommendations into place:

* Investments by consumers and businesses in efficient furnaces, buildings, and equipment that are powered by natural gas
* A large-scale program for solar hot water to replace natural gas
* A tax on excess use of natural gas for boiler fuel
* A program to steadily supplement and replace natural gas with renewable hydrogen for home heating and peak power production

A growing role for hydrogen-fueled cars in the next twenty years is possible but, to be realistic, we must count on biofuels, the plug-in hybrid, and all-electric vehicles using renewable electricity and renewable biomass to do most of the job of getting us off oil. I've learned the hard way that hydrogen will come later. But not too much later, I hope.

Renewable Hydrogen

The share of our energy supply fueled by natural gas today must continue for several decades. Within the next thirty years, we should be able to transition ourselves off coal and oil. The next transition will be to move off natural gas. The replacement can best be made by renewable hydrogen.

Renewable hydrogen is also the ideal fuel to power aircraft because it is so much lighter than petroleum jet fuel. A pound of hydrogen has three times the energy of jet fuel so that airplanes could fly nonstop around the world on hydrogen. The Soviet Union actually built the prototype for such a plane in 1988.

Just because we may have a couple of decades left of natural gas supply is no excuse for not launching a hydrogen program now.

Unless we lay out a long-term program for developing renewable hydrogen at once, we will not be able to complete the transition without serious energy shortages and continued pollution.

First, we must demonstrate that it is practical to convert solar and wind power—our huge resources—into hydrogen. The only way to do that is to do it! A good way to start would be for the U.S. government to procure a significant quantity of renewable hydrogen only by open bid each year for its own use in motor vehicles, power production, the space program, and other areas.

The demonstration project I propose would be to build a large solar power complex with electrolysis machines to convert the solar power to hydrogen. A parallel demonstration would show the feasibility of the decentralized approach of renewable electricity in the home. Solar cells in a resident's own backyard with a small-scale electrolysis system that separates the hydrogen, stores it, and dispenses it to run either a hydrogen IC automobile or a hydrogen fuel cell could be built, whichever is ready for mass production.

These demonstrations won't take place without direct federal funding, which is needed.

CONCLUSION

This is no time for theoretical arguments about the role of business versus government. Protecting the security of the country is the government's job. We must not confuse General Motors with Uncle Sam. We are in a fix because the status quo isn't working. We face a crisis far more severe and deeply embedded in our way of life than the threat of terrorists. To combat it requires us to act the way people express their collective will in a democracy: by passing laws to require what needs to be done.

WHAT YOU CAN DO

Consumers have been inundated with laundry lists of things they can do to "save the planet." Thankfully, many of these same actions to protect the environment will also help secure the nation and free our foreign policy from the shackles imposed by our oil dependency.

It is helpful to distinguish the "rabbits" from the "elephants." Turning off the lights when you leave the room is fine, but it is nothing compared to what kind of car you buy. So, I would like to suggest the purchases/actions a person can make or take that could really advance America toward an efficient, renewable energy economy.

1. By far the most important action consumers can take involves the kind of motor vehicle an individual or company purchases. Consumers need to demand a plug-in hybrid or flex-fuel car and use biofuels for the internal combustion engine. If your car dealerships don't have one to sell, tell them you are not buying a new car or fleet till they or someone else offers one. The people, collectively, have the purchasing power, and withholding it until you get what you want can be a very effective tool for change.

2. The other biggie is the kind of electricity you buy. Every American should demand green power (electricity made from renewable sources). Tell that to your utility—write it on your bill when you pay. E-mail your state's Public Utilities Commission that you want your utility to offer you green power and tell you how to get it. If enough people demand it, the utilities will respond. The Appendix contains a form letter that you can send to your state Public Utilities Commission.

3. When you buy any electric appliance, buy the Energy Star model.

4. If you have a natural gas or oil furnace, replace it with an Earth-source heat pump or a more efficient model furnace—it will pay off over time.

5. If you live in a house, check out how you can install solar panels or solar hot water or a heat pump. In a new home, insist on incorporating efficiency and solar panels.

6. Plant trees to offset the carbon you emit. Plant as many as you can afford.

7. Get on your human resources committee at work and suggest ways that your company can be run more energy efficiently, and make sure your company follows through.

8. These are the biggies, but perhaps bigger than them all is to lobby for tax incentives for plug-in hybrids and a ban on new coal and nuclear power plants. Contact your elected public officials at all levels of government and support candidates who will commit to these ideas. The Appendix contains a form letter you can send to your congressional representative. Talk to your friends and share the ideas presented in this book as well as your own ideas about what might work better.

America can go green. The people can make it happen.

✳✳✳

1 Thomas Friedman, "The Energy Mandate," *International Herald Tribune* (October 14–15, 2006).
2 Hybrid batteries achieve about four miles per kWh. The average mpg for vehicles, according to the Department of Transportation, is twenty-four. So, 6 kWh is about equal to one gallon gasoline. Using three-dollar-a-gallon gasoline and eight-cents/kWh electricity, the electricity is forty-eight cents per gallon equivalent, or about six times less in cost than gasoline. Note that plug-in hybrids also use a gasoline engine backup, so the combined cost is typically estimated at one-dollar-a-gallon gasoline equivalent.
3 Bob Egelko, "U.S. Court Puts PG&E Nuclear Permit on Hold Until Terror Review," *San Francisco Chronicle* (June 3, 2006).
4 Donald L. Barlett and James B. Steele, "Why U.S. Is Running Out of Gas," *Time* (July 21, 2003).

13 THE NEXT TEN YEARS

{The Time for Transition} ✳✳✳

IN 1974, I WROTE IN A BOOK ENTITLED *Energy: The New Era:* "The next ten years—the period through 1984—probably will be decisive for our high energy civilization."[1] It was. I advocated and advanced a policy of "energy thrift" that helped the nation achieve zero growth in energy while gaining healthy growth in the economy. The result: we bought some time in the energy field, although the earth was then and still is on an escalating path of global warming. It just wasn't as well publicized.

Now it is thirty-three years later and we've used up all the time we saved. Without a dramatic commitment to efficiency and a strong shift to renewables, the energy troubles we confront will do massive and irrevocable harm to the people on Earth today and for generations to come.

So again we face a decisive decade. The hope for a good outcome has a solid foundation, but people are not fully aware of the problems posed by imported oil, carbon-rich coal, and radioactive nuclear power. The pain at the pump got their attention, and the American people can now focus on getting to the bottom of the mess we are in.

The policymakers in Washington, D.C., today correctly say that our energy woes can't be solved overnight. True enough. But these energy problems can be dramatically alleviated in the next ten years if we take decisive action now and stick with it.

> **THE POLICYMAKERS IN WASHINGTON, D.C., TODAY CORRECTLY SAY THAT OUR ENERGY WOES CAN'T BE SOLVED OVERNIGHT**

The most visible problem is imported oil: its price, the local air pollution, the global warming it causes, and the stranglehold on our foreign policy it has created. Here we can mount a two-step effort that will turn the tide. I realize this chapter might seem repetitive, but the timetable necessary for these direct actions to take place needs to be reinforced.

STOP GROWTH OF OIL CONSUMPTION

First, we must and can stop the growth of oil consumption in America. For example, gasoline consumption in 2006 was about the same as in 2005.[2] This is a beginning. It was a direct result of higher prices. This slightly downward trend should continue in 2007 as the longer-term impact of Americans buying more efficient cars begins to be felt. Sales of SUVs in 2006 were down and ordinary hybrids were selling better.[3] All this is a good start but, if history is any guide, in the absence of sustained government action, people will adjust to the higher prices.

It will take more than higher prices to bring gasoline consumption down to a safe level. Demand is growing rapidly as the over 2 billion people in China and India begin to buy cars—even small cars—and guzzle gas (America has only 300 million people).

Furthermore, our level of imports—over 60 percent of our present consumption—is so large and growing so rapidly that simply stopping the growth in consumption is a recipe for disaster.

Up to now the debate over reducing oil consumption has focused on tightening the federal fuel efficiency standards. In 2006 that debate has gained a new life. There has been a shift in the position of the auto companies, from outright opposition to changes that give the appearance of progress. There was a major change in Congress and with it came a renewed interest in energy policy. That change made President Bush take notice and broaden his scope on our national energy situation and his policies.

Legislation to tighten the overall standards is necessary and can now be enacted if made a priority. Originally I supposed that legislation would have to wait until a new president and Congress in 2008. It could happen sooner. But the standards alone can only help trim the consumption of gasoline. America must do much more in the next decade, and get started now.

As I see it, we have, at most, a three-year window for plug-in hybrids and flex-fuel cars (cars that can run on either biofuel or gasoline, or a blend of both) to start being offered for sale and sold in large numbers. Otherwise, the overall world growth in oil consumption will present the U.S. and the world with fearsome pollution and foreign policy problems far greater than those we are currently experiencing. Chapter one explained the urgency with which the U.S. and the world needs to act and act now.

Our experience with the auto industry is that it may well require both the force of law, monetary incentives, and the enthusiastic demands of potential customers to make it happen.

The auto, oil, coal, and nuclear lobbies are formidable opponents. But the auto companies know that plug-in hybrids can be adapted to cars they are already making with minor adjustments.

It is time to change the debate from whether there *should* be governmental action to *what* action is needed today to get these vehicles mass-produced and sold. Let's make the debate about avoiding pain at the pump, something car-loving Americans will relate to. And let's use something the auto companies can readily agree to: incentives from their government.

What has been missing in the debate about getting off oil is the possibility of monetary incentives, not just for consumers but also for the nearly broke automakers. Perhaps in the past when the auto companies seemed invulnerable financially they couldn't be "bribed to do good," but maybe now is the time for incentives that will help rescue our failing auto industry. If we focus on plug-ins and flex-fuel cars, I believe we can be successful.

A plug-in hybrid enables a car to go on average 80 miles on a gallon of gas and some electricity. That is three times today's average mileage.[4] If half of the 14 million new cars sold each year were plug-in hybrids or flex-fuel ten years from now, they would start reducing gasoline consumption about 2 to 3 percent per year as they displace the older gas-guzzling vehicles.[5] But this can happen only if we begin mass-producing plug-in hybrids and flex-fuel cars well within the next ten years. And by mass-production I mean millions of such cars sold each year. Gasoline consumption could be reduced by at least 50 percent in twenty years.

WHAT HAS BEEN MISSING IN THE DEBATE OF GETTING OFF OIL IS THE POSSIBILITY OF MONETARY INCENTIVES NOT JUST FOR CONSUMERS BUT ALSO FOR THE NEARLY BROKE AUTOMAKERS

Why do I emphasize plug-in hybrids and flex-fuel vehicles, rather than hydrogen fuel-cell cars, or just fuel efficiency across the board? There are several reasons:

* Hybrids and flex-fuel cars are a known commercial technology that's already on the market. We are merely asking the automakers to add a simple plug-in feature which, combined with additional batteries, will provide 80 to 100 miles on a gallon of gasoline.
* The automakers are already mass-producing hybrids and there is no other major technology that is on the near horizon to achieve comparable results.
* When the hydrogen fuel-cell vehicle is developed, and its cost has come down to make it affordable for average Americans, it will be a perfect fit with the plug-in hybrids and flex-fuel vehicles. Its day of debut is farther off, and we need to lower oil consumption now.
* The plug-in hybrid does not need a new, costly "hydrogen highway" infrastructure to begin lowering the nation's gasoline consumption.
* The plug-in hybrid is the perfect partner with ethanol or other forms of biomass to make it a car that uses virtually no oil at all. It is our ordinary car that can run on 85 percent ethanol (E-85) and can switch to gasoline if needed as a backup.
* The plug-in and flex-fuel technology may be one area where party politics can be put aside and all Americans can agree that is should be developed.
* Congress has already provided a limited subsidy for hybrids. This subsidy needs to be increased for plug-ins and flex-fuel cars, given unlimited funding, and a five-year life, after which they will become a standard feature of motor vehicles.

Be part of the "my next car will be a plug-in hybrid" club. As millions of Americans get excited about new technology and saving money, they will put pressure on auto companies and the government. I hope that by the time you read this book, one or more of the large auto companies will be selling plug-in hybrids.

ELECTRICITY FROM RENEWABLES

The other battlefield in this "war on energy" is to clean up electric power production. If we are to substitute electricity for oil, we sure as hell need to be sure the electricity is made from renewables and not inherently dirty coal or radioactive atoms.

What's needed now is to give the electric utility companies clear orders. They have always been regulated and now it's time to send them on the road to a renewable future.

Remember that the utility industry embraced nuclear power in the 1960s and 1970s. But back then, nuclear was a government initiative; the federal government funded nuclear research as well as a series of demonstration plants. The utilities went along but they were not the agents of change; it took direct federal action (through decisive leadership) to bring in a new source of energy.

Most economists, who seem to have an almost religious faith in the marketplace, ignore the fact that in the energy business, higher prices have not encouraged the development of alternative sources. Even with five and six dollar a gallon prices in Europe, cars still run on gasoline.

However, price does impact consumption and encourages more efficient use of the same resource. If we want to develop the Big Solar alternative to coal and nuclear for electricity, the government must subsidize its initial entrance into the commercial market. It will also require long-term strict rules to require the utilities to utilize cleaner alternatives, on an urgent timetable.

Except in California and Texas, the utility industry today is only flirting with renewables. Their hearts and wallets are still with the big plants running on coal or atomic power.

First, we need to create 1,000-kilowatt installations for the competing concentrated solar technologies to make sure they perform as predicted. Then we can move quickly to large-scale projects.

> I had a conversation in 2001 with representatives from the Duke Power Company—one of the more enterprising utilities—when I was "energy czar" for the state of California. I asked them, "Why aren't you guys in the solar business?" They said bluntly, "We don't do kilowatts. In fact we don't do megawatts. We don't do projects unless they are *hundreds* of megawatts in size."
>
> There you have it. Major companies are now engaged in wind power farms because they can aggregate to 100,000 to 200,000 kilowatts. But the solar field still focuses on less than 10 kilowatt installations on rooftops. Big solar is still largely stuck at pilot projects or on blueprint paper.

If such a program were developed, Big Solar could be available in whatever quantities are needed five to ten years from now. With Big Solar, wind, and biomass plants, electricity could be available to replace coal and nuclear and fuel the plug-in hybrids with green power. It would also be available to fuel the all-electric vehicles that I hope will make a comeback within the next decade.

The next decade will be the time when electric power must begin to make the transition from coal, nuclear, and natural gas to one that has green power as its core. Natural gas plants will be used for fewer and fewer hours, and in time they will only be used as a backup to ensure the system remains reliable.

The first step in that transition is, just like with oil, for the U.S. to mount an efficiency effort that will offset growth. The regulatory process is capable of mandating that to happen, but here consumers can engage in self-help. The opportunities for saving electricity and saving money need to become household habits.

The important lesson for consumers is to invest in equipment and devices that save electricity automatically. Don't depend on your memory to turn off the lights or adjust the thermostats—you may well forget. It is cost effective to invest in Energy Star air conditioners, refrigerators, etc. The Energy Star label assures that you are buying the most efficient model available, and the labels inform the consumer of the amount of the savings. Yet in the next decade there are opportunities for massive new savings that go beyond simply substituting the most efficient new equipment for what's worn out.

MANY EXPERIMENTS WITH SMART METERS ARE UNDER WAY AND THE TECHNOLOGY IS NOW COMMERCIAL

Load management is not conservation, but it is important. Your home electric bill covers fuel and the cost of the equipment to generate and deliver electricity. Utilities must have enough equipment to serve everyone, especially on the hottest days and hours of the year. Load management means that if a customer can do without the electricity when everyone else needs it, there is a reduction in the equipment the utility needs to purchase and run. With load management, utilities pay a customer not to use electricity during heavy-use hours. Of course the utility must be able to rely on the customer cutting back during peak use, and that is done by installing load-shedding devices.

Let me give an example: your air conditioner can stop running for fif-teen minutes and you don't notice the difference. It doesn't save energy, but implementing this practice with many people in rotation cuts down on the utility's peak load, ensures steady power, and reduces the amount of equipment a utility needs to run. It works the same for businesses.

These kinds of savings can come about only as utilities install twenty-first-century meters for residential and commercial use that can manage all the loads in the house or business and measure the capacity as well as the total kWh used.

Many experiments with smart meters are under way and the technol-ogy is now commercial. Traditionally, utilities have financed meters and included them in the cost of service. The same should be true for modern meters, resulting in an average 10 percent reduction in utility bills.

Consumers need to know about smart meters and demand that they get one.

The other large opportunity for saving that is virtually unknown is excess voltage. Voltage is the electric power industry's deep dark secret. The perfect voltage for an electric system is 114 volts. The industry has adopted 120 as its minimum, but in order to achieve 120 at the end of its distribution system most customers receive power at above 120.

Let me reveal that I am on the board of directors of a company that manufactures voltage reduc-tion machines that can return the excess energy above 114 volts to the nearest transformer and thus save the consumer anywhere from 5 to 10 percent of their bill.

> I had a good reputation for keeping the lights on, even during energy shortages. In 2000, I was the Jewish guy in L.A. who made certain the Christmas lights stayed on at city hall's forty-foot tree while the rest of the state suffered from blackouts. I am not about to recommend an energy transition that runs the risk of blackouts in winter or summer.

Without focusing on any particular device, the next ten years should see consumers doing something about the fact than they are being sold more electricity than they need. Also, the higher voltage has the impact of wearing out motors and other equipment faster than necessary. The utilities can fix this and should be made to do so by order from the state utility commission.

Investments in efficiency and load management can enable the electric power industry to reliably supply a growing economy. The real test of the

next ten years is to work out the process of saying goodbye to the old patterns of growth and hello to the new ones. I have already discussed the
crucial step that must be taken to stop building any new coal or nuclear
plants or even additions to old ones.

It is too late to leave the energy transition to chance or market incentives that may or may not work. We are dealing with a monopolized, regulated industry that needs to be told to stop adding to the world's poisons.

Every utility should be required to supply its utility commission with a
thirty-year plan of action that has the following priorities:

* Investments in efficiency and load management
* New renewable capacity and energy to meet growth and
  replace existing coal and nuclear

If any utility can show it needs additional power and it cannot acquire
sufficient renewable power on its own, it should buy additional power on
the open market to avoid blackouts. The nation does not have uniform
needs and we need to be firm but realistic in our implementation plan.

Our goal should be that in a decade the companies now building wind
power, solar power, geothermal, and biomass will be the electric generating companies that dominate the business. There will be no new business for coal or nuclear plants, and with government help for large-scale
demonstrations these renewable resources will be available in whatever
quantity they may be needed five to ten years from now, and we'll have a
mass of new green jobs, too.

CONCLUSION

By 2017, the United States can be in control of our energy future. Our goals
need to be clear and attainable. They are:

* Large-scale solar power plants and wind turbines will be the
  state of the art in electric power plants.
* It is likely that we can harness the continuous wind power at
  30,000 feet about the earth and deliver that around-the-clock
  electricity at a favorable price.
* Utilities will be "selling" efficiency as their highest priority
  product.

* Every customer will have a smart meter.
* Plug-in hybrids and flex-fuel cars will be standard equipment and available for all model cars.
* Ethanol and biofuels will supply 10 percent of our automotive fuel.
* A "hydrogen highway" will be well underway and the infrastructure economically available to all fleet owners in selected cities.
* Hydrogen IC and fuel-cell cars will be offered for sale to fleets and the general public in selected cities.
* Oil imports will be at least 20 percent lower than today.
* Carbon emissions will be 10 percent below 2007 levels.

If we can do all that, and we can, America will have turned the corner. We will be well on our way to a cleaner and safer world. We can do it.

***

1   Freeman, 1974.
2   U.S. EIA "Pertoleum Navigator," (October 2006).
3   As of January 2006, hybrid sales were up by nearly double from 2005, while the sale of SUVs had declined by 14 percent between February and March 2006. www.treehugger.com, "Sales of Full-Size SUVs Take a Dive in February" (March 5, 2006), and "Hybrid Sales Keep Going Up, Up, Up" (February 24, 2006).
4   Bureau of Transportation Statistics, "National Transportation Statistics 2006."
5   When compared to regular vehicles, flex-fuel vehicles use about 20 percent of the gasoline, and HEV 60 would use about 30 percent. Assuming an equal amount of flex-fuel and HEVs, the average fuel consumption would be 25 percent of a regular vehicle. Seven million vehicles per year is 3.5 percent of the total vehicles in the U.S., and would result in an overall decrease in petroleum consumption of about 3.7 million gallons per year, for a 2.6 percent reduction.

14

2017 AND BEYOND

{A Clean-Energy Economy} ✳✳✳

WHAT THE FAR FUTURE HOLDS depends mightily on what we do in the next ten years. The most important lesson to be learned is that fundamental changes in energy sources require decades of ramp-up time. Unless there is serious, sustained action in years one, two, and three, there will not be success in years twenty-one, twenty-two, and twenty-three.

We must embark on the journey to an all-renewable energy supply today if 2017 and beyond are going to be peaceful and prosperous in a livable environment. Let's look at what is possible within twenty years with 2027 as our end goal.

During the next twenty-year period, America's automobile fleet will essentially be replaced, most home office and factory equipment will be renewed, a good fraction of housing will be built or remodeled, and old power plants will be retired. In other words, a sizeable opportunity looms for us to replace inefficient energy-using equipment with more efficient versions. Simultaneously, we can replace coal and nuclear power with solar and wind and use that electricity and biomass to cut oil consumption by more than half.

Commercialization of a clean, green suite of home and business equipment and vehicles in the next ten years will lead to mass production (translation: more domestic jobs) and use in the ten years that follow.

That's fine as an overview, but what exactly are we talking about?

> A SIZEABLE OPPORTUNITY LOOMS FOR US TO REPLACE INEFFICIENT ENERGY-USING EQUIPMENT WITH MORE EFFICIENT VERSIONS

RENEWABLE HYDROGEN

Let's review renewable hydrogen. Being a realist as well as a visionary, I believe if we leave it to market forces, hell will freeze over before America runs on hydrogen. There has been big talk about hydrogen by political leaders including President Bush and Governor Schwarzenegger, but nothing much has happened except the U.S. Energy Department has handed out alternative energy funds to their favorite "charities," such as General Motors.

There needs to be a federally funded effort to build a national network of hydrogen fueling stations starting at once. After World War II, the U.S. government decided to build a national interstate highway program, and we did. The same can happen for hydrogen.

The ultimate answer to getting off oil and natural gas is renewable hydrogen—that is, separating the hydrogen atom from water using electricity. Research is now needed to learn how such separation can be achieved chemically or thermally instead of relying only on electricity. But until those advances are made, we must assume that we will use electricity from solar, wind, and biomass to separate hydrogen from water twenty years from now.

It may at first glance appear to be quite a waste to convert solar electricity into hydrogen rather than using the electricity directly to run a plug-in hybrid. And that is exactly the reason the plug-in hybrid is a choice for the first ten years. And an all-electric car would be even better. We need all the options we can get to replace coal, nuclear power, oil, and natural gas. Airplanes, for example, need hydrogen to replace jet fuel. Natural gas, which supplies 23 percent of all our energy, will begin to peak within twenty years. Heating oil must be replaced by hydrogen, or at least a heat pump backed up by hydrogen storage. We need hydrogen to power backup generators and office buildings so the generators can be used without polluting the air on hot-air alert days when electricity use is at its peak.

Today is not 1908, when Henry Ford took a risk and built the Model T. The Wharton MBAs that run Ford today wouldn't dream of taking risks like that.

Developing a renewable hydrogen infrastructure is vital to this nation's long-term security and quality of life. But that means the government must treat hydrogen as if it were a major weapon system. We must build this system as if our nation's life depends on it, because it does. It is foolish to assume that the auto industry, the oil industry, or any other industry will do it.

It is entirely possible that the hydrogen infrastructure can be in place by 2027, but only if we start in 2008 and stay with it for twenty straight years. And it need not emerge full blown all at once. It could be that we will find that developing hydrogen as a way to store renewable energy and use it in fuel cells or combined-cycle plants is all we will need. But if the U.S. government doesn't begin a comprehensive effort at once, it will always be twenty years away.

Americans deserve as many choices as possible, and hydrogen-fueled cars that don't compete with the food chain—as biofuels might in the future—need to be a choice. Hydrogen can be burned in an internal combustion engine or it can be converted to electricity in a fuel cell via a chemical reaction that is truly pollution free and fairly efficient. The current attitude of treating hydrogen as purely a research project virtually assures that it won't get us off oil soon enough to avoid irreparable damage to our nation and the entire planet.

DEVELOPING A RENEWABLE HYDROGEN INFRASTRUCTURE IS VITAL TO THIS NATION'S LONG-TERM SECURITY AND QUALITY OF LIFE

There is every reason to believe that by 2017, a critical mass of hydrogen infrastructure for city fleet operations can be available to service a sizeable number of hydrogen IC and fuel cell cars. The technology at least for the hydrogen IC car and the hydrogen hybrid are available today. The sizeable tax credit I recommend for both the car owner and manufacturer should be persuasive, with proper promotion and infrastructure in place to make hydrogen cars a reality.

The real challenge beyond 2017 is to start building the renewable hydrogen production centers to replace natural gas and to make hydrogen available to motorists throughout the nation.

It is not necessary to predict whether central production of hydrogen in the sunny desert or at the wind farm will prevail. It may be that a decentralized approach of making hydrogen in small quantities anywhere there is water and electricity—which is almost everywhere—will be best. Imagine a solar-panel-powered electrolysis machine and hydrogen storage tank and dispenser in your backyard. You can drive where you need to go during the day, "fill 'er up" at night, and never have to stop at a service station again. With the perfection of low-cost, thin-film solar panels within our reach, this option can become a way of life in ten to twenty years. But people must know that it is possible and we must have government programs to jump-start the process.

It seems obvious that both options will be useful. Certainly, huge solar-hydrogen complexes will be needed to fuel the huge quantities of hydrogen slated to replace natural gas and oil heating, and to fuel aircraft. They can and should be built between 2017 and 2027.

The United States needs to lay out a twenty-year renewable hydrogen plan with milestones established one year at a time. The very feasible goal is for hydrogen cars to be a commercial option of sizeable proportions by 2017 with mass production starting before or shortly thereafter.

THE ELECTRIC CAR

That brings up the future of the all-electric car. By now it is clear that the auto companies made a tragic mistake when they stopped their electric car program over the angry protests of their customers. GM and the rest may be guilty of killing off their electric "baby," but my opinion is that the electric vehicle is not dead or forgotten, and it can make a sizeable and profound comeback.

With existing lead-acid batteries, electric vehicles can only travel short range—less than a hundred miles for a sizable car. As a country western singer may put it, "You can't go to heaven in an electric car because the gosh darn car won't go that far." But with advances in battery technology, we can surely extend the range these cars can travel and help liberate ourselves from oil dependence. The new Tesla Motors electric car with lithium ion batteries goes 250 miles between charges. After seeing the incredible jumps in technology that computers have made, we cannot even begin to envision the type of batteries that will be on the market in ten to twenty years.

Today, high gasoline prices have given new life to the electric car. If the existing auto companies don't come to their senses and restart their electric car programs they will find American entrepreneurs and Chinese manufacturers doing to them just what Nissan and Toyota are doing to GM, Ford, and Chrysler right now—eating their lunch, so to speak.

The California Air Resources Board (CARB) gave birth to the electric car in 1990 with a government program requiring the auto companies to make more and more of them during that decade. But, by the year 2000,

CARB caved in to industry pressure and revised its program to become, quite frankly, an accomplice to the demise of the electric car.

But high-priced gasoline, global warming, and worsening air quality on California's streets and highways provide a basis for CARB to correct its mistake. And the program doesn't just affect California, which has 10 percent of the nation's auto market. New York and others can piggyback on the California program. CARB can reinstate the program by requiring plug-in hybrids to be sold in California in rapidly increasing numbers. Extra credit can be given to all-electrics. The electric car can live again and be mass-produced by 2017. CARB can be a hero and restore its reputation by finishing the job it started.

POWER GENERATION

Beyond 2017, we can expect steady product improvement in solar and wind technologies. The new processes for converting municipal waste and other biomass to useful energy will have been demonstrated and built in large numbers as routinely as gas turbines are built today.

The renewable family as we know it today should reach maturity. The question is, will there be any newcomers to the field?

Let us be clear on nuclear power. Many, including myself in the past, have spoken of "inherently safe nuclear plants." Mark my words—there is no such thing. Even if a power plant were meltdown-proof, the problem remains that the fuel cycle—the steps to make the fuel—are the same steps one takes to make a bomb.

Proliferation of nuclear weapons is the most fearsome threat to life on earth. It must be our goal to eliminate it, not perpetuate it. There is no such thing as a peaceful atom, except perhaps for medical uses. Another twenty years is not apt to solve the problem of how to store the radioactive wastes to assure their safety for eternity.

I trust America will continue the market-imposed moratorium on new nuclear plants for the next decade and witness the renewables come of age. By then no one will be urging that we return to nuclear power any more than the people in my hometown of Chattanooga, Tennessee, will want to go back to coal furnaces in their homes.

But there could be newcomers to the energy scene twenty years from now. The potential newcomers include fusion power, solar in the sky, tidal or ocean current power, and magnetic power.

When I was an early "energy czar" in the White House Science Office in 1970, I sent a memo to Dr. Glenn Seaborg asking whether, if he had adequate funding, fusion power would be a reality by 1980. He replied yes, there would be scientific feasibility by 1980. Well, they did have adequate funding and it is now 2007 and they haven't yet built a fusion machine that gets more energy out of it than they put in.

Fusion power continues to hold promise of being free of the radiation concerns that we face with current reactors. And as Glenn T. Seaborg, former head of the Atomic Energy Commission and the inventor of plutonium used to say, "[Fusion is] the equivalent of a Pacific Ocean full of oil."

I'm sure fusion power will continue to be funded, but it is foolish to count on duplicating the sun's heat here on Earth and getting enough power out of it to "keep the lights on." Instead we will do well to continue the steady technological improvements occurring in the solar commercial market.

The idea of a solar satellite above the clouds seemed too risky thirty years ago. But advances in space technology have given this old idea new life.

I do not count on the solar satellite option as being essential to a solar energy future, but it no longer seems that far out. In a decade, it may seem as practical as solar on the ground is today. High in the sky the sun's rays are six or seven times as intense, there are no cloudy days, and microwave beams could deliver the electricity to Earth. Let's file this energy source and not forget it.[1]

The tides and ocean currents are always mentioned as potential energy sources. I've followed the subject for over forty years and seen a lot of articles but few commercial projects of any size. With the technology at hand to pursue solar, wind, and biomass, it is difficult to suggest that tidal power or ocean currents will become a serious source given the environmental concerns they pose. The enormous resource potential of the sun and the wind is more than adequate and seems a better bet for the foreseeable future.

Magnetic power is the real sleeper in our energy future. To date, magnetic power has been left to the mystics and the psychics with supposed supernatural power. In a sense magnetic power is where atomic energy was a hundred years ago, an undiscovered sleeping giant.

We know there are tremendous magnetic forces that surround the Earth. We know the strength of magnets. We know that some materials are well suited for becoming magnets. But there has never been the perceived need to harness magnetic power. There was no need to harness atomic power until scientists warned President Roosevelt that it was possible and that if we didn't do it the German Nazis would succeed first and blow us off the face of the earth.

People need an energy source that not only does not threaten our lives but will ensure our current way of life. We have it in the sun, wind, and biomass, but wouldn't it be great to add another option to our energy family that didn't pollute and had huge capacity?

We have a set of energy-related problems that are at least "the moral equivalent of war." Perhaps humanity will find that magnetic power can be harnessed in a chain reaction comparable to atomic power but with no residue. That is another possibility for a safe energy future.

***

1   The solar satellite would collect solar energy twenty-four hours/day, four times more than solar collectors on Earth (six to seven hours/day). Solar insolation on the earth's surface is about 200 watts per square mile, when averaged over twenty-four hours. Solar radiation outside the atmosphere is 1,300 watts per square mile .

15 A BROADER PERSPECTIVE

{THE JOY OF MAKING THINGS LAST} ✳✳✳

I BELIEVE THAT THE LONG-TERM SOLUTION to the energy-related problems the United States is facing will require profound changes to the material-growth mentality that is now so prevalent in this country. Different individuals will, of course, see our national situation differently and propose different courses of action. This chapter briefly sets forth my personal assessment.[1]

CONTINUING THE STATUS QUO

One option we always have is to continue our consumption habits and patterns that were formed in the past era of abundance. To satisfy such demands, an all-out effort to develop domestic energy sources must be mounted at once. This course assumes that enough renewable energy can be produced and efficiently used to continue our energy-intensive lifestyles and economy unrestrained. Such a course, with an ever-growing appetite for more material affluence, reflects quite a risky challenge. It places a greater priority on owning more things and subordinates the environmental and foreign policy problems inherent in sustaining our accustomed rate of growth far into the future. It further assumes that we will be able to build all the new technology necessary to supply this growth indefinitely no matter how large it is and also control any further contamination of the environment.

The primary purpose of such an approach is to preserve and expand the key features of present-day, middle-class American life—unrestricted use of large family cars, comfortable enjoyment of an oversized suburban home far from mass transit and shopping districts, and expansion of an economy geared to producing material goods. The highest priority for this kind of policy is to enlarge the supply regardless of direct and indirect social and ecological costs. Such a policy recognizes no limits on material growth.

No one can be certain that such a future is not possible indefinitely. Yet the assumption that we can continue the energy growth rates of the past is actually very risky. Such a policy rests on the belief—amounting to a perilous act of faith—that unlimitied material growth poses no serious threat to our well-being.

A CONSERVATIVE PARADIGM

Another alternative, at once more conservative and realistic, is to reduce our material growth to the level of supplies that we can reasonably and safely expect to have available now and into the future. This approach of intelligent austerity will require a willingness to make rather fundamental changes in our economy and our values. It may not be sufficient merely to squeeze the energy waste out of our present way of life with efficiency measures.

Increases in energy consumption reflect population growth as well as an increase in the number and size of the things we own—and of the things that own us, or at least claim a large part of our time and attention. As long as the United States continues to assume that "more is better," all our efforts at increased energy efficiency—hybrid cars, mass transit, industrial re-engineering—will result in securing ten or perhaps fifteen years of additional time. Thereafter, the demand for energy, minerals, and material goods in America will resume its former rate of exponential growth and we will soon be confronted with the same problems we sought to escape; they will have just been deferred and intensified.

The energy policy issue is fundamental and demands that we reassess our definition of "growth," our criteria of individual and collective well-being, and even our ideal of the American way of life. Many times in our history we have changed, adjusted, and matured, emerging stronger from the process. Now we are entering another time of change, another test of our intelligence and maturity.

My study of energy policy has led me to the most difficult and trouble-some conclusions. It is imperative that the United States economy intensi-fies the fundamental restructuring already under way in order to balance our energy and materials budget. If we are to reach a stable level of energy consumption, the mix of the nation's GNP must undergo continuous change. (Note: "zero energy growth" is a misleading phrase—zero growth will require huge and increased quantities of energy to sustain America at even current levels of consumption.) Yet a policy of stability does imply that we are fast approaching the saturation point for material goods. Our economic growth must accelerate the shift to services and occupations that do not require as much energy as manufacturing, a trend that is already under way.

The United States sets the pace and determines the shape of the energy growth curve throughout the world. Therefore, the problems posed by a U.S. energy demand that grows by even 2 percent a year are enormous, especially since we dare not consider our needs in isolation. The global energy needs of billions of people are at issue, and our supply is very much in doubt. The cruel impact of skyrocketing oil prices on the African continent merely foreshadows the tragedy of global energy shortages that are guaranteed in the years ahead.

A basic reason for changing the pattern of our economic growth and reducing energy consumption is to forestall hazards such as global warming, air pollution, and the ravaging of our coastlines and countryside.

Placing a limit on material growth may be desirable as well as necessary. Already, Americans have voluntarily reduced birthrates drastically. And, since Americans consume six times the resources as the worldwide average, this trend is of great importance.

Even now, a growing number of Americans are finding that happiness does not depend on more and more material goods. Of course, many Americans have yet to attain a decent standard of living, much less a life of affluence; and most people in the world are in poverty. For them, economic growth is an urgent necessity. But for Americans who embrace a Voluntary Simplicity lifestyle, as advocated by author Duane Elgin,[2] they realize they have reached a saturation point in per-capita consumption, and more growth does not mean more happiness and fulfillment.

HAPPINESS DOES NOT DEPEND ON MORE AND MORE MATERIAL GOODS

Politicians, social theorists, and ordinary citizens throughout the developed world are beginning to question the familiar material growth ethic. More people are becoming critical of the headlong rush for "more things," and they are seeking a more orderly and balanced concept of national development and individual fulfillment. For these and other fundamental reasons, the growth rate in U.S. energy consumption in the decades ahead is very much an open question.

In my view, a realistic and desirable objective for the U.S. would be a full-employment, knowledge-intensive, food- and service-oriented economy that would be fueled at a fairly stable level of energy consumption using renewables. Such a society would contain a high degree of material affluence and consume huge quantities of energy each year. But the U.S. would be able to demonstrate how much affluence is enough and give other nations an opportunity to use more energy and catch up.

A moral constraint should be added to the environmental and political constraints on our growth in energy production. If all the people on Earth are eventually going to enjoy an adequate level of material well-being, we will need to adopt a new ethic which regards waste as a form of theft. If we continue a self-indulgent, disposable society in which the cycle continually is to dig, burn, build, and then discard, we are stealing from our children and grandchildren the planet's resources.

An all-renewable energy supply will in some ways accelerate the pace of growth in the disposable "stuff" that requires energy to run. Our energy appetite and its consequences should cause us to question the whole structure of our material-oriented, energy-intensive pattern of industrial production, and at bottom, the basis of our civilization.

WE MUST QUESTION THE SYSTEM THAT MEASURES PRODUCTIVITY BY THE UNIT COST OF PRODUC- TION TO THE MANUFACTURER, RATHER THAN THE UNIT COST OF SERVICE TO THE CONSUMER

A root fallacy in the present organization of American economic life is vividly demonstrated by the manner in which we measure productivity. Mass production is the overriding criterion. Success is determined by the number of automobiles or shoes or lightbulbs produced per unit of investment in capital and labor. Yet, if we think about it, the number of lightbulbs a worker can produce in a day and the total manufacturing cost of a bulb are not the decisive tests at all. What is more important is how long the bulb will last and its cost per hour of use for the consumer. We must question the system that measures productivity by the unit cost of production to the manufacturer, rather than the unit cost of service to the consumer.

Emphasis on quantity rather than quality and durability dominates our contemporary society. As long as the supply of material goods and the energy to produce them seemed infinite and the environment was a free garbage can in which to dispose of them, the system made sense. But we have been misled by a very incomplete accounting system. Consumers have always subsidized the production costs of industry because these costs do not include such items as the damage to the environment and human health. Nor does the price tag reflect the cost to society of disposing of poorly built automobiles, toasters, or tricycles after they fall apart. We do not even calculate the cost to dispose of one-time-use items such as paper napkins, disposable diapers, fast-food wrappers, or the plastic packaging used ubiquitously at drugstores, mini-marts, and box stores.

Our economic system is geared to make it profitable for the production of new goods to increase. The system has performed quite well in achieving our current standard of living. But we can now perceive a need to conserve our resources and protect the environment. Therefore, it is time to examine the new incentives that would encourage industry to make products that last longer, are repairable, and can be recycled and reused. To be sure, people enjoy buying new things and often items are discarded not because they wear out but because a better camera or similar item has been developed. Yet much of what America buys does wear out quickly. The lightbulb is only the most conspicuous example. Often items are discarded because there is no easy way to repair them.

Achieving greater durability in the products of industry would affect the demand for energy in a very fundamental way. If energy-intensive industrial products lasted twice as long as they do now, then annual energy requirements for those industries could be cut in half.

Changes in the manufacturing process to achieve such savings need not seriously disrupt the economy. Economic efficiency still would be the test, but it would be measured over the life of the product and on the basis of the full cost to society. The objective would be to make products last as long as possible, be easy to repair, and be susceptible to recycling or reuse. Innovation would not be stifled but redirected. New models just for the sake of change would no longer be in style. Mass-production techniques would not necessarily be abandoned, but jobs would of necessity be structured to provide the worker with enough variety and interest that he could take satisfaction in performing his tasks and in turning out a durable, high-quality product. In some instances this might mean completely mechanizing an operation and replacing the current human "robots" with machines overseen by people.

An important starting point in moving toward more durable industrial products is to educate consumers to think more in terms of costs over the useful life of the items they buy. If all manufactured goods were accurately labeled to reveal their expected (or better still, guaranteed) life span and their cost per unit of useful service, we might see a new kind of product competition, i.e., winning a public reputation for quality, longevity, and craftsmanship. Another important step would be to put the tax laws to work to encourage durability and reuse. A tax incentive that increased with the length of time a product was guaranteed to last might be a very effective incentive. Regulations would be needed to require that autos and other products were built so that the materials they contain could be 100 percent reused. Equitable freight rates for transporting recycled materials could complete the package.

> **AN IMPORTANT STARTING POINT IN MOVING TOWARD MORE DURABLE INDUSTRIAL PRODUCTS IS TO EDUCATE CONSUMERS TO THINK MORE IN TERMS OF COSTS OVER THE USEFUL LIFE OF THE ITEMS THEY BUY**

I believe that the concept of making quality and durability the hallmarks of industrial production should have strong appeal to a nation concerned with solving the shortage of energy and protecting the environment against damage from the rapid growth of energy-intensive industries, which are also often pollution intensive. The concept should have appeal to consumers who get too little service and satisfaction for their money from present industrial products. Workers in the plants whose aspirations for human dignity are subverted by the mindless drudgery of their jobs have a direct and vital stake.

A common "bogey man" is that conserving will reduce employment. Here it is important to distinguish between planned conservation and a sudden unexpected shortage. Obviously if industry is suddenly deprived of the energy it has counted on, production slows down and jobs are lost. But the gradual shift to better-insulated homes, more efficient cars, and less-energy-intensive industrial production is no threat to employment. To be sure, the postindustrial society does mean fewer people working in factories that produce goods, but it also means more people who are better paid for providing skilled services including repairs and servicing of products. If worker productivity (as traditionally measured) were to decline in order to achieve quality and durability, the net effect would be fewer blue-collar jobs in industry. But there would be an off-setting factor: many more jobs would be created for individuals to maintain and repair the longer-lasting industrial products and to work in the industries that reclaimed and recycled materials—the result, green-collar jobs. Another offsetting factor could be a shorter industrial work-week; the material needs of society could be satisfied with fewer human hours of work per hour of useful service to the consumer. Furthermore, the new growth industries—education, farming, manufacturing, and solar-system installation—would be more labor intensive, creating additional and more rewarding jobs than those lost in the energy-intensive industries.

I do not mean to minimize the difficulties of achieving and maintaining full employment in the years ahead. We have fallen short of achieving this goal in times much less uncertain. Yet if we move in a planned and orderly manner, our shift to an economy in which energy and materials are used more frugally poses no threat to employment opportunities for Americans.

I also recognize that the role of government—at least in terms of providing leadership—will need to be more sharply defined. New programs will have to be initiated if the changes outlined in this chapter are to be achieved. But those who attempt to depict such a conservation-oriented society as coercive or stagnant are drawing a false picture. There is nothing coercive about a society in which buildings do not leak heat and people get to work by rapid transit rather than by driving single-passenger cars; where short trips are taken by high-speed rail rather than by driving or flying; and in which the products of industry are built to be durable and recyclable. It is a matter of reordering priorities and channeling investments into energy-saving activities rather than building more power plants and refineries. And such a society is not stagnant. Recreation, education, performing arts, farming, health care, research and development, and high technology are some of its growth industries.

These conservation measures would be a part of a much broader restructuring of our economy and changing of our values, especially as they relate to material goods. The quick fix of buying something new would give way to the joy of purchasing something that is well made, a pleasure to use, and built to last.

We could shift our preoccupation from possessions to intellectual and human concerns. We would have time to do more things with our hands, things we like to do. I do not foresee a hard or Spartan life in a slower, more frugal America. Indeed, our energy requirements, though fairly stable, would be sufficient to provide comfortable housing, pleasant indoor temperatures the year round, and basic conveniences such as a washing machine for everyone. But these material goods would move toward the background of our lives. Our satisfaction and growth would come more from our minds, spirits, and relations with other people and our communities.

As we develop a more human-centric society and aspire to new challenges we will not give up our material comforts. From any worldwide, long-term perspective this means that huge increases in the amount of energy will be required to achieve a desirable standard of living for all people, and these levels must be sustained. The future of humanity requires the development of renewable sources of energy. Only then will it be possible to aspire to improving quality of life and flourishing civilization into the distant future.

There can be no more urgent task for humanity than to find, as rapidly as possible, alternatives to burning the limited fossil fuels on Earth. It is not simply that an energy crisis is approaching. Any long-term projection of the need for hydrocarbons as an industrial raw material should convince us that lavish and wasteful consumption of fuel must quickly cease. Petroleum may be increasingly useful to prevent starvation on Earth. In the long run, fossil fuels may serve humanity better as a source of protein than as fuel to take three trips to the mall in one day.

The world of energy has progressed steadily to more and more concentrated and sophisticated sources. The progression has been from wood to coal to petroleum and now to the atom. The next and perhaps ultimate step is to harness the sun directly. Once such an inexhaustible source of energy is available, we would have the physical means to eradicate poverty. For it is clear that with inexhaustible and relatively clean and economical energy, we can satisfy the basic need for food and material comforts for all people inhabiting the Earth. But first, Americans must recognize and value a limit on personal material affluence.

THE FUTURE OF HUMANITY REQUIRES THE DEVELOPMENT OF RENEWABLE SOURCES OF ENERGY

My study of energy policy thus leads me to serious questions about America's present growth pattern as well as the urgent need for cleaner and more abundant sources for an energy-starved world. As our government begins to grapple with these fundamental concerns, I am confident that the American people will respond vigorously to the challenge.

The energy crisis is an opportunity for greatness and service. We can serve not only the future generations of Americans but also people throughout the world. In coming decades they can be brought out of darkness and hopelessness into a global community where food and shelter are no longer a daily struggle and there is time for the recognition of human dignity and the pursuit and enjoyment of shared values.

✳✳✳

1　The ideas for this chapter are substantially the same since the author introduced them in his 1974 book, *Energy: The New Era*.

2　Duane Elgin, *Voluntary Simplicity* (New York: Harper, 1998).

REFERENCES

✳ ✳ ✳

Albright, David and Kimberly Kramer. "Plutonium Watch: Tracking Plutonium Inventories." Institute for Science and International Security, June 2004.

American Wind Energy Association (AWEA). "Comparative Cost of Wind and Other Energy Sources." 2001.

———. "Wind Web Tutorial: Wind Energy Basics." 2005. http://www.awea.org/faq/wwtbasics.html.

Apollo Alliance. August 2006. http://www.apolloalliance.org.

Archer, Christina and Mark Z. Jacobson. "Evaluation of Global Wind Power." Stanford, CA: Department of Civil and Environmental Engineering, Stanford University, 2004.

"Arrêté du 7 juillet 2006 relatif à la programmation pluriannuelle des investissements de production d'électricité." Décrets, arrêtés, circulaires, Textes généraux, Ministère de l'économie, des finances, et de l'industrie—industrie, *Journal officiel de la République française*, 17, 65, July 9, 2006.

Barlett, Donald L. and James B. Steele. "Why U.S. Is Running Out of Gas." *Time*, July 21, 2003.

California Air Resources Board. "2005 Estimated Annual Average Emissions, Los Angeles County." http://www.arb.ca.gov/app/emsinv/emseic1_query.php.

California Energy Commission. "Integrated Energy Policy Report 2005." November 2005.

———. "Renewable Resources Development Report." 2003, Appendix C.

California Fuel Cell Partnership. 2005. http://www.cafcp.org/fuel-vehl_map.html.

Carter, Jimmy. "The Crisis of Confidence." July 15, 1979.

Center for American Progress and *Foreign Policy Magazine.* "The Terrorism Index: A Survey of the U.S. National Security Establishment on the War on Terror." Panel presented on June 28, 2006.

"China is World's Leading Investor in Renewable Energy." *Xinhua News Agency,* May 17, 2006.

Clayton, Mark. "Carbon Cloud over a Green Fuel." *Christian Science Monitor,* March 23, 2006.

Clendenning, Alan. "Brazil Leading Effort to Boost Ethanol Use." *The Associated Press,* March 10, 2006.

Doyle, Alister. "Iceland's Hydrogen Buses Zip to Oil-Free Economy." *Reuters,* January 10, 2005.

Egelko, Bob. "U.S. Court Puts PG&E Nuclear Permit on Hold Until Terror Review." *San Francisco Chronicle,* June 3, 2006.

Eisenhower, Dwight D. "Atoms for Peace." Speech given to General Assembly of the United Nations on Peaceful Uses of Atomic Energy, New York City, December 8, 1953.

Electric Power Research Institute. "Comparing the Benefits and Impacts of Hybrid Electric Vehicle Options for Compact Sedan and Sport Utility Vehicles." July 2002.

Elgin, Duane. *Voluntary Simplicity.* New York: Harper, 1998.

Elliott, D. L. and M. N. Schwartz. "Wind Energy Potential in the United States." Pacific Northwest Laboratory. September 1993. http://www.nrel.gov/wind/wind_potential.html.

Elliot, Larry. "No! It Was Not the Hydrogen." *H2 Nation,* November/December 2003.

Ellison, Katherine. "Turned Off by Global Warming." *New York Times,* May 20, 2006.

Embassy of the People's Republic of China in Australia. "A Rising China and the Flourishing China–Australia Relationship." July 11, 2005. http://au.china-embassy.org/eng/zggk/t203070.ht.

Energy Policy Project of the Ford Foundation. "A Time to Choose: America's Energy Future." 1974.

Energy Policy Research Institute. "System Level Design, Performance, Cost and Economic Assessment—San Francisco Tidal In-Stream Power Plant." Energy Policy Research Institute (EPRI), June 10, 2006.

Environmental and Energy Study Institute. "Ethanol, Climate Protection, Oil Reduction." Environmental and Energy Study Institute, 9, May 25, 2000.

Ericsson, Karin and Lars. J. Nilsson. "International Biofuel Trade—A Study of the Swedish Import." Division of Environmental and Energy Systems Studies, Lund Institute of Technology, 2004.

European Wind Energy Association. 2005. http://www.ewea.org.

Fabiola, Anthony. "Turn off the Heat—How Japan Made Energy Saving an Art Form." *The Guardian,* February 17, 2006.

Freeman, S. David, Jim Harding, and Roger Duncan. "Solar Cells Change Electricity Distribution." *Seattle Post-Intelligencer,* August 10, 2006.

Freeman, S. David. *Energy: A New Era.* New York: Vintage Books, 1974.

Fridleifsson, Ingvar B. "Geothermal Energy for the Benefit of the People." United Nations University—Geothermal Training Programme, 2003.

Friedman, Thomas. "The Energy Mandate." *International Herald Tribune,* October 14–15, 2006.

Greene, Nathaniel. "Growing Energy: How Biofuels Can Help End America's Oil Dependence." Natural Resources Defense Council, December 2004.

"Gulf Wind: Harnessing Offshore Wind off the Coast of Texas." *REFocus, Elsevier Ltd.,* January/February 2006.

Hanssen, Greg, of Edrive Systems. From personal conversation on May 13, 2006.

Hawken, Paul, Amory Lovins, and Hunter L. Lovins. *Natural Capitalism: Creating the Next Industrial Revolution.* Boston: Little, Brown and Company, 1999: 248.

"Health Risks from Exposure to Low Levels of Ionizing Radiation." National Academy Press, 2005.

Heitz, Eric and Patrick Mazza. "The New Harvest: Biofuels and Windpower for Rural Revitalization and National Energy Security." The Energy Foundation, November 2005.

"Hybrid Sales Keep Going Up, Up, Up." February 24, 2006. http://www.tree hugger.com.

Intergovernmental Panel on Climate Change. "Climate Change 2001: Synthesis Report: Summary for Policymakers."

International Energy Agency. October 12, 2005. http://www.oja-services. nl/iea-pvps/isr/22.htm.

"Israel's Experience in Sustainable Energy." United Nations Environmental Program, January 2006.

Journal of Petroleum Marketing, The, June 1998.

Kammen, Daniel. "An Integrated Hydrogen Vision for California." Energy Resources Group, July 9, 2004.

Kanellos, Michael. "Solar Panel Shortage to Continue through 2006." CNET News.com, April 10, 2006.

———. "With Hefty Funding, Solar Start-up Takes on Big Guns." CNET News.com, June 21, 2006.

King, Waytt and L. Hunter Lovins. "Boom, Bust and Efficiency." *Fueling the Future.* Toronto, Ontario: House of Anansi Press, 2003.

Kutscher, Charles F., United States National Renewable Energy Laboratory. "The Status and Future of Geothermal Power." August 2000. http:// www.nrel.gov/geothermal/pdfs/28204.pdf.

Laumer, John. "Sweden Raises The Renewable Energy Bar." January 24, 2006. http://www.treehugger.com /files/2006/01/sweden_raises_t.php.

Lawrence Berkeley National Laboratory, Environmental Energy Technologies Division, Heat Island Group. April 2000. http://eetd.lbl.gov/ HeatIsland/CoolRoofs/.

Lee, Mike. "Iceland: the First Country to Try Abandoning Gasoline." *ABC News,* January 18, 2005.

"Let's Get Serious About Alternatives to Oil." *Wall Street Journal,* April 18, 2005.

Li, Zijun. "China Aims to Build Energy-Efficient Society in Next Five Years." Worldwatch Institute, October 20, 2005.

Link-Wills, Kimberly. "Plasma Power." *Georgia Tech Alumni Magazine,* 2002.

Lipman, Timothy. "What Will Power the Hydrogen Economy? Present and Future Sources of Hydrogen." Prepared for the Natural Resources Defense Council, July 12, 2004.

Little, Amanda Griscom. "Warts and Ethanol." *Grist Magazine,* May 26, 2006.

Liu, Yingling. "Made in China, or Made by China? Chinese Wind Turbines Struggle to Enter Own Market." Worldwatch Institute, May 19, 2006. http://www.worldwatch.org/features/chinawatch/stories/20060519-2.

Los Angeles Times, August 18, 2006, B-1.

Luhnow, David and Geraldo Samor. "As Brazil Fills Up on Ethanol, It Weans off Energy Imports." *Wall Street Journal,* January 9, 2006.

"Marketbuzz 2006." *Solarbuzz,* March 15, 2006.

Mattias, Karen. "Sweden, a Leader in Renewable Energy, Aims to End Oil Dependency by 2020." *Associated Press,* February 2, 2006.

McLaren, Warren. "Gorbachev Sounds Off on Nuclear vs. Renewables." April 27, 2006. http://www.treehugger.com/files/th_exclusives/celebrities/ index.php?

Mehos, Mark and Richard Perez. "Mining for Solar Resources: U.S. Southwest Provides Vast Potential." National Renewable Energy Laboratory, Summer 2005.

National Wind Technology Center. "Wind in a Minute." 1999.

Nuclear Energy Institute. http://www.nei.org/documents/Energy_Bill_2005.pdf.

"Plug in Hybrids." *Consumer Reports*, May 2005.

"Portugal Starts Huge Solar Plant." *BBC News*, June 7, 2006.

Public Policy Institute of California. "Special Survey on Californians and the Environment." PPIC Statewide Survey 2004.

Quaid, Libby. "Ethanol Dazzles Wall Street, White House." *Associated Press*, June 3, 2006.

Reece, Eric. "Moving Mountains: The Battle for Justice Comes to the Coal Fields of Appalachia." *Orion*, January 9, 2006.

Ristau, Oliver Ristau. "The Photovoltaic Market in Japan: Unquestioned Leadership of World Market." *The Solarserver*, September 15, 2001. http://www.solarserver.de/solarmagazin/artikelseptember2001-e.html.

Romm, Joseph. E-mail to Felix Kramer from "Gas-Optional and Green." Blog reposted by James Cacio on June 14, 2005. http://www.worldchanging.com/archives/002891.html.

Rother, Larry. "With Big Boost from Sugar Cane, Brazil Is Satisfying Its Fuel Needs." *New York Times*, April 10, 2006.

"Sales of Full-Size SUVs Take a Dive in February." March 5, 2006. www.treehugger.com.

Schueger, Matt. "Midwest Wind Power Development." Wind on the Wires Presentation on February 11, 2004.

Set America Free. "A Blueprint for U.S. Energy Security." http://www.setamericafree.org/.

Shears, John, Center for Energy Efficiency and Renewable Technologies. Private conversation.

Spadro, Jack. "Mountaintop Removal: Mining Practices Must Change or the Ecosystem Will Be Destroyed." *The Charleston Gazette*, February 21, 2005.

Steenkamp, Willem. "SA Solar Research Eclipses Rest of the World." IOL. February 11, 2006. http: //www.iol.co.za.

Stenzel, Jennifer and Jonathan Trutt. "Flying Off Course: Environmental Impacts of America's Airports." Natural Resources Defense Council, October 1996.

Tennessee Valley Authority. "Watts Bar Nuclear Plant." http://www.tva.gov/
   sites/wattsbarnuc.htm.
"Toyota Takes Green Car to China." *BBC News*, Sept. 15, 2004.
Tremlett, Giles. "BP Joins Bank in Record Solar-Power Project." *The Guardian*,
   April 22, 2006.
U.S. Bureau of Mines, 1995.
U. S. Bureau of Transportation Statistics. "National Transportation Statistics
   2006." September 2006.
U.S. Central Intelligence Agency. CIA World Fact Book. 2004. http://www
   .cia.gov/cia/publications/factbook/.
U.S. Department of Agriculture, Economic Research Service. November 1,
   2006. http://www.ers.usda.gov/data/.
U.S. Department of Energy (DOE), Energy Efficiency and Renewable Energy,
   Wind and Hydropower Technologies Program. September 8, 2006.
   http://eereweb.ee.doe.gov/windandhydro/wind_potential.html.
———. "United States—2005 Year End Wind Power Capacity (MW)."
   Windpowering America, January 25, 2006. http://www.eere.energy.
   gov/windandhydro/windpoweringamerica/wind_installed_capacity
   .asp.
———. "Wind Energy Potential." September 15, 2006. http://www1.eere
   .energy.gov/windandhydro/wind_potential.html.
U.S. DOE, Energy Information Administration. "Annual Electricity Outlook
   2006 With Projections to 2030."
———. "Annual Energy Outlook 2006." December 2005.
———. "Basic Electricity Statistics." 2004. http://www.eia.doe.gov/neic/
   quickfacts/quickelectric.html.
———. "Coal Production and Number of Mines by State and Type." 2003.
   http://www.eia.doe.gov/cneaf/coal/page/acr/table1.html.
———. "Country Analysis Briefs." August 2006.
———. "Petroleum Navigator: Product Supplied." October 2, 2006. http://
   tonto.eia.doe.gov/dnav/pet/pet_cons_psup_dc_nus_mbbl_a.htm.
———. "State Energy Data 2002: Comparison." http://www.eia.doe.gov/
   emeu/states/sep_sum/html/pdf/rank_use_per_cap.pdf.
———. "Summary Statistics for the United States." November 9, 2006.
   http://www.eia.doe.gov/cneaf/electricity/epa/epates.html.
———. "U.S. Primary Consumption by Source and Sector." 2004. http://
   www.eia.doe.gov/emeu/aer/pdf/pecss_diagram.pdf.

U.S. Department of the Interior. "Technology White Paper on Wind Energy Potential on the U.S. Outer Continental Shelf." May 2006. http://ocsenergy.anl.gov/documents/docs/OCS_EIS_WhitePaper_Wind.pdf.

U.S. Departments of Energy and Agriculture. "Biomass as Feedstock for a Bioenergy and Bioproducts Industry: The Technical Feasibility of a Billion-Ton Annual Supply." April 2005.

U.S. Environmental Protection Agency and DOE. "Compare Hybrids Side-by-Side." November 3, 2006. www.fueleconomy.gov.

U.S. Environmental Protection Agency. "National Totals of SO2, NOx, CO2, and Heat Input for Coal Fired and Non-Coal Fired Title IV Affected Units for 1996–2001". 2001. http://www.epa.gov/airmarkets/emissions/score01/table1.pdf.

U.S. National Renewable Energy Laboratory (NREL). "Hydrogen Production and Delivery." http://www.nrel.gov/hydrogen/proj_production_delivery.htm. November 20, 2006.

———. "How Much Land Will PV Need to Supply Our Electricity?" January 2004. http://www.nrel.gov/ncpv/pvmenu.cgi?site+ncpv&idx=3&body=faq.html.

U.S. Public Interest Research Group (PIRG), "Making Sense of the Coal Rush: The Consequences of Expanding America's Dependence on Coal." July 2006.

U.S. PIRG Education Fund. "Up in Smoke." July 1999.

West, Larry. "Sweden Aims to be World's First Oil-Free Nation." February 2006. http://environment.about.com/od/renewableenergy/a/oilfreesweden.htm.

Yen-Nakafuji, Dora. "California Wind Resources." California Energy Commission Staff White Paper CEC-500-2005-071-D, April 2005.

Zakaria, Fareed. "Mile by Mile, Into the Oil Trap." *The Washington Post*, August 23, 2005.

Zwaniecki, Andrezej. "U.S–China Cooperation Could Advance Mutual, Global Energy Goals." April 2005. http://usinfo.state.gov/eap/Archive/2005/Apr/04-622583.html.

APPENDIX

∗∗∗

WEB RESOURCES

Alternative Vehicles and Fuels Information and Incentive Programs

* Plug-In America (latest info on plug-in and electric cars)—www .pluginamerica.com
* Plug-In Partners National Campaign—www.pluginpartners.org
* Alternative Vehicle Incentives and Information—www.eere .energy.gov/fleetguide/
* Federal and State Incentives and Laws for Alternative Vehicle Fuels—www.eere.energy.gov/afdc/laws/incen_laws.html
* Federal Fuel Economy—www.fueleconomy.gov

Renewable Energy and Efficiency Tips, Information and Incentive Programs

* Database of State Incentives for Renewables and Efficiency—www .dsireusa.org
* Flex Your Power (CA)—www.fypower.org
* DOE Energy Savers (U.S.)—www.energysavers.gov

Your Carbon Footprint

* Sustainable Travel International—www.carbonoffsets.org
* Safe Climate Carbon Calculator—www.safeclimate.net/calculator/

Other Resources

* United States Geological Survey—www.usgs.gov
* United States Department of Energy—www.doe.gov

* National Renewable Energy Laboratory—www.nrel.gov
* Energy Efficiency and Renewable Energy Program—www.eere .energy.gov
* University of California, Davis, Institute of Transportation Studies—http://its.ucdavis.edu/
* University of California, Berkeley, Energy and Resources Group— http://socrates.berkeley.edu/erg/index.shtml
* U.S. House of Representatives—www.house.gov
* U.S. Senate—www.senate.gov

LETTER TO SENATOR OR REPRESENTATIVE

Dear _____,

I am writing to urge you to take decisive action that will enable America to regain its independence from the oil-producing nations, prevent global warming, and reduce the dangers of nuclear bombs falling into the hands of terrorists.

These dangers are the war we must win and, to do so, I urge you to reject the false propaganda of the energy lobby and take decisive action.

The essential actions the Congress must take are the following:

* Outlaw any new coal or nuclear electric power plants.
* Enact a $5,000 tax credit to each consumer who purchases a plug-in hybrid, and a $1 billion tax credit to the first company that sells 200,000 plug-in hybrids.
* Require all electric power companies to achieve 30 percent renewable energy by 2020.
* Increase the standards for fuel efficiency in motor vehicles by one mile per gallon (mpg) each year for the next twenty-four years to double today's mpg standard.
* Authorize a ten-year program with funding to build hydrogen service stations throughout the nation to service hydrogen-fueled motor vehicles.

As your constituent and a citizen of this country, I urge you to take action on these important items.

Sincerely,

_____

LETTER TO YOUR STATE PUBLIC UTILITY COMMISSION

Dear _____ ,

I am writing to urge that you adopt policies and make decisions that will move the electric power companies under your jurisdiction along the path of investments in energy efficiency and renewable energy. To this end, I urge you to take the following steps:

* Ban any new coal or nuclear-powered power plants or any additions to existing plants.
* Require your utilities to give investments in cost-effective energy efficiency measures the highest priority by requiring each utility to adopt efficiency programs that will at least offset project growth in energy use.
* Require the utilities you regulate to present a program for your approval to achieve a steadily increasing share of its power from renewables, with a minimum of 20 percent by 2020 and 30 percent by 2040.
* Promote decentralized power sources with rates that increase with increased usage, net metering, reasonable backup rates, and fast approval of interconnection agreements.
* Promote the use of plug-in hybrid cars with promotional off-peak rates, fleet purchases, and advocacy of tax credits.

Please respond to this letter.

Sincerely,

_____

INDEX

***